# Why Life Speeds Up As You Get Older

Is it true, as the novelist Cees Nooteboom once wrote, that 'Memory is like a dog that lies down where it pleases'? Where do the long, lazy summers of our childhood go? Why is it that as we grow older time seems to condense, speed up, elude us while in old age significant events from our distant past can seem as vivid and real as what happened yesterday? In this enchanting and thoughtful book, Douwe Draaisma, author of the internationally acclaimed *Metaphors of Memory*, explores the nature of autobiographical memory. Applying a unique blend of scholarship, poetic sensibility and keen observation he tackles such extraordinary phenomena as déjà vu, near-death experiences, the memory feats of idiots savants and the effects of extreme trauma on memory recall. Raising almost as many questions as it answers, this fascinating book will not fail to touch you at the same time as it educates and entertains.

DOUWE DRAAISMA is Professor of History of Psychology at the University of Groningen, The Netherlands. He is the author of *Metaphors of Memory* (Cambridge, 2001). The original Dutch version of this current book, entitled *Waarom het leven sneller gaat als je ouder wordt* (2001), has won several scientific and literary awards.

# Why Life Speeds Up As You Get Older

## How Memory Shapes Our Past

DOUWE DRAAISMA

Translated by Arnold and Erica Pomerans

CAMBRIDGE UNIVERSITY PRESS

PUBLISHED BY THE PRESS SYNDICATE OF THE UNIVERSITY OF CAMBRIDGE
The Pitt Building, Trumpington Street, Cambridge, United Kingdom

CAMBRIDGE UNIVERSITY PRESS
The Edinburgh Building, Cambridge, CB2 2RU, UK
40 West 20th Street, New York, NY 10011–4211, USA
477 Williamstown Road, Port Melbourne, VIC 3207, Australia
Ruiz de Alarcón 13, 28014 Madrid, Spain
Dock House, The Waterfront, Cape Town 8001, South Africa

http://www.cambridge.org

Originally published in Dutch as *Waarom het leven Sneller gaat als je ouder wordt. Over het autobiografische geheugen* by Historische Uitgeverij 2001
and © Douwe Draaisma 2001

First published in English by Cambridge University Press 2004 as *Why Life Speeds Up As You Get Older. How Memory Shapes Our Past*
English translation © Cambridge University Press 2004

This translation was supported by a grant from the Foundation for the Production and Translation of Dutch Literature.

Fourth printing 2005

Printed in the United Kingdom at the University Press, Cambridge

*Typeface* Sabon 10/14 pt.     *System* LaTeX $2_\varepsilon$  [TB]

*A catalogue record for this book is available from the British Library*

*Library of Congress Cataloguing in Publication data*

Draaisma
[W                              der wordt. English]
                                w memory shapes our past / by
Douwe Draaisma ; translated by Arnold and Erica Pomerans.
    p.  cm.
  Includes bibliographical references and index.
  ISBN 0 521 83424 4    1. Autobiographical memory.  I. Title.
BF378.A87D7313 2004
153.1'3–dc22   2004049441

ISBN 0 521 83424 4 hardback

# Contents

# Illustrations

# Acknowledgments

I am greatly indebted for their encouragement, criticism and help to my friends and colleagues Ann Boer, Trudy Dehue, Maarten Derksen, Yvette Draaisma, Ellis Ellenbroek, Goffe Jensma, Gerrit Krol, Sarah de Rijcke, Willem Wagenaar and Anne Wolff. Also thanks to Patrick Everard, who has been such a valuable coach in writing this book. I owe a special word of thanks, or rather gratitude, to Arno and Erica Pomerans. Translating is partly rewriting and this they have done with so much sensitivity, delicacy and elegance that I am proud to have worked with them. Thanks, finally, to Sarah Caro. This is our second book together; again she was my trusted guide on matters of style, taste and common sense.

# 1 'Memory is like a dog that lies down where it pleases'

Our memory has a will of its own. We tell ourselves, 'This is something I must remember, this is a moment I must hang on to, this look, this feeling, this caress', yet within a few months, or even after just a couple of days, we find that the memory can no longer be summoned up with the colour, smell or savour we were hoping for. 'Memory', says Cees Nooteboom in *Rituals*, 'is like a dog that lies down where it pleases.'

Nor does our memory take much notice of our order *not* to preserve something: if only I had never seen that, experienced it, heard of it; if only I could just forget all about it. But it's no good, it keeps turning up at night, spontaneously and uninvited, when we cannot fall asleep. Then, too, memory is a dog; it retrieves what we have just thrown away, wagging its tail.

Since the 1980s psychologists have been referring to the part of our memory in which we store our personal experiences as our 'autobiographical memory'. It is the chronicle of our lives, a long record we consult whenever someone asks us what our earliest memory is, what the house we lived in as a child looked like, or what was the last book we read. Autobiographical memory recalls and forgets at the same time. It is as if you are having the notes of your life taken by an obstreperous company secretary, who meticulously documents those things you would rather forget and during your finest hours pretends to be industriously at work when actually he still has the cap of his pen screwed on.

Autobiographical memory obeys some mysterious laws of its own. Why does it contain next to nothing about what happened before we were three or four? Why are hurtful events invariably recorded in indelible ink? Why are humiliations remembered for years on end with the precision of a charge sheet? Why is it invariably set in motion at sombre moments and during sombre events? Depression and insomnia transform our autobiographical memory into a tale of woe: every unpleasant memory is linked to other unpleasant memories by an oppressive network of cross-references. Now and then we are taken by surprise by our own memory. A smell suddenly reminds us of something we haven't thought about for thirty years. A street we last saw when we were seven seems to have shrunk beyond all recognition. Memories of youth can seem clearer in old age than they were at the age of forty. And these are mere common or garden recollections. You might also want to know why you still remember exactly where you were when you heard that Princess Diana had been killed, how having a déjà vu comes about and why life seems to speed up as you grow older.

It seems odd that psychologists should not have identified something like an 'autobiographical memory' until fairly recently. This is because the ability to store your personal experiences and recall them later is precisely what is meant by 'memory' in common speech. What else could your personal memory possibly contain except 'personal experiences'? This question is, however, based on a misunderstanding. Every psychology textbook distinguishes between dozens of different types of memory. Some forms of memory refer to the duration of the memory storage, for instance short- or long-term memory; others refer to the sense with which different types of memories are linked, for instance auditory or iconic memory, and yet others to the type of information stored, for instance semantic, motor or visual memory. All these types of memory have their own laws and characteristics; you remember the meaning of a word differently from the way you remember the movements you make with your feet when driving a car, Pythagoras' theorem differently from the first time you went to school. On further reflection it is therefore not so remarkable that it was not until the early 1980s that among all the different forms of memory a special technical term was introduced for storing memories of personal experiences. Quite another question is why the study of autobiographical memory should have got under way when it did. *Why so late in the day?*

## In London and Berlin

It could easily have happened a century earlier. The first experiments with what is now called autobiographical memory were made in about 1879 and were conducted by the English scientist Sir

Francis Galton (1822–1911), who had become interested in his own associations. While on a stroll along Pall Mall, he fixed his attention on the objects he saw and at the same time noted the associations they called to mind. He was surprised to find how varied his associations were and that they often reminded him of things about which he had not thought for a long time. In observing the operation of his own mind, incidentally, Galton was faced with the 'difficulty of keeping watch without embarrassing the freedom of its action'. Galton solved this problem by allowing his mind to play freely for a while, quietly waiting until a couple of ideas had passed through it. Then he suddenly turned his attention upon them 'to scrutinise them, and to record their exact appearance'. It resembled a sudden arrest and search. After his walk, Galton decided to repeat his experiment in a more systematic fashion. He drew up a list of seventy-five words that seemed suitable to him, like 'carriage', 'abbey' and 'afternoon', wrote them on sheets of paper and laid one of the sheets under a book in such a way that he could read the next word only by leaning forward. The experiment had a fixed procedure. Galton leaned forward, read the word, pressed a small 'chronograph' or stopwatch, waited for a few associations to rise in his mind and stopped his chronograph. He then made a note of his associations and recorded the time it had taken to form them. 'I soon got into the way of doing all this in a very methodical and automatic manner', Galton explained, 'keeping the mind perfectly calm and neutral, but intent and, as it were, at full cock and on hair trigger, before displaying the word.' This is not to say that Galton enjoyed the experiments; on the contrary, he found them extremely irksome and trying. He had to summon all his resolution to carry on. Galton went through the list on four separate occasions, with intervals of about a month and under very different circumstances. He ended up with a total of 505 associations taking up a total time of 660 seconds. This amounted to a rate of fifty in a minute – 'miserably slow', Galton felt, compared to the natural speed of association in reverie. The number of *different* associations was considerably lower than the original list of 505: a mere 289. This surprised Galton and it certainly diminished his admiration for the variety he had noticed in his first experiment, strolling along Pall Mall. His associations seemed to behave like actors staging an endless procession by marching off on one side and running back behind the stage to join the procession again on the other side. All this repetition proved that 'the roadways of our minds are worn into very deep ruts'.

Another discovery was that so many of his associations went back to his youth – no fewer than 39 per cent. Several words had made him recall how, as a boy, he had been allowed to poke around for a couple of days in the laboratory of a chemist he knew. Recent events gave rise to considerably fewer associations – just 15 per cent. Moreover it was, above all, the 'old' associations that were responsible for all the repetitions: a quarter of the youthful associations came up four times, that is, ran back three times. Education and training had a marked effect on adult associations. Although Galton had seen a great deal of the world and had made his name as an explorer, he was struck by the fact that his associations had remained typically English; indeed when he examined the list, he also found that they were characteristic of the social background in which he had been born and had grown up.

At the end of his experiments, Galton was a satisfied man. He had demonstrated that fleeting associations can be recorded and registered for statistical analysis, that they can be sorted, dated and categorized. He had penetrated the 'obscure depths' of his mind. What he had seen there was not always fit to print. Associations, he wrote, 'lay bare the foundations of a man's thoughts with curious distinctness, and exhibit his mental anatomy with more vividness and truth than he would probably care to publish in the world'. The general impression his experiments had left upon him 'is like that which many of us have experienced when the basement of our house happens to be under thorough sanitary repairs, and we realise for the first time the complex systems of drains and gas and water pipes, flues, bellwires, and so forth, upon which our comfort depends, but which are usually hidden out of sight, and with whose existence, so long as they acted well, we had never troubled ourselves'.

With his research, Francis Galton might well have become the founder of a promising psychology of autobiographical memory. He was the first to demonstrate the 'reminiscence effect': the fact that, as we approach the age of sixty – Galton was fifty-seven – our associations tend to turn to our youth. He was also the first to devise a method for gaining access to compartments of the mind that

4

had never before been opened to systematic research. Yet his experiments had no significant sequel. The reason was that, at the same time, in about 1879, someone else was busy conducting memory experiments, again with lists of words and a stopwatch. That man was a German.

Hermann Ebbinghaus (1850–1909) was a philosopher. After working in England and France as a private tutor, he was called to Berlin to teach Prince Waldemar at the Prussian court. The lessons came to an abrupt end when Waldemar died of diphtheria in 1879. Ebbinghaus then decided to try his luck as a private university lecturer in philosophy. His thesis was devoted to the experiments that he had begun while still at the Prussian court. Just like Galton – but independently of him – he had investigated the workings of his own memory.

Ebbinghaus designed his own cues. He inserted one vowel between two consonants, obtaining a stock of 2,300 syllables such as 'nol', 'bif' and 'par'. He next wrote these syllables – often called 'nonsense syllables', although some of them were real words – on cards. The average experiment went as follows: at a fixed time of day, Ebbinghaus would place his watch on the table and pick up the supply of cards, select a number of them randomly and copy the syllables into a notebook. Next, he would run a piece of string with wooden beads, every tenth bead being coloured black, through his fingers. Then he would start to read the series of syllables to himself at great speed – two or three syllables per second – until he knew the series by heart. Later, after an interval that could vary from twenty minutes to six days or even a whole month, he would repeat the test using the same set of syllables. By deducting the number of repetitions needed to relearn the series from that needed to learn it, Ebbinghaus obtained an index of what he called 'saving': relearning demands fewer repetitions than learning, but how many fewer depends on the interval between learning and relearning.

With this method, Ebbinghaus discovered an indirect path to the quantification of the memory. You cannot measure directly what you have forgotten but you can determine the number of repetitions needed to relearn it. In particular, Ebbinghaus was able to express his discovery that people forget more as the time interval since they learned it increases by means of a curve that dips very quickly during the first twenty minutes, slopes a little less steeply after an hour, and after a day flattens out – Ebbinghaus's famous 'forgetting curve'. Another of his discoveries was that the number of repetitions required increases disproportionately with the number of syllables used. If the series consisted of up to seven syllables, Ebbinghaus was able to learn it in one attempt, but with twelve syllables he needed as many as seventeen repetitions, and with sixteen syllables the figure shot up to thirty. This disproportionate increase is now known as the 'Ebbinghaus law'.

In 1880, Ebbinghaus presented the report of his experiments as a *Habilitationsschrift*, the thesis required of candidates for a university lectureship, to the physicist and mathematician Hermann von Helmholtz. Helmholtz's opinion was favourable: he praised the approach and the statistical treatment, thought the results 'not particularly impressive' but acknowledged that this was something you could not tell in advance, and recommended the appointment of this 'bright fellow' as an unsalaried lecturer. With the desired appointment successfully negotiated, Ebbinghaus repeated his experiments and complemented them with new research. He continued to be his own guinea pig. There was no other way. The concentration required, he wrote, the patience the experimental subject needs in order to submit for months to so utterly boring a task as learning series of syllables by heart – these are qualities that in all good conscience you cannot expect of anyone else. So he himself would sit every morning muttering his syllables as the string and the beads ran through his hands. The results of this donkeywork appeared under the title of *Über das Gedächtnis* (On memory) in 1885.

In their experimental approach, Galton and Ebbinghaus had much in common. They both studied their own memory. They both set to work systematically and tried to arrive at precise answers, in quantifiable form, in percentages. And the chief similarity: both were delighted that memory had been opened up successfully to experimental research. Galton wrote that with his experiments he had penetrated the obscure depths of hidden mental processes; Ebbinghaus thought himself fortunate to have discovered a place where 'the two mighty levers of natural science, experiment and measurement' could do their work.

Yet there was also a difference between them. Both series of experiments dealt with the memory, *but Galton's alone dealt with memories.*

From his 'forgetting curve' nothing could be deduced about Ebbinghaus's youth, nothing about what went on in the obscurity of his mind, or what could be found under the cellar floor. The very associations Galton welcomed so hospitably before suddenly arresting them and 'booking' them were kept out of Ebbinghaus's experimental protocol from the very outset. The syllables he proffered to his memory were intentionally without any meaning; the laws of learning and relearning, saving and forgetting, could only be brought to light in a bright and unoccupied room, free of all distractions. The best material does not recall or release anything, is nothing but a short series of meaningless stimuli. What served Galton as the object of his researches was no more than an interfering factor for Ebbinghaus. But thanks to that restriction, Ebbinghaus's research has a quality that Galton's lacked. What Ebbinghaus reproduced from his memory, he could compare with what he had presented to himself. He could express his own exploits in terms of proportions: the influence of the time interval between learning and relearning, the length of the list of syllables, the effect of lists learned earlier, in short, all of that lent itself to very precise quantification, thanks to the fact that the stimuli were recorded. In Galton's scheme that was impossible. No doubt his associations went back to what had entered his memory at some time. He could not have recalled his days in a laboratory had he not been there in his youth. But the associations did not admit of numerical comparisons. Ebbinghaus was able repeatedly to do just that. What he lost in meaning and content with his artificial syllables, he made up for with tests and precision.

Francis Galton and Hermann Ebbinghaus greatly appreciated each other's work. Had they been able to look twenty or thirty years ahead in 1885 and to take a bird's-eye view of the landscape of memory research, they would have been dumbfounded. Their own experiments differed in design and methodology, but were of equal value, each with its own merits and shortcomings. A generation later that equivalence had entirely disappeared. The experimental work in Ebbinghaus's style quickly created a riverbed into which more and more tributary streams flowed, until finally it became the main stream.

Fig. 1  Memory experiment in the Ebbinghaus style.

Memory experiments assumed a form that a photograph from *Aus der Werkstatt der experimentellen Psychologie und Pädagogik* (1913) typifies. It was taken in a German laboratory; the place and date are not given. It would not have made a great deal of difference if they had been; the experimental protocols had become so well established that not only the instruments and the course of the experiments but even the laboratories were interchangeable to some extent. While Ebbinghaus had performed his experiments at his desk at home, with no more equipment than a series of cards with syllables, a string with beads, and a pocket watch, his successors did their experiments in laboratories with refined measuring apparatus. The two men and the girl in the photograph show that the roles of experimenter and experimental subject, still fused in Ebbinghaus, have become separated. It is the memory of the girl that is being put to the test, while the experimenters devote all their attention to operating the instruments. The memory experiment has been subjected to rigorous mechanization. Learning material is being offered with the help of all sorts of 'mnemometers' and other 'memory instruments', one of which has been placed before the girl on the table. Inside the small box is a mechanism ensuring that she is being fed the stimuli at standardized intervals. She is part and parcel of a closed circuit of equipment. The moment the cue appears, the chronoscope in the bell jar to her left starts to run. It stops as soon as she responds to the word: a sensitive membrane in front of her picks up the vibration of her voice and switches the chronoscope off. The chronoscope used to be the very icon of precision in psychology; it carefully captured the reaction time in milliseconds. The wall chart depicts the electric circuitry of a Hipp chronoscope.

Thirty years after Ebbinghaus's muttering of syllables in a Berlin study everything had changed: the experimental site, the distinction between experimenter and experimental subject, the advanced apparatus and the standardization of the experiments. The fact that the experiment with the girl is placed firmly in the Ebbinghaus tradition is to do with what she has been asked to memorize: still that one vowel between two consonants, that cue without a meaning: 'kad'.

## The eclipse

The fate of Galton's association experiments is quickly told. His findings were overshadowed by the rise of a memory psychology that was an extension of Ebbinghaus's work. This was true not only of the methods and approach, but also, and logically so, of the research objects: any craftsman will tell you that your tools largely determine the use to which you can put them. The new trend has helped to turn the psychology of memory into an authentic science. Most textbooks confirm that a great deal of knowledge about learning and remembering, recognizing and reproducing, has been accumulated during the past century. Research with syllables is still undertaken, but such studies are now part and parcel of a varied repertoire of techniques, applied to the most diverse types of information. What has remained is a predilection for questions that lend themselves to *precise* quantitative answers. And hand in hand with that is the attempt to account for what goes into the memory. The possibility of a numerical comparison of inputs with outputs, as the material we have learned and reproduced has since come to be called, remains a self-evident requirement of memory research.

The price paid for this approach has been that topics difficult to access by experiments and measurement were kept off the research agenda, either temporarily or for good, with crucial repercussions on research into autobiographical memory. Our personal fortunes do not happen to be recorded first in a notebook, nor do they have the ease in use of 'bif' or 'kad'. Under normal circumstances, memories cannot be expressed as ratios, simply because one half of the equation is missing.

It was not until the 1970s that a counter-current emerged. It would be taking us too far afield to outline the background of that turn of events, but one important factor was the disturbingly great distance between the topics in which the main stream of memory research was interested and the questions that can arise concerning the operation of memory in everyday life. Investigators such as Loftus, Neisser, Baddeley, Rubin, Conway, and in Holland Wagenaar, shifted their attention to topics which Neisser classified as 'everyday memory', that is, the working of the memory under natural conditions. The most striking expression of the new approach was the speedy increase in research into autobiographical memory.

The unexpected irony of this development is that experimental methods, once applied to autobiographical memory, should have turned out to be so productive. To take a few examples: the psychologists Crovitz and Schiffman wondered if Galton's method of eliciting associations could not be slightly adapted to their own research. They presented just under a hundred students with twenty words, together with a request that they note down the first memory each word evoked and date it as closely as possible. The result was that the frequency of memories was found to decrease regularly with time: most of the memories were of very recent events, expressed in terms of hours and days; thereafter the number decreased rapidly. Crovitz and Schiffman wrote that in view of the age of their experimental subjects, no meaningful comparisons with Galton's own results were possible, but viewed in retrospect this turned out to be one of the major surprises of their experiments: their twenty-year-olds did *not* hark back to 'old' memories. Crovitz and Schiffman's study was published in 1974 in the *Bulletin of the Psychonomic Society*, the focus more or less of quantitative and experimental psychology. Their article marked the beginning of what has become known as the 'Galton cuing technique', nowadays a frequently used experimental approach to autobiographical memory.

Another example is Wagenaar's 'diary study'. At the age of thirty-seven, Wagenaar began to study his own memory, a project that would take him six years to complete. Every day he recorded one event in his personal life, noting *what* had happened, *who* had been involved and *where* and *when* it had occurred. He also recorded on a five-point scale his own emotional involvement and to what extent the events recorded had been remarkable or pleasant. In addition he put down one critical detail that had to serve as a test of whether or not he really remembered the event. Between 1979 and 1983 Wagenaar assembled 1,605 brief reports of personal happenings. A year later, he chose one of the cues – who, where or when – at random and tried to recall the event. If he did not succeed with just one cue he picked a second and if necessary a third, until he could remember the incident. Wagenaar – like Galton and Ebbinghaus before him – found this part of the experiment tiresome. He could cope at most with five events a day, which explains why he took a whole year over the experiment. Among the cues, 'who was involved' and 'where' proved the most effective; 'when' was of little use. However important dates may be in social terms, in the memory they turned out to be of small weight. Wagenaar noticed that, in the short term, he remembered pleasant events better than unpleasant ones, but that this difference was lost with time. Forgetting – defined as the number of cues he needed to recall an event – seemed to reflect a rule that had been known since Ebbinghaus: in the beginning one forgets relatively much more than one does later on; even with autobiographical memory, the curve dips steeply at first, later to level off. An important difference, Wagenaar noted, was that Ebbinghaus had as good as forgotten his syllables after a month, while he himself was able to reproduce every event in the long run, be it with great difficulty and with the help of others who had been present.

Thus research into autobiographical memory combines the oldest with the newest findings. It employs methods originating in the nineteenth century, but processes the results with the most advanced statistical methods. It is based on questions that were being asked even before the rise of experimental psychology but have since been assigned a firm place in research. That the results cannot always be expressed in decimals is inevitable. Anyone studying memories, in the old, common, full significance of the word, is dealing with what Ebbinghaus had been forced to sacrifice for the sake of accuracy, namely meaning and content.

## Why life speeds up as you get older

Autobiographical memory is our most intimate companion. It grows up with us. It behaves differently when we are five, or fifteen or sixty, though the changes are so gradual that we hardly notice them. The questions thrown up by autobiographical memory must be fitted on to a time axis – in life as well as in this book. Between our first memories and the forgetfulness of old age, between the formation of the memory and the erosion of memories, between the not yet and the no longer being able to remember, lie questions that are bound to arise in each one of us, simply *because* we have a memory. It is impossible *not* to look astonished at something that has been our companion all our life. The answers must be sought in a form of research that is rapidly growing in scale, enthusiasm and scope – the study of autobiographical memory.

But not there alone. For many psychologists – and I am no exception – it has become second nature to give preferential treatment to questions suited to the instruments at our disposal. The experiments are designed accordingly, along with the questionnaires, the measurements of associated physiological and neurological processes, and also more recently such representational techniques as the

PET-scan and a handful of other instruments. These methods define the limits of our field of study. What lies outside is something we prefer not to bother with. It does not fit into our type of research.

At least that was our initial reaction.

*Why Life Speeds Up As You Get Older* is an attempt to resist that reaction. Much of what we experience with our memory is played out on a timescale admitting of no experimental research. Some phenomena are too fleeting to be recorded. Déjà vus suddenly appear, and by the time you realize that you are having one, the wonderful sensation of repeating part of your life has gone again. By contrast, the illusion that time speeds up as you get older is far too protracted a phenomenon: it is not possible to conduct experiments covering the entire scale of a human life. Yet other experiences occur under conditions that do not allow of experimental research. Some people who have suddenly found themselves in a life-threatening situation report later that they saw a whole series of images flash by. How could that sort of thing possibly be tested under laboratory conditions? The dilemma is clear: either one puts such questions to one side, or else the answers are sought outside the experimental sphere. My own choice is reflected in the title of this book. Even where direct experimental research is impossible, one can often collect data that provide at least part of the answer. Sometimes the answer cannot be found in psychology alone: neurologists and psychiatrists have also written about memories, as have writers and poets, biologists and physiologists, historians and philosophers. Sometimes the findings transcend the bounds of *contemporary* psychology, and it is the colleagues preceding Ebbinghaus who, in all innocence and with no other resources than their personal experiences and observations, have written on questions that will no longer be encountered in a modern research programme.

In an introduction, reader and writer face in opposite directions. For the reader, the book lies in the future, for the writer it lies in the past. In retrospect, this writer can see that his book has turned out more in the spirit of Galton than of Ebbinghaus, and that 'old' associations often led his thoughts back to the early years of psychology. It is for this reason that *Why Life Speeds Up As You Get Older* has itself become the expression of a reminiscence effect. A lovely time was had by all.

## BIBLIOGRAPHY

Benschop, R., and D. Draaisma, 'In pursuit of precision: the calibration of minds and machines in late nineteenth-century psychology', *Annals of Science* 57 (2000) 1, 1–25.

Crovitz, H. F., and H. Schiffman, 'Frequency of episodic memories as a function of their age', *Bulletin of the Psychonomic Society* 4 (1974), 517–18.

Ebbinghaus, H., *Über das Gedächtnis*, Leipzig, 1885.

Galton, F., 'Psychometric experiments', *Brain* 2 (1879), 149–62.

Nooteboom, C., *Rituals*, translated by Adrienne Dixon, Baton Rouge, 1983.

Schulze, R., *Aus der Werkstatt der experimentellen Psychologie und Pädagogik*, Leipzig, 1913.

Traxel, W., and H. Gundlach (eds.), *Ebbinghaus-Studien* 1, Passau, 1986.

Wagenaar, W. A., 'My memory: a study of autobiographical memory over six years', *Cognitive Psychology* 18 (1986), 225–52.

# 2    Flashes in the dark: first memories

We shall have to wait and see if our life ends with memory loss; what is certain is that it starts with it. Most people date their first memories back to somewhere between the ages of two and four, although there are extensions in both directions. And these first memories do not mark the end of that memory loss; rather they emphasize it. They are snatches, disconnected images; not only does nothing precede them but often nothing follows them for a long time either. 'In probing my childhood', Nabokov wrote in *Speak, Memory*, 'I see the awakening of consciousness as a series of spaced flashes, with the intervals between them gradually diminishing until bright blocks of perception are formed, affording memory a slippery hold.'

But where does the darkness between the flashes come from? The memory of three- or four-year-olds, who have already learned and remembered all manner of things, seems to work well enough. It is at this very age that their vocabulary explodes. They chatter non-stop about what has happened to them, and their reactions tell us that they think about their experiences and that some incidents have made a great impression upon them. For children, the past is still a very long and undifferentiated 'yesterday', but there is no doubt that they remember it. And yet, within a few years almost all these memories have disappeared and nothing but flashes in the dark remain.

Freud called this form of memory loss 'infantile amnesia'. In his scheme, 'infantile' ran from birth to the age of six or seven. It is the kind of term that originally had a neutral, technical significance, but assumed other connotations in everyday speech. The standard term today is childhood amnesia. Freud held that we disregard it far too easily: 'There has not, in my opinion, been enough astonishment over this fact.' For if it is true that the first years are crucial for the development of an individual, why is it that we later forget them almost completely? Freud was the first to pose this question clearly; it is one that has stimulated research since the beginnings of psychology – the first investigation dates back to 1895 – and has never lost its appeal. The various fashions and schools in psychology that have emerged during the last century are all reflected in the different theories on childhood amnesia.

Most of the research, incidentally, has been devoted to the flashes, not the darkness. The reason for this is obvious: we hope that the nature of our first memories may throw some light on the causes of our memory loss. For Nabokov there was no doubt that his first recollections and the gradual piercing of the dark were linked to the dawn of some awareness of time. It must have happened on a day in August 1903, he recalled in *Speak, Memory*, on his mother's birthday. A scene bathed in sunlight. Flanked by his parents, he was walking down a lane on their country estate near St Petersburg. He had learnt to count a little and had just asked about his own age and that of his parents. As he took in the replies, the realization that he was four and that his parents had ages just like him caused 'a tremendously invigorating shock'. 'At that instant, I became acutely aware that the twenty-seven-year-old being, in soft white and pink, holding my left hand, was my mother, and that the thirty-three-year-old being, in hard white and gold, holding my right hand, was my father.' It was as if until that moment his parents had been present incognito in his vague infantile world. For several years afterwards, 'I remained keenly interested in the age of my parents and kept myself informed about it, like a nervous passenger asking the time in order to check a new watch.'

## A bowl of ice

In 1895, the French psychologist Victor Henri and his wife Catherine had a questionnaire on first memories printed in five of the leading international psychological journals. It was the first attempt to gather adequate material for a comparative study. The replies were to be sent to Leipzig, where Victor was studying with Wilhelm Wundt. A year later, the Henris published their findings in *L'Année Psychologique*. They had received 123 replies, including seventy-seven from Russia (where a professor of philosophy at the University of St Petersburg had asked his students to participate in the work) and thirty-five from France. The number of replies from Britain and the United States was negligible. One hundred people wrote that they could identify a specific memory as their first; twenty respondents had two or three early recollections and could not tell which of them was the earliest. The Henris started by tabulating the age at which the first memory had occurred. One individual wrote that at the time he was less than one year old. From eighteen months on, the figure increased rapidly. The peak came after the second birthday. Roughly 80 per cent of first recollections occurred between the second and fourth years, although it was not unusual for a first memory to date from the ages of five, six or even seven. With most respondents, there was a fairly long interval between their first and a second or third memory – sometimes as much as a year. Only from about the age of seven or more did memories begin to combine into coherent stories, with a clear sequence and direction. Often the beginning was marked by an event that could be dated, such as 'when we moved to X' or 'when I went up to Form Y'.

The Henris also kept an account of the emotions that were reportedly connected with first memories. The largest category mentioned happiness or elation (10 times). Next came distress (6) and pain (6). Surprise (5), too, was mentioned as the first memory, and so were feelings of fear of being left alone (5 in all). Shame, regret, curiosity and outrage were each mentioned once or twice. A classification of first recollections of particular events demonstrated that the birth of a baby brother or sister made a great impression (6). The second-largest category was connected with deaths (5). A visit seems to have given rise to as many first memories as sickness or fire (4). Brightly lit festive celebrations (3) were also mentioned, more often, in fact, than the first attendance at school (2).

First recollections, the Henris noted, were almost invariably described as pictures, not as smells or sounds. People remembered the appearance of others, sometimes even every word they had spoken, but not their voices; they recalled the lights at parties, not the music; the panic after an accident, not the screams. Among all the recollections there was just one connected with a sound. One respondent remembered that she was playing with her dolls when she heard that she had a little sister. The news had come by letter, her father had read it out to her and told her that the little girl was called Hortense. Every time she recalled the event, the sound of that name would resound in her memory.

Shortly after the Henris' investigation, several reports of similar studies were published. The American psychologist F. W. Colegrove interviewed a hundred predominantly older people and came to the conclusion that first recollections are mainly of a visual kind. He was struck by the fact that memories of smells were few and far between, even later in life. In a survey about the early memories of a hundred students, Elizabeth Bartlett Potwin found the same overrepresentation of visual memories. In almost all first recollections, she established further, the subject appeared as someone who had done or experienced something, not as a spectator. The particular merit of such surveys is that they constitute an inventory and a classification of first memories. The Henris, too, did not process their material to any extent, so that we cannot tell whether responses such as surprise predominate in early or in late first memories, or how the frequency of first memories of given events is related to the frequency of the events themselves. Nor did they state whether young respondents report other or earlier first memories than older respondents. However, in the margin of their report they made two important comments. The first was that many respondents saw themselves in their recollections. 'I am standing by the edge of the sea and my mother takes me in her arms; I am watching this scene as if standing outside it.' Or, 'I can see myself during my illness like someone who is standing outside.' 'One *sees* oneself as a child', the Henris concluded. 'One sees something in which a child appears and one *knows*: I am that child.' The second important comment was that not all first memories involve strong emotions; it seemed almost inexplicable why some incidents were recalled while other events from the same period, far more visually striking perhaps for children, were completely forgotten. A professor of philology wrote that one of his first recollections was of standing before a laid table with a bowl of ice on it. It was at about the time that his grandmother died. His parents told him that he had been very upset. He could remember none of that: neither the funeral, nor his parents' grief, only the bowl of ice. Both of these comments by the Henris attracted the attention of a reader in Vienna.

## The difference between *m* and *n*

A twenty-four-year old man reported the following scene as his first memory: 'He is sitting in the garden of a summer villa, on a small chair beside his aunt, who is trying to teach him the letters of the alphabet. He is in difficulties over the difference between $m$ and $n$ and he asks his aunt to tell him how to know one from the other. His aunt points out to him that the $m$ has a whole piece more than the $n$ – the third stroke.' So much for his recollection, an innocent scene when he was four; nothing special about it. But why does he happen to recall so trivial an incident? Is the banal character of the recollection not an indication that something important had been swept under the carpet? The real significance of the scene only came to light when it became clear that this memory was symbolic of 'another of the boy's curiosities. For much as he had tried to fathom the difference between $m$ and $n$, so he tried later to discover the difference between boys and girls.' He then discovered 'that the difference was a similar one – a boy, too, has a whole piece more than a girl; and at the time when he acquired this piece of knowledge he called up the recollection of that parallel curiosity of his childhood'.

This is what Freud said.

As early as March 1898, shortly after he had read the Henris' article, Freud suggested in a letter to his friend Wilhelm Fliess that the forgetfulness of the first years of life had the same cause as the formation of neurotic symptoms; its purpose was to prevent painful memories and impulses from reaching our consciousness. He elaborated this idea at various times in lectures, articles and books, beginning in 1899 with his paper called 'Screen memories'. The example of the little boy with his aunt comes from *The Psychopathology of Everyday Life*. What we take for our first recollection is in reality a much later reconstruction, a radically edited version. That, according to Freud, follows from the very fact that we see ourselves in the memory, as the Henris specified. We could never have witnessed the incident in that form, so that the recollection cannot be considered a faithful reproduction of a real event. Equally suspect is the fact that so many of our early recollections 'cannot justify their survival'. They are often so commonplace and insignificant that we wonder why the memory should take the trouble to hang on to them. On closer investigation, or more precisely after psychoanalysis, it emerged that these memories serve to cover up other memories – they are 'screen memories'. Like dreams, they have a predominantly visual character. They are linked to the repressed recollections by associative processes. Freud's interleaved copy of *The Psychopathology of Everyday Life* contained a sheet of paper with notes on the origin of such associations. Thus ice, he explained, 'is in fact a symbol by antithesis for an erection: something that becomes hard in the cold instead of – like a penis – in heat (in excitation). The two antithetical concepts of sexuality and death are frequently linked through the idea that death makes things stiff. One of the Henris' informants instanced a piece of ice as a screen memory for his grandmother's death.'

That is not, of course, how the Henris' unsuspecting informant put it at the time, but the example makes clear what Freud himself meant. A three- or four-year-old child is an intensely sexual being. It demands, desires, seeks satisfaction and pleasure; in later years, when the impulses have been subjected to personal and social control, the recollections of that phase are found to be painful and shaming so that our consciousness puts up a screen to protect itself. The few memory snatches that manage to escape that memory loss and to enter consciousness owe it to their ostensibly innocent nature: the aunt pointing out to him that the *m* has an extra stroke, a bowl of ice.

It is remarkable – but also characteristic of Freud's relaxed treatment of the evidence – that he treated as hard evidence what the Henris' presented as an exception. According to the Henris, first memories were, in the great majority of cases, bound up with events that had evoked strong emotions; in only a few persons did a first recollection bear upon something unimportant. Later investigations, such as those by Blonsky (1929), the Dudychas (1933) and Waldfogel (1948), have confirmed this view. The study by the Muscovite educationalist Blonsky was a direct response to the psychoanalytic explanation of memory loss – his own findings pointed more or less in the opposite direction. Blonsky collected 190 first memories from his students and elicited another eighty-three first memories from children aged about twelve. The children had earlier first memories than the students, who were aged between twenty and thirty; it seemed as if during the first ten years of their life all recollections of what had happened before the subjects were three had vanished, and during the next ten years, of what had happened to them between the ages of three and five as well. But what in particular surprised Blonsky was the high percentage of recollections of menacing situations. The most powerful 'mnemonic factor', as he called it, was fear, or shock. Almost three quarters of the first memories were bound up with frightening experiences – being left alone, losing sight of their mother in a busy market, getting lost in a wood, coming face to face suddenly with a large dog, being left alone at home when a storm broke. The next most powerful mnemonic factor was pain, the first recollection in that case being of falling out of bed, having one's tonsils removed, being burnt or being bitten. (The accidents mentioned in the older surveys help to date them: nineteenth-century children still fall out of their nanny's arms; half a century later they fall off a swing, and nowadays recollections are being stored of what future investigators will perhaps consider a typical domestic accident, tumbling off a jungle gym.) Starting from first recollections, Blonsky showed that children have a good memory for situations causing fear, shock and pain. Quite a few adults attributed their fear of dogs or storms to their first memories, as if the acute shock they felt then had been turned into a less violent but chronic form of anxiety.

Such findings, Blonsky contended, cannot be reconciled with Freud's conception of memory loss; rather do they bear out the evolutionary theory that the human memory helps self-preservation. To avoid painful, dangerous and alarming situations in the future, we have to remember them. In no way are they pushed into the unconscious to dissolve in the darkness of memory loss; on the contrary, they are often among the very first images our memory has stored. Nor is there much that can be called symbolic in the pictures: the association between your present-day fear of dogs and the recollection of the dog that flew at you when you were four does not call for any psychoanalytic interpretation. Many first recollections are simply too nasty to be considered credible screen memories.

In *Histoire de ma vie* (1855), Georges Sand writes about her first memory. The incident must have taken place in 1806: 'I was two years old, a nursemaid dropped me from her arms onto the corner of a chimney-piece, I was frightened and had a cut on my forehead. This blow, which shook my nervous system, made me feel that I was alive, and I clearly saw, and still see, the reddish marble of the chimney-piece, blood, and the shocked expression of my nanny.' This recollection fits into what Blonsky considered the biggest category of our memories: fear, pain, dismay, the very opposite of the insignificant, innocent recollections that, according to Freud, escape from memory loss. The fact that such first memories, like that of Georges

Sand and of the majority of Blonsky's respondents, should have such disastrous consequences for Freud's theory of infantile memory loss reflects a hidden irony. Until the last quarter of the nineteenth century, 'trauma' was a strictly medical term. It meant what it still means in the traumatology department of a hospital: a physical injury or wound. But in everyday parlance, trauma has shifted from general medicine to psychiatry and psychology. Nowadays, it refers to a psychological injury, a mental scar. Freud played a large part in that shift: he psychologized traumas. Thanks to him, many people have come to share the idea that memories of traumatic events can be pushed out of consciousness as an aid to self-preservation. The same repressive mechanism, according to Freud, serves as the basis of memory loss in infancy. The irony is that so many first recollections appear to involve injuries, accidents, wounds, bruises, burns, bites – events, in short, that are traumatic in the nineteenth-century sense of the word. Far from being repressed, they happen to be the very first recorded autobiographical memories.

## The language of first memories

Few of the students of education who took part in Blonsky's survey can be alive today. If they were, they would be in their nineties, further removed than ever from their first memories. Theirs are not just pictures of their personal life, but also reflect the circumstances in which they arose. These subjects used to be children who shared with their parents and siblings the thrill of listening to the first radio broadcasts. No less nostalgic is the fact that Blonsky introduced a special category of first memories of 'exciting things that father does': he talks about infinitely great numbers; he turns up suddenly with a jet-black dog; he keeps a strange collection of red pencils in the drawer of his desk; at night he plays the violin in the quiet house.

Anyone reading more recent studies of first memories will come across further examples, different categories, different analyses, but above all a completely different methodological approach. In the modern literature, the traditional questionnaires have made way for questions the answers to which can be verified and quantified. The results are expressed in graphs, in histograms and curves that were completely absent from the work of the Henris and of Blonsky and were few and far between before the sixties. The memories themselves have all but disappeared, what remains of them sometimes reduced to a short list of keywords in a note. Many studies examine the 'reliability' of first memories, their 'validity', as it is called in Anglo-Saxon literature; experimental psychologists use the same term when judging whether a test measures what it sets out to do.

According to the psycholinguist Katherine Nelson, the results of the older studies, with such methods as lists of questions and interviews, have retained their validity. Studies allowing the examination of first memories reflect, by and large, the same age patterns and types of recollection. The study by the psychologists Usher and Neisser is a model of research, using, as it were, the opposite approach: they first identified four events that could be clearly dated and verified – the birth of a brother or sister, admission to a hospital, the death of a family member, moving house – and went on to analyse the recollections of these events with the help of a questionnaire. Their subjects had to answer seventeen questions, such as, 'Who looked after you during your mother's confinement?', 'Who told you that it was a boy or a girl?', 'Where did you first see the baby?', 'Who fetched your mother from hospital?' Though one event elicited somewhat 'earlier' recollections than another (early for birth and admission to hospital, late for deaths and moving house), the general pattern nevertheless turned out to be what was already known from the earlier studies: memories before the second year of life are extremely rare; for most children their first memory does not appear before their third year or later. Once formed, first memories seemed – after enquiries from relatives – to remain pretty accurate. The question of the 'reliability' of first recollections, moreover, is not always relevant: the recall of an incident that, according to others, was quite different, is a recollection for all that.

It is, for that matter, an established fact that first memories can be completely unreliable. Jean Piaget, the Swiss developmental psychologist, was fortunate enough to have an exciting first memory going back to his second year. 'I was sitting in my pram', he recalled, 'which my nurse was pushing in the Champs Elysées, when a man tried to kidnap me. I was held in by the strap fastened around me while my nurse bravely tried to stand between me and the thief. She received various scratches, and I can still see vaguely those on her face.

Then a crowd gathered, a policeman with a short cloak and a white baton came up, and the man took to his heels. I can still see the whole scene, and can even place it near the tube station.' When Jean was about fifteen, his parents received a letter from his former nurse. She wrote that she had been converted to the Salvation Army and wanted to confess her sins from the past. She had made up the story of the robbery, faking the scratches. The nurse returned the watch that she had received as a reward for her brave defence. Apparently Jean had heard the story as a child and transformed the scene silently into a memory. It became, in Piaget's own words, 'a memory of a memory, but false'.

First memories cannot always be separated from stories circulating in the family. In an autobiographical novel by Nicolaas Matsier, the narrator, Tjit, tells us about an incident; he is unable to decide whether it is his first memory – as he himself would like to think – or an anecdote, told many times by his mother. In the first version, the memory, he is standing in the doorway; the milkman has just poured three measuring jugs into his mother's pan and while she is going back inside to fetch the money, the milkman says:

'Well, now, my boy. And what is your name?'
I look him straight in the face.
'Hendrik.'

When his mother has paid, she shuts the door and says, flabbergasted, 'Hendrik?' In his mother's version, however, it was not the milkman but the grocer and she did not go back into the house in order to fetch money but to find out what she needed. A little while later, the narrator is no longer certain about what happened: didn't his mother's version actually take place in the grocer's *shop* in Noorderhoofd Street?

This sort of confusion is quite frequently to be found with first memories, and for that matter with later memories as well. But the same confusion between story and recollection also focuses attention on one factor that, according to Nelson, is essential for the formation of autobiographical memory. The first recollections and the gradual diminution of childhood amnesia coincide with the development of linguistic skills. The vocabulary grows rapidly in size. Children begin to grasp grammatical connections and to make use of them. They learn that a verb in the past tense refers to something that has already happened. The ability to talk about past events has the same effect as repetition: it increases the chance of remembering such events. Nor does that always have to take the form of telling others: in her study of 'crib talk', the babbling of toddlers before they fall asleep, Nelson noticed that they like to tell themselves what they have been experiencing. Together with the development of language – and partly as a result – other abstracting skills, too, are helped to mature. Children begin to arrange their experiences in categories. They form memories that relate to similar experiences and not to particular events.

The effect of these developments on autobiographical memory is twofold. Many recollections and particular events become fitted into schemes and routines. A toddler who is taken to the zoo for the first time on his third birthday is likely to have vivid memories of the visit for some time. But if the same toddler returns to the zoo a few months later with his grandparents, and for the third time still later during a school outing, his memories of the separate visits will fuse into a general impression of 'going to the zoo'. The formation of more abstract schemes thus has an erasing effect on memories. In this respect, autobiographical memory in early life behaves no differently from the way it does in later years, when memories of – say – holidays in Brittany merge unnoticed into more or less general images of small harbours, bays, walks along the cliffs and striped jerseys. However, the same process also conjures up its opposite: what is stored up all the better is the deviations, the exceptions, the surprises. The crucial point in this explanation is that our first memories demand a background of repetition and routine – something that does not occur until about the third year of life.

Childhood amnesia has often been attributed to neurological causes. The human brain – and in particular the hippocampus, which studies of lesions have shown to be essential for the memory – is thought to be still so immature during the first years of life that it cannot possibly retain the traces of early experiences. The fact that children actually can remember much from a very early age is hard to reconcile with this neurological explanation, while it is a prelude in the explanation proffered by Nelson: *memories are present in fact* but they are later absorbed into more abstract structures and can then no longer be recalled individually. Childhood amnesia is due not to inadequate wiring or some other 'hardware' problem, as psychologists liked to put it in the eighties, but to the programs, to the 'software'.

The fact that later abstractions rob memories of some of their power, ultimately causing them to disappear altogether, is something that has been alluded to earlier, albeit not in a psychological journal. In the spring of 1939, two years before her death, Virginia Woolf started her autobiography, *A Sketch of the Past*. The book was published posthumously. Her sister Vanessa had told her to start writing her memoirs in good time, unlike the unfortunate Lady Strachey, who at a ripe old age started her autobiography, *Some Recollections of a Long Life*, but did not manage to write more than a dozen pages. Virginia began with the beginning: her first memory. 'This was of red and purple flowers on a black ground – my mother's dress; and she was sitting either in a train or in an omnibus, and I was on her lap. I therefore saw the flowers she was wearing very close, and can still see purple, red, and blue, I think, against the black; they must have been anemones, I suppose.' A bit further on in her *Sketch* there is another memory ('which also seems to be my first memory'), of herself lying in bed in the nursery of their holiday home in St Ives, listening to the sound of the waves breaking on the beach. The odd thing about the two memories, Virginia Woolf wrote, was that they were so simple: 'Perhaps this is characteristic of all childhood memories; perhaps it accounts for their strength. Later we add to feelings much that makes them more complex, and therefore less strong; or if not less strong, less isolated, less complete.' It is precisely these additions, as a result of which these memories are rendered less independent, which increase the chances of their disappearance as memories.

## The veil and the kiss

Explanations of early memory loss can be put into two groups. The first contends that no memories at all are stored during the first years of life. The hypothesis that the brain is still immature at the time and does not preserve lasting traces is one example, and so is the hypothesis that language is needed for storing memories. The second group contends that though memories are stored, they later become inaccessible. Different theories point to different causes of this inaccessibility. According to Freud, early memories are repressed; according to others they become inaccessible owing to fusion with general, schematic conceptions or because the way in which an adult perceives and interprets reality differs too radically from the perception and interpretation of a toddler for any later associations to lead back to these early memories. The world seen at knee height has disappeared. Even if an adult returns to a room left unchanged since he was a small child, that room is no longer the room it used to be. The interior with chair legs at eye level and tables that have nothing but an underside has vanished.

The most recent explanation of the veil drawn over the first few years places the cause in the child's lack of self-consciousness. As long as there is no 'I' or 'self', experiences simply cannot be stored as personal recollections. The psychologists Mark Howe and Mary Courage believe that a young child must first accumulate a critical mass of insights about itself as a separate 'I' before it can develop something like an autobiographical memory. A memory without an 'I' is as unthinkable as an autobiography without a leading character. The first indications that self-consciousness is beginning to dawn in a child can only be observed well after the first birthday. Children at a very young age react to their image in a mirror; they reach out for it and smile and babble at it. As they approach their first birthday, they get an inkling of the properties of mirrors and begin to turn round for the objects they see in the glass. But it is only when they are about eighteen months old that they grasp that they themselves are being reflected in the mirror; it is only then that they reach out in surprise for their *own* nose in their mirror image when the nose has secretly had a smear of rouge applied to it. Tests with Bedouin children who have never seen themselves in a mirror before the experiment demonstrate that experience with mirrors makes no difference. It is also not until they are about eighteen months old or even later that children can point to themselves in a photograph. If the child's development is slowed down – for instance owing to a mental handicap or to autism – a delay in self-recognition inevitably follows. Only at a mental level of eighteen months, regardless of calendar time, does a child develop an understanding of itself as an 'I'.

Another indication of self-awareness is the use of the words 'I' and 'me'. These are the first personal pronouns a child makes its own, followed a few months later by 'you'. But the correct use of these words is complicated. In just the way as a place that was 'there' changes into 'here' when the child walks up to it, so 'I' and 'you' keep changing with the speaker's perspective: the same two-year-old is 'I' when he says something and 'you' when somebody says something to him. The fact that there are many people in the world who are also 'I' is equally confusing. The correct use of these pronouns presupposes a grasp of the difference between oneself and others. Almost all children have solved the problem by the time they are nearly two and can distinguish 'I', 'you' or 'me' at any given moment.

Only if there is an 'I' that combines experiences into the memories of one person can an autobiographical memory develop. Once opened, the record will go on to comprise the entries of someone who is author and leading character combined. What the hypothesis of Howe and Courage has in common with that of Nelson is that it is not the memory itself which changes, but the way in which memories are arranged and stored. Questions of priority – does self-knowledge give rise to autobiographical memory or vice versa? – are of secondary importance; they are processes that lack a clear beginning, that do not proceed in one direction and whose predominant direction may even be impossible to determine. What is certain is that in many autobiographical texts the first memory is linked to an understanding of one's own identity. For Nabokov, the first flash in the dark was the discovery that he and his parents were of different ages; that understanding, he wrote, was linked to 'the inner knowledge that I was I and that my parents were my parents'. According to the writer Edith Wharton, her memory emerged simultaneously with 'the birth of the conscious and feminine ego', one bright winter's day in New York. In her autobiography, *A Backward Glance*, she wrote:

> The little girl who eventually became me, but as yet was neither me nor anybody else in particular, but merely a soft anonymous morsel of humanity – this little girl, who bore my name, was going for a walk with her father. The episode is literally the first thing I can remember about her, and therefore I date the birth of my identity from that day.

She had been put into her warmest coat and wore a splendid bonnet of white satin with 'a gossamer veil of the finest Shetland wool'. During the walk her father met his cousin Henry with his son, Daniel. 'The little boy, who was very round and rosy, looked back [at me] with equal interest; and suddenly he put out a chubby hand, lifted the little girl's veil and boldly planted a kiss on her cheek. It was the first time – and the little girl found it very pleasant.'

It could not have begun more charmingly. A veil lifted up like a revelation, a memory that was kissed awake.

## BIBLIOGRAPHY

Blonsky, P., 'Das Problem der ersten Kindheitserinnerung und seine Bedeutung', *Archiv für die Gesamte Psychologie* 71 (1929), 369–90.

Colegrove, F. W., 'Individual memories', *American Journal of Psychology* 10 (1899), 228–55.

Dudycha, G. J., and M. M. Dudycha, 'Some factors characteristic of childhood memories', *Child Development* 4 (1933), 265–78.

Freud, S., *Screen Memories*, translated by J. Strachey, Standard Edition, vol. 3, London, 1974.

 *The Psychopathology of Everyday Life*, translated by J. Strachey, Standard Edition, vol. 6, London, 1974.

Henri, V., and C. Henri, 'Enquête sur les premiers souvenirs de l'enfance', *L'Année Psychologique* 3 (1896), 184–98.

Howe, M. L., and M. L. Courage, 'On resolving the enigma of infantile amnesia', *Psychological Bulletin* 113 (1993), 305–26.

Matsier, N., *Gesloten huis*, Amsterdam, 1994.

Nabokov, V., *Speak, Memory*, London, 1951.

Nelson, K. (ed.), *Narratives from the Crib*, Cambridge, Mass., 1989.

 'The psychological and social origins of autobiographical memory', *Psychological Science* 4 (1993) 1, 7–14.

Piaget, J., *The Child's Construction of Symbols*, London, 1945.

Potwin, E. B., 'Study of early memories', *Psychological Review* 8 (1901), 596–601.

Sand, G., *Histoire de ma vie*, Paris, 1855.

Usher, J. A., and U. Neisser, 'Childhood amnesia and the beginnings of memory for four early life events', *Journal of Experimental Psychology: General* 122 (1993), 155–65.

Waldfogel, S., 'The frequency and affective character of childhood memories', *Psychological Monographs: General and Applied* 62 (1948), 1–38.

Wharton, E., *A Backward Glance*, New York, 1933.

Woolf., V., 'A sketch of the past', in *Moments of Being: Unpublished Autobiographical Writings*, London, 1976, 61–137.

# 3   Smell and memory

Anyone writing about smell and memory, it seems, is obliged to start by taking tea with Marcel Proust. Every treatise on the psychology of smell contains a reference to a scene from *A la recherche du temps perdu*. The depiction is often at the umpteenth hand, three lines long at most and whittled away until almost unrecognizable: the narrator drinks a cup of tea, dunks a piece of cake in it and suddenly the smell takes him back to his youth in Combray. In the original version by Proust, the scene covers a good four pages. His is a subtle, introspective account of the trouble it costs him to come to grips with his feelings. One cold winter's day he comes home feeling depressed. His mother offers him a cup of tea, and one of the small fancy sponge cakes called 'petites madeleines'.

> And soon, mechanically, weary after a dull day with the prospect of a depressing morrow, I raised to my lips a spoonful of the tea in which I had soaked a morsel of the cake. No sooner had the warm liquid, and the crumbs with it, touched my palate than a shudder ran through my whole body, and I stopped, intent upon the extraordinary changes that were taking place. An exquisite pleasure had invaded my senses, but individual, detached, with no suggestion of its origin.

The narrator tries to discover where the sudden delight had come from, but fails in his attempt. He senses that it is somehow connected with the taste of the tea and the cake. He takes another sip and then another, but the third sip tells him even less than the second. 'It is time to stop', he tells himself, 'the potion is losing its magic.' It is as if something in him has been aroused that he has not quite grasped. He puts the cup down. He traces his thoughts back to the moment he sipped the first spoonful of tea. He tries to banish every distraction, every other thought from his mind, holds his hands to his ears so as not to hear noise from the room next door. But all in vain. Then he relaxes and thinks of other things, to allow his concentration to recover, and makes a last attempt. Deep down he feels something 'start within me, something that leaves its resting-place and attempts to rise, something that has been embedded like an anchor at a great depth; I do not know yet what it is, but I can feel it mounting slowly; I can measure the resistance, I can hear the echo of great spaces traversed'. What is trying to emerge, he now feels certain, is the image, the visual memory linked to the taste of the tea and the madeleine. But that image keeps slipping away into the depths of his being, and he has to repeat the experiment no fewer than ten times.

> And suddenly the memory returns. The taste was that of the little crumb of madeleine which on Sunday mornings at Combray (because on those mornings I did not go out before church-time), when I went to say good day to her in her bedroom, my aunt Léonie used to give me, dipping it first in her own cup of real or lime-flower tea. The sight of the little madeleine had recalled nothing to my mind before I tasted it; perhaps because I had often seen such things in the interval, without tasting them, on the trays in pastry-cooks' windows, that their image had dissociated itself from those Combray days to take its place among others more recent; perhaps because of those memories, so long abandoned and put out of mind, nothing now survived, everything was scattered.

The moment the narrator recognizes the taste, other memories come back to him as well. He sees again the little house that had been built onto the back of his aunt's house, the town, the square; he remembers the streets where he ran errands, and the road along which he used to go for walks in good weather.

> And just as the Japanese amuse themselves by filling a porcelain bowl with water and steeping in it little crumbs of paper which until then are without character or form, but, the moment they become wet, stretch themselves and bend, take on colour and distinctive shape, become flowers or houses or people, permanent and recognizable, so in that moment all the flowers in our garden and in M. Swann's park, and the water-lilies on the Vivonne and the good folk of the village and their little dwellings and the parish church and the whole of Combray and of its surroundings, taking their proper shapes

32

and growing solid, sprang into being, town and gardens alike, from my cup of tea.

In the psychology of memory, the 'Proust phenomenon' has come to stand for the ability of smells to call forth early memories. It is often presented as a quick, almost instantaneous process. In that sense, the scene with the madeleine is anything but a Proust phenomenon; it took the narrator a great deal of time to associate his spoonful of tea and the crumbs of the cake with remembered images. What emerged from one moment to the next was the association with a *feeling*, a feeling of delight; the remembered image itself was still a long way in coming. Strange, too, is the fact that the sensation Proust described should have lived on as the classical association between *smell* and memory, when the narrator was actually *tasting*, not smelling, the cake and the tea. This is an understandable mistake. For taste, we have only four receptors – for sweet, sour, bitter and salt; the rest of the taste palette is added by smell. In the main we taste what we smell. On the other hand, some psychologists doubt whether such a thing as a Proust phenomenon really exists. Precisely what it involves is as unclear. Is it primarily *early* memories? Or memories that can only be accessed through smell associations? Or memories we have apparently forgotten? These are small but essential differences in definition, and the results of research into smell and memory are not equally cogent for each of the versions of the Proust phenomenon.

## Fresh sawdust

That smells can evoke youthful memories used to be something of a piece of conventional wisdom long before Proust. Ackerman tells us that Charles Dickens 'claimed that a mere whiff of the type of paste used to fasten labels to bottles would bring back with unbearable force all the anguish of his earliest years, when bankruptcy had driven his father to abandon him in the hellish warehouse where they made these bottles'. Hazy memories such as these bring back not only images but also moods; a sense that one was happy at the time, or that one was not. To assemble a more reliable set of data, the Psychological Laboratory at Colgate University sent out a questionnaire in 1935 to 254 'men and women of eminence', among them writers, scientists, lawyers and ministers. On average they were in their early fifties. The result, published by Donald Laird in *Scientific Monthly*, is a pleasure to read, not least because of all the personal experiences with smells and the memories they evoke. The great majority of the respondents declared that it was smells above all that took them back to their youth. Many reports are similar to the experiences of Dr Walter E. Bundy:

> The smell of fresh sawdust invariably takes me back to the sawmill where my father worked when I was a small boy. The sight of sawdust does not call up these boyhood memories, but the odor of fresh sawdust never fails to reconstruct a series of pictures so graphic that for the moment I live the scenes again. If I try to reconstruct these memories of the sawmill by conscious mental effort, I can locate this object and that, this person and that, in the scene, but the memory thus reconstructed lacks life and is hazy. But the odor of fresh sawdust, especially when the odor reveals its presence, before I have seen the sawdust, calls up the whole picture as real as life itself.

Bundy added that no stimulus breaks his train of thought so abruptly as a smell. This seemed to be a common experience. One of the correspondents wrote that as a young boy he had had much to do with horses and stables. 'At twenty years of age I one day was walking along a country road, and a cart, laden with stable manure, was some 100 yards in front of me. The odor caused a sudden shock of memory of the years of my childhood, which thrilled me into *immobility*.' Some associations last for a lifetime. A seventy-three-year-old Connecticut insurance agent wrote that smells carried him back to his fourth year, 'the time of the occupation of Norfolk [Virginia]'. (A seventy-three-year-old remembering his fourth year in 1935 does indeed take us back to the last year of the American Civil War.) Odours can produce sudden mood swings that strike us as being quite mysterious. 'On the train once', a woman wrote, 'in the midst of happy circumstances, I suddenly felt discouraged, awkward, unhappy. As soon as I recognized the perfume used by a fellow traveller, I saw very vividly a large dancing class, a French dancing master, and felt again my girlish dismay at his attitude toward my poor attempts to learn the steps he was trying to teach me.' Another correspondent was reading a book and suddenly felt overwhelmed by a sense of loneliness. She came to realize that as a child all her books were printed in London, and that English and American print have very different odours. Smells evoke not only incidents or scenes, but also the mood associated with them at the time, indeed the emotional colour of part of one's youth. A woman wrote that the smell of lilacs revived recollections from the years from twelve to eighteen, 'particularly the emotional flavour of those years, with a great deal of its intensity'. The association is generally pleasant, although sometimes unpleasant, but it is never neutral. These are feelings you re-experience with pleasure; some correspondents make sure that they have the smell close to hand. An attorney who grew up in a small mining town in Nevada later moved to a damp and rainy part of the country. From then on he suffered 'a perpetual nostalgia for the sun, warmth, clean air, the peculiar lemon desert fragrances and the great panoramic vistas and strong colours'. When he spent a summer in the Tahoe district he brought home a bunch of sage brush and put it carefully in a receptacle. Each time he smells the sage, 'visual and emotional sensations arise within me in considerable clarity of the desert scene. A slight sniff doubles and redoubles the tranquil nostalgia.'

Various respondents were intrigued by the age of remembered smells. One of them wrote that new associations can arise temporarily, but that ultimately the earliest always reassert themselves. He always associated the smell of wool with his Uncle Lem, who had died when the respondent was a small boy. Uncle Lem had just started to practise as a doctor and was wearing a new woollen overcoat. Later one of the respondent's friends bought just such a coat and the smell of wool became associated with memories of that friend. Later still, the friend acquired his 'own' odour, that of pipe tobacco and cigarettes, and the odour of wool became associated with the familiar smell of Uncle Lem once again. The same respondent suggests that smells which are encountered very frequently – 'as, say, Turkish cigarette odor' – may get associated with so many memories that they cancel each other out. In the long run, he argued, the earliest connection will prevail: 'I believe that men of my age and older are especially apt to recall early memories through odor associations, because the interim associations have become so numerous that they are lumped together and ignored.'

Apart from a mixture of lime-blossom tea and madeleine crumbs, the smells of paste, sawdust, manure, perfume, sage, lilac and wool can call forth emotionally coloured memories. This seems to happen in two ways. Sometimes, as with Proust, it takes two phases. Somebody comes across a smell, often without realizing it, notes a sudden change of mood in himself and, surprised, tries to discover what memory is responsible for the mood. Only if he succeeds in doing that can he associate the odour with a memory. In other cases, it all happens so quickly that there seems to be a direct association between smell and memory, without mood changes as a link between the two. In such memories, smell seems to prevail over all other senses. Whenever sight and smell can both stimulate memories – for instance, a pile of fresh sawdust or a few sprigs of sage – it is smell which has the greater effect; it is not enough to look at the sage, the herb must be smelled. The look of the sawdust is probably not so effective for the same reason that Proust gave for the madeleines he had frequently seen in the pastry-baker's shop: the image may later have become associated with fresh memories and have become isolated from the old association as a result.

## Smell and memory in the laboratory

Are memories that are elicited by smells really older and more vivid? Are they more closely associated with our mood than memories we associate with what we see, hear and feel? Donald Laird's respondents thought just that, but perhaps they were merely giving voice to a prevailing view that did not stand up to closer examination. Laird and his associates did not enquire into the age of the memories or into memories elicited by sense stimuli other than smell. Modern psychologists like to classify personal experiences like those of Laird's respondents (and, indeed, also those of the man who lent his name to the term 'Proust phenomenon') under the heading of 'anecdotal evidence', which commands little respect. For more reliable measurements, tests and comparisons it would be more useful to reproduce the Proust phenomenon in the laboratory, where it can be manipulated experimentally. Attempts to do so have had mixed fortunes.

David Rubin and some of his colleagues presented their subjects with either smells or the name of smells – for instance the smell of mothballs or the word 'mothballs' – as stimuli. All in all they used fifteen stimuli, including the smell of (and the words) coffee, baby powder, mint, peanut butter and chocolate. After every stimulus, the subjects were asked to write down the earliest memories called forth by each odour or word. They were instructed to use a seven-point scale to record how vivid or clear a particular memory was and how pleasant or unpleasant it felt to them, both in the present and at the remembered moment. They also had to record whether or not they saw themselves in the memory – according to Freud, proof of the reconstructed nature of early memories; whether the memory was one that had been recalled previously; and how long ago it was since they had last recalled it. Next, the subjects had to date their memories as closely as possible, in such terms as 'last week', 'last year' or 'when I was ten'.

The experiment was specifically designed to test the Proust phenomenon, and Rubin and his colleagues expected to find that the memories elicited by smells would be more vivid, more pleasant, and – above all – older than the rest. Perhaps, as additional proof of their age, they would be memories in which the experimental subjects saw themselves. But nothing of the sort happened. The only way in which memories of smells differed from the rest was that there was a slightly greater chance that they bore on an event the subjects had not been thinking about recently or that the experiment had made them remember for the first time. As experimental proof of the Proust phenomenon, this was a poor result.

Does the Proust phenomenon really exist? Rubin's tests are no proof that it does *not*. With his experimental set-up, the chance of eliciting Proustian memories was not favourable from the start. Associations between smells and old memories are particularly personal. For one subject the smell of apple pie will call forth memories of Sunday lunch; for another, who grew up next door, it is the smell of plums and custard. The same Sunday feeling, of a hot meal in the middle of the day, can thus be released by various smells. It is unreasonable to blame Rubin for not including these smells on his list, but if the Proust effect exists then his experiment failed to bring it out. Even Proust himself would have done poorly in this experiment. Not

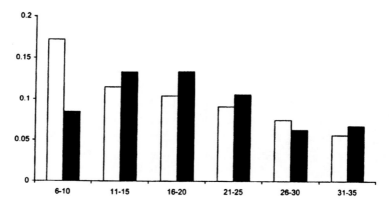

Fig. 2 Histogram of the average share of autobiographical memories by age. The white rectangles represent memories elicited by smells; the black rectangles represent memories elicited by words.

so much because the lime-blossom tea and madeleine were missing, but because it took him so long to recapture the memory that the experiment would have been over before he could start writing about Combray.

The psychologists Chu and Downes were more successful using a different approach. Earlier experiments using the cue word method had shown that older subjects, aged about sixty, brought up a disproportionately large number of memories of their youth and early adult years. This 'reminiscence effect' produces a memory bump between the ages of about fifteen to twenty-five years in histograms representing the percentage of memories by age. Chu and Downes used the same procedure as Rubin: experimental subjects were presented with smells such as vinegar, talcum powder, ink, cough syrup, lavender, or with the names of these smells. The crucial difference between their experiments and Rubin's was the age of the experimental subjects: with Rubin it was about twenty; with Chu and Downes the average was seventy. The results varied markedly. Memories elicited by the names of smells took the form of the reminiscence effect in older subjects: they were overrepresented between eleven and twenty-five years. The distribution had a clear bump, with a rise, a peak and a fall. Matters were different with memories elicited by the smells themselves: a peak between the ages of six and ten and then a gradual fall. That is a considerable shift. From the moment memories exist, that is, directly after the period of childhood amnesia, smells call forth almost twice as many memories in older people as the names of smells.

There is something paradoxical in this finding. In seventy-year-olds the ability to distinguish smells is literally no more than a fraction of the power they enjoyed earlier, a few per cent at most. After the age of twenty, our sense of smell declines drastically – by an estimated factor of two every ten years. The perception threshold keeps getting higher. And yet it is smells that release early memories in older people. According to some authors this is no paradox at all, but rather a part of the explanation. It may well be that the 'old' associations are intact because they are no longer disturbed by fresh impressions. We can smell less and less and that is why that part of our memory remains untouched for forty, fifty or sixty years. Other experiments, too, have shown how obdurate are the traces smells leave in our memory. With almost everything we store in our memory any new addition has a disturbing effect on what was there before. With smells this happens to a much lesser extent. Thus learning to identify a new series of smells has hardly any effect on the smells we learned to identify earlier. Once laid down, the trace persists in the memory for a very long time, perhaps throughout life.

A variant of this explanation is that we cease to encounter certain smells and tastes. Much as some notable cars disappear unheeded from our streets and you only remember them when you happen to spot one still on the road – a Beetle with a split screen for instance – so smells and tastes can vanish from your life, sometimes for a while but sometimes forever. That can happen with such typical baby food as rice pudding with mashed banana and orange juice, but also with dishes that you used to eat perhaps every week as a child and then never again. You left home, or the style of cooking changed or a new range of desserts ousted the familiar old ones almost overnight. With the advent of fruit yoghurts and flavoured custards the smells and tastes of barley gruel, buttermilk porridge, sago and tapioca disappeared. And what certainly did not come back was the taste of your pudding blended with the high tidemark of tomato left in your bowl to remind you of the earlier soup course of the meal. If later, by some curious coincidence, we do encounter the same taste and smell, the old associations prove to have remained intact and lead us effortlessly to early memories.

## The anatomy of olfaction

It sometimes happens that neurological discoveries run in such close parallel with observations made a very long time ago in an entirely different field that a hypothesis which combines both sets of findings may appear ineluctable, not least because the two corroborate each other. That is the case with what is currently the most widely accepted explanation of the Proust phenomenon. Its clarification calls for a few introductory remarks on the evolutionary history of the sense of smell and of the brain.

In evolutionary respects, smell is a primitive sense. It developed from two bulges of the neural tube, the olfactory bulbs. The younger parts of the brain, such as the neocortex, then folded over them. The bulbs account for less than a thousandth part of the total brain volume. The path covered by the smell stimuli between the nasal mucosa and the bulbs is short. High up in the nose lies the olfactory epithelium, two small yellow-brown patches each measuring 1 cm². The olfactory epithelium contains from 6 million to 10 million sensory cells, a number that seems insignificant when compared not only with the 220 million cells of the sheepdog but also with the roughly 200 million light-sensitive cells in the human retina. The olfactory epithelium owes its colour to the cilia of the olfactory cells; in the words of Diane Ackerman, 'they stick right out and wave in the air current like anemones on a coral reef'. The cells of the olfactory epithelium transmit the signal from the stimulus to both bulbs lying close behind it. The connecting nerves run through the perforations of the ethmoid bone. No other sense is as close to the place in the brain where sensory information is analysed. Phrased in anatomical terms, it seems as if two small parts of brain have dropped down into the nose to meet the stimuli.

The pathway following the two bulbs is short and easy to trace. The bulbs have direct links to a deep-seated part of the brain, the limbic system. Other branches – to the neocortex, for instance – are few. The limbic system is also a phylogenetically primitive part of the brain, consisting of a set of structures involved in vigilance and emotions. There are direct links too between the sense of smell and the hippocampus, a structure essential for the storage of memories. Smell is not a particularly speedy sense: following the first distinction

40

between pleasant and unpleasant odours, a moment or two goes by from stimulus to identification, but the route between arrival and storage is short and without any side paths. It is as if the olfactory stimulus, like the suspect of a sensational crime, were being brought to court out of sight of the curious.

The price of this privileged route is lack of contact with the parts of the brain responsible for our grasp and production of speech. Once brought to court, the olfactory stimulus falls silent. Smell is known as the 'silent sense'. Smells are hard to describe, and generally involve references to the objects that produce them. What we can *see* of an orange is readily expressed in words and explained to others: round, orange in colour, some three inches in diameter, small pits in the skin. What we can *smell* of an orange, however, can only be described as an orange odour. More general descriptions of smells, such as sweet or sour, are borrowed from descriptions of taste, or else they refer to reactions to the smell: delightful, disgusting, delicious or dreadful. In the eighteenth century, Linnaeus came up with a classification of the smells plants exude, with the pleasantness or unpleasantness of the smell as his main criterion. His scale ran to seven classes, from aromatic and fragrant, via ambrosial, pungent or garlicky, stinking or goat-like, to repugnant and disgusting. In many descriptions the suffix 'like' does staunch service. An arresting fact is that blind people can identify and name smells better than sighted persons, even though their sense of smell is no more acute. The probable reason is that they find it more difficult to localize the source of the smell and are therefore forced to concentrate on the qualities of the smell itself. All in all, our vocabulary for smells is extremely limited, restricted to the source of the smell, and lacking classification and abstraction. Smelling eschews language.

The formation of autobiographical memory, as we saw in the previous chapter, goes hand in hand with the development of speech. The recording of personal memories seems to call for certain abstracting abilities, perhaps for language itself or perhaps for something that develops as a side effect of language. From the age of three or four the fog of amnesia seems gradually to lift, but even after the 'first memories' it still takes several years before a closer chronological course of memories emerges. The histogram of Chu and Downes is characteristic of the results of most investigations: it is only from about the age of ten that autobiographical memory truly fills out. The same investigators found that, when it comes to memories elicited by smells, a peak occurred several years earlier. The cause might well be that memories from that period owe their presence to the fact that they did not involve the use of language. Thanks to the special 'wiring' of the sense of smell in the brain they are led straight to the hippocampus, and after that they can only be resuscitated along that particular route. This may explain why a smell often conjures up no more than an ambience, a mood difficult to express in words, and that it is not until later, sometimes with a great deal of effort, that we can find the memory responsible. This course of events fits in well with the evolutionary task of the sense of smell: a quick first reaction associating the smell with danger, a sense of wellbeing or tension, followed by the somewhat more time-consuming closer identification. In this view, the Proust phenomenon is a conspiracy between evolution and neurology.

## The faithful persistence of taste and smell

A convincing explanation is to the existence or absence of a certain phenomenon what a motive is to a crime; it must not be confused with a proof. Some psychologists will only accept that there is such a thing as a Proust phenomenon if it can be convincingly demonstrated under laboratory conditions. Their scepticism is not entirely unfounded. Whether smells call forth older memories than other sensory associations can only be established by a comprehensive comparative study. Anyone choosing the right stimuli can access early memories even through other senses. In an autobiographical novel by Nicolaas Matsier, the narrator looks at a photograph of his brother Jan, who died at an early age, smiling and dressed in his striped pullover knitted from left-over scraps of wool. He can see the buttons on the left shoulder. 'On the left shoulder, is that right? Surprised, I put my hands up to the spot and take in the appearance of my forty-seven year old fingers. Yes, now I remember the manoeuvre with which we would worm the last three or four buttons through their loops – you couldn't really call them buttonholes.' Here it is a gesture, a feeling in the fingers that evokes a long forgotten detail from the author's youth. At a jumble sale, the mysterious green light of an old-fashioned radio may suddenly bring the name of the Swiss station 'Beromünster' back to mind. On another occasion a tracing wheel emerges from a needlework box and you see your mother copying patterns from the magazine *Women's Weekly* on the table she has specially cleared for the purpose. The associations are passing, the stimuli accidental. What they have in common is that they can hardly be elicited in experimental ways. They are too fleeting, too personal, too closely bound up with a particular age group or social circle. Conclusions in decimals are unlikely to express the Proust phenomenon.

Not even with Proust does smell hold a monopoly over early memories. Much later on in *A la recherche du temps perdu*, the narrator jumps out of the way of a tram, almost loses his balance, and recalls the asymmetric tiles in a Venetian church he had visited long ago. Or he wipes his lips with a starched napkin and is immediately reminded of the towels in the hotel in Balbec where he spent his summer holidays as a boy. Even so, it was smells that carried the memory back furthest, and that is why the sense of smell always held pride of place in Proust's musings. Directly after the memory of Auntie Léonie's madeleines dunked in tea came back to him, he reflected: 'But when from a long-distant past nothing subsists, after the people are dead, after the things are broken and scattered, still, alone, more fragile, but with more vitality, more unsubstantial, more persistent, more faithful, the smell and taste of things remain poised for a long time, like souls, ready to remind us, waiting and hoping for their moment, amid the ruins of the rest ... '

BIBLIOGRAPHY

Ackerman, D., *A Natural History of the Senses*, New York, 1990.
Chu, S., and J. J. Downes, 'Long live Proust: the odour-cued autobiographical memory bump', *Cognition* 75 (2000), B41–B50.
Delacour, J., 'Proust's contribution to the psychology of memory. The *réminiscences* from the standpoint of cognitive science', *Theory and Psychology* 11 (2001), 255–71.
Laird, D. A., 'What can you do with your nose?', *Scientific Monthly* 45 (1935), 126–30.

Matsier, N., *Gesloten huis*, Amsterdam, 1994.

Murphy, C., and W. S. Cain, 'Odor identification: the blind are better', *Physiology and Behavior* 37 (1986), 177–80.

Proust, M., *Du côté de chez Swann*, 1913. Quoted from *Swann's Way*, translated by C. K. Scott Moncrieff, London, 1922.

Rubin, D. C., E. Groth and D. J. Goldsmith, 'Olfactory cuing of autobiographical memory', *American Journal of Psychology* 97 (1984), 493–507.

Schab, F. R., 'Odors and the remembrance of things past', *Journal of Experimental Psychology: Learning, Memory and Cognition* 16 (1990), 648–55.

'Odor memory: taking stock', *Psychological Bulletin* 109 (1991), 242–51.

Vroon, P., A. van Amerongen and H. de Vries, *Verborgen verleider: psychologie van de reuk*, Baarn, 1994.

# 4    Yesterday's record

When I was about fourteen, I used to play draughts for my school, the Christian High in Leeuwarden. I was not particularly good but I played with great enthusiasm, even if with little expertise or talent. Early on I had drawn unwelcome attention to myself by falling into the opening-move traps which the boys who belonged to a draughts club had been warned about at their first lesson. Our best player was Johan Capelle. He would take the first board, the next-best player would take board number 2, and so on. The weakest ('the weediest') player sat at the lowest board.

One day we were due to play against one of town's higher-grade schools. Their number one board was taken by Harm Wiersma, thirteen years old but already a legend in Friesland. Before we started the match our team leader called us together. He had a plan. 'This Wiersma is so good', he explained, 'that it would be a shame to waste our strongest player on him, because whoever plays him is bound to lose. Johan'll do better taking on their second board.' We allowed the logic to sink in. 'But then, following that argument, the one who, uh ...' someone started; he did not have to finish his sentence. Five or six members of our team turned as one towards me. I went bright red, nodded that I understood and took my seat at the first board.

Why do we have such a horribly good memory for our humiliations?

Ask someone if he can call to mind a moment in which he felt humiliated and you are likely to get an answer so detailed, so graphic, that it is as if his memory had kept a special account of it. Insults are inscribed in indelible ink. They never fade with age. As we grow older they travel with us in time so that hardly a day seems to have passed between the event and its recall.

When, after a long and industrious life, Wilhelm Wundt wrote his autobiography, *Erlebtes und Erkanntes*, at the age of eighty-eight, what he recalled most vividly of his first years at school was being bullied by his classmates. Again, thinking back over his years at high school, he remembered one of the teachers snapping at him, before the entire class, that not every child of educated parents (Wundt came from a family of clergymen and academics) was suited to an intellectual life. Perhaps a career as a postman would show Wilhelm to best advantage. Three quarters of a century later, Wundt still remembered it as if it had happened yesterday.

After years of studying the diary records of his own memory, Wagenaar made a special analysis of recollections of particularly unpleasant events, in which he himself was the prime mover ('my worst sins'). These are events that cause the same red faces as humiliations and in a sense they are just that – affronts to one's self-image. Among the 1,605 events he recorded during the four years of his experiment, there were eleven that fell into this embarrassing category. Wagenaar mentions the time that he loftily reprimanded a woman who had parked her car in front of his house: she turned out to be disabled, with a special permit, and on a visit to his neighbours. The memories in this category proved to be easier to recall than any other types – easier than their opposites, the particularly pleasant memories in which he himself was the prime mover and also easier than the particularly unpleasant memories in which he had not been the prime mover. While Wagenaar tended in general to forget unpleasant memories faster than pleasant ones, his most unpleasant memories seemed to have been carefully retained.

Wagenaar assumed that keen memories of such events played a role in updating our self-image and that our memory is particularly good at storing those events that are hardest to reconcile with our self-image. They ensure that our self-image does not stray too far from the reality. In that sense, our 'worst sins' have a secret productivity, which they share with humiliations. The latter sometimes have an effect that, as it were, guarantees their preservation. Some affronts do more than moderate our self-image – they bring about a critical change in our lives and are then accommodated in the memory with appropriate respect. But even memories of affronts that are not assigned so prominent a place in the review of our life have a few peculiar characteristics.

When people describe affronts, it is as if the events have been stored in the memory in real time. Recalling and reporting them takes just as long as the events themselves: 'This bloke walked in without knocking, came and sat himself down on the edge of my desk, I can see him now, and, cool as a cucumber, he said...' Such memories are reminiscent of the early years of the cinema, when editing to give the story some momentum was still in its infancy. Where the passage of time may sometimes lend shape and meaning to less emotional memories, affronts run like so many early films – Lumières – through the projector of our memory.

The special timescale on which you remember your affronts also gives your body every chance to re-experience the physical reactions you had at the time. I have seen old people flush at an insult they received seventy years earlier. Even after more than half a century people will still tremble with rage or hit the arm of their chair in anger. You cannot talk about truly embarrassing events without wanting to cover up your eyes once again or avert your face from your listener.

There is yet another odd thing about memories of affronts. *You can see yourself.* Recall a humiliation and you will see your own red face, your attempt to hide your feelings of hurt; you will see others laugh and their pitying looks. It is as if you had not recorded the scene yourself but were one of the actors in it. I can still see myself nodding and walking up to the first board. Wundt must have seen himself back at his school desk when he recalled that unsolicited career advice. Anyone feeling humiliated immediately sees himself from the outside.

Perhaps that also explains the vividness of such memories. You have introspective access to the embarrassment, the rage and the confusion, all the feelings you know from the inside and remember as such. But the same event is also stored as a registration of an outside event. The record sets down how others – or so you think – looked at you when it happened to you. Everything is stored in duplicate. In one record the humiliation, in the other the weediest player who took his place at the first board.

## BIBLIOGRAPHY

Wagenaar, W. A., 'Remembering my worst sins: how autobiographical memory serves the updating of the conceptual self', in M. A. Conway, D. C. Rubin, H. Spinnler and W. A. Wagenaar (eds.), *Theoretical Perspectives on Autobiographical Memory*, Dordrecht, 1992, 263–74.

Wundt, W., *Erlebtes und Erkanntes*, Stuttgart, 1920.

# 5  The inner flashbulb

If you are asked where you were on a day five or six years ago chosen at random, say 31 August 1997, what you were doing at the time, whom you were with and what the weather was like, the odds are that you will not be able to come up with the answer. And it is unlikely that you will find such exhortations as 'try and remember, it was a Sunday', or the like particularly helpful. That day, like most days a long time ago, seems to have been consigned to oblivion.

But all that changes with the knowledge that 31 August 1997 was the day on which you heard that Princess Diana had been killed in a car crash. If you think back to that moment, you probably still know who told you the news – a member of your family or a television or radio announcer, and you also remember where you were, who else was there, what you were doing, what your first reaction was, and how the people around you reacted.

Memories not only of the report of an event but also of the setting are known as 'flashbulb memories', an expressive phrase coined in 1977 by the psychologists Brown and Kulik. They observed that on receiving shocking news, people not only remembered the report itself but also details of the circumstances surrounding the report. The classic example is the death of President Kennedy. At every anniversary of the assassination, American newspapers and journals publish articles in which people set down their personal flashbulb memories of the moment when they heard that he had been shot. The genre is so familiar in the American media that light-hearted treatments of the subject also appear: the animals in the forest tell one another where they were when they heard the news that Bambi's mother had been shot.

No doubt the strangest flashbulb memory of Kennedy's death was that of one Derek Waken, a teacher at a boarding school. At the end of the school day he had taken a group of students to the shooting range for practice. After a while, Waken decided to go back to the school to prepare for the next day. Breaking all the rules, he asked the shooting instructor, a young colleague called Cameron Kennedy, to lock up. He gave him the keys to the gun cabinet and the ammunition store and left. When he was back at school working at his desk the door was suddenly flung open. A student yelled: 'Sir! Sir! Kennedy has been shot!' In fear and trembling he ran to the school hall where students and teachers were standing about talking agitatedly. The headmistress walked up to him with a serious face and told him that President Kennedy had been shot. Derek Waken breathed a sigh of relief: 'I still had my job and felt very pleased.'

Although the term 'flashbulb memory' was not coined until 1977, the phenomenon itself is as old as the hills. One of the earliest studies of autobiographical memory appeared in 1899, revealing that the assassination of Abraham Lincoln had had much the same effect: of the 179 people questioned, 127 were able to say where they were and what they were doing when they heard of his death. The reports, recorded in 1899, that is, thirty-three years after the event, all have the characteristics of flashbulb memories. A woman of seventy-six remembered that she was standing by the stove preparing the evening meal when her husband walked in and told her the news. A man of seventy-three: 'I was busy repairing our fence and can even show you the place where I was standing. Mr W. came past and told me. It was about nine or ten o'clock in the morning.' Some people remembered the event almost like an internal film. In slightly abbreviated form:

> My father and I were on the road to A— in the State of Maine to purchase the 'fixings' needed for my graduation. When we were driving down a steep hill into the city we felt that something was wrong. Everyone looked so sad, and there was such terrible excitement that my father stopped his horse, and leaning from the carriage called: 'What is it, my friends? What has happened?' 'Haven't you heard?' was the reply – 'Lincoln has been assassinated.' The lines fell from my father's limp hands, and with tears streaming from his eyes he sat as one bereft of motion. We were far from home, and much must be done, and we finished our work as well as our heavy hearts would allow.

With their flashbulb analogy, Brown and Kulik did not mean to imply that a memory is like a photograph on which you can study all sorts of details well after the event. Rather, they meant that a memory can often comprise, apart from a picture of the circumstances, the sorts of details that, as it were, get on to the photograph by accident, details that would otherwise have been long since forgotten, for instance that the person who brought you the news fiddled nervously with a loose thread in his sweater. It is, Brown and Kulik wrote, as if somewhere in your brain a 'Print now!' mechanism is being activated, one that captures the entire scene indiscriminately.

With some events, such as the assassination of President Kennedy or the death of Princess Diana, this kind of flashbulb seems to light up in people all over the world. There are also events that lead to national flashbulb memories only, for instance the murder of Olaf Palme in Sweden (1986), or the resignation of Margaret Thatcher in Britain (1990). Others again are personal, for instance when you receive bad news about someone you love. In their first investigation, Brown and Kulik examined ten events that seemed to elicit flashbulb memories. These included assassinations such as those of President Kennedy, Robert Kennedy and Martin Luther King, abortive murder attempts such as those on President Ford, and natural deaths such as that of General Franco. Not all these events caused the same number of flashbulb memories. Thus only half the persons interviewed seemed to have a flashbulb memory of the death of Robert Kennedy. The ethnic background of those interviewed – forty black and forty white Americans – seemed also to make some difference.

The murder of the militant black activist Malcolm X produced flashbulb memories in a larger number of black than of white Americans. The same was true of the assassination of Martin Luther King. The difference was greatest in the case of Medgar Evers, a black fighter for equal rights who was shot dead in 1963 by a white racist: not a single white person had a flashbulb memory of that event. With the attempted assassination of President Ford and the death of Franco the proportions were the other way round. At first sight it is curious that the unsuccessful attempt to kill George Wallace, an extreme right-wing politician, should have led to a greater number of flashbulb memories in black Americans than it did in white. The likely explanation is that Wallace's campaigns had more serious and threatening consequences for blacks than they did for whites.

Why does the mechanism responsible for flashbulb memories exist in the first place? Why do we not, as in most things we hear and see, simply remember the report of the event in question? Brown and Kulik looked for the explanation in neurophysiology: the sudden rush of emotion tells the brain to store more details in a short space of time than it normally does. They suggested that the 'Print now!' command is an evolutionary vestige preceding the development of language or other more abstract forms of communication: if you are thrown from one moment to the next into a situation in which you have to absorb information with far-reaching consequences, it is important to remember as many aspects of the situation as possible, if only so as not to finish up in that situation for a second time. What argues against this explanation is that if people end up in a truly life-threatening situation, for instance as victims of an armed hold-up, their vision will often seem to have been narrowed, so that they can later report, say, a nervous rise and fall of their Adam's apple, but not whether or not their attacker was wearing a coat.

Brown and Kulik were unable to assess the reliability of their subjects' flashbulb memories. Yet reliability became the most important aspect of the study following their first publication. Are flashbulb memories really such photographically faithful copies as the analogy suggests? And are they really proof against forgetfulness and distortion? The psychologist Neisser denies both assertions. According to him, flashbulb memories rest not on a special method of encoding information, as the 'Print now!' mechanism suggests, but on the manner in which we process such memories. It is precisely with shocking news and events that there is a good chance that we recall them and discuss them with others. Such repetition ensures that we store the memory carefully away so that we can access it easily in future. The memory is thus not an internal photograph, but rather a story we tell ourselves and others so often that we do not forget it. That, according to Neisser, also explains why the memory gradually assumes the structure of a narrative: where did it happen, who told me about it, who was present, how did I react – the very elements of a well-told story.

Stories, even the stories we tell ourselves, keep changing. Let us look at just one flashbulb memory. In January 1986, when Challenger exploded, Neisser and his colleague Harsch handed a questionnaire to over one hundred students within twenty-four hours of the disaster. The students were asked how they had heard the news, where they had been at the time and what they had been doing. When they were asked again thirty-two months later, considerable differences from their first account were detected, even in the answers to the questions about from whom they had heard the news and who else had been present. A common mistake was that whereas no more than nine persons had stated in their first report that they had seen the news on the television, the number had risen to nineteen in the second report. Clearly the many repetitions of pictures of the exploding Challenger had been interposed into the flashbulb memory. One quarter of the students got all the main facts wrong. Flashbulb memories, Neisser concluded, do not differ from other autobiographical memories, and are as likely to be forgotten.

Martin Conway, one of the best-known researchers of autobiographical memory, disagrees with Neisser's conclusions. In his book, *Flashbulb Memories*, he presents an overview of the studies of flashbulb memories during the preceding ten to fifteen years. What Neisser's theory fails to explain is the persistence of memories of unimportant details, the chance events Brown and Kulik had already remarked upon. There is no doubt that the flashbulb memories associated with personal events, such as women's recollection of their first menstrual period, comprise all sorts of irrelevant but graphic minor details which are absent from other autobiographical memories. And flashbulb memories, Conway writes, strike us more as a coherent whole than 'ordinary' memories, which often consist of part reconstructions and interpretations. Eliciting autobiographical memories is usually a recall of recollections that gradually grow sharper and more complete; flashbulb memories – like photographs, in fact – are at our direct disposal.

It would seem therefore that for once our intuitions are correct. Recalling the moment when we heard of Princess Diana's death, we know again where we were and perhaps even if we were standing, sitting or lying down. All that is included in the image our brain was busy storing away while we digested the news. The internal photograph – or rather, short film – is perhaps not immune to oblivion, but it is certainly more durable than most other memories. What were you doing on 30 August or 1 September 1997?

**BIBLIOGRAPHY**

Brown, R., and J. Kulik, 'Flashbulb memories', *Cognition* 5 (1977), 73–99.

Colegrove, F. W., 'Individual memories', *American Journal of Psychology* 10 (1899), 228–55.

Conway, M., *Flashbulb Memories*, Hillsdale, 1995.

Neisser, U., 'Snapshots or benchmarks?', in U. Neisser (ed.), *Memory Observed: Remembering in Natural Contexts*, San Francisco, 1982, 43–8.

Neisser, U., and N. Harsch, 'Phantom flashbulbs: false recollections of hearing the news about *Challenger*', in E. Winograd and U. Neisser (eds.), *Affect and Accuracy in Recall: Studies of 'Flashbulb Memories'*, Cambridge, 1992, 9–31.

# 6  'Why do we remember forwards and not backwards?'

One of the pleasures of non-computerized literary searches is the chance discovery. You page through an entire year of a periodical, allow your fingers to run through the table of contents, look up various entries in it or in the index, and in the unpredictability of this archaic search process, you come up with an unexpected find, sometimes more valuable than what you were searching for. A short while ago I was riffling through the pages of the 1887 volume of *Mind*, looking for a particular review, when I saw the title of an article flash by: 'Why do we remember forwards and not backwards?' This question produced a kind of intellectual double take: I had already left the library with a copy of the review I had originally come for when the subtlety of the question suddenly struck me and I retraced my steps to read the whole article.

It ran to less than four pages and had been written by Francis Herbert Bradley (1846–1924), an Oxford philosopher of the idealist school. Bradley needed no more than a few paragraphs to demonstrate that you cannot always give a simple answer to a simple question.

The simple answer concerning the direction of our remembering is that your memory replicates the course of events: first there was X, then there was Y, and you might expect to remember them in that order. But on closer inspection it turns out to be not quite so obvious, and that is what made me retrace my steps in the library, for why should the sequence of *retrieving* parallel that of storing events up? When recalling the events you invariably enter from the other side, so to speak: in the filing system of your memory the most recent event lies right on top, like bank statements in a folder, and if you page back you will find Y before X. But why then do we remember forwards and not backwards?

Now, it is an incontrovertible fact that we remember events forwards. I think back to Maradona's second goal against England in 1986, at the World Cup in Mexico. Maradona was in his own half, just outside the centre circle. He received the ball, two English players were on to him in a flash, he made a tight turn, quickly wrong-footing them, and was off towards the penalty area. Driving the ball forward with short flicks of his left foot, he passed two defenders and deceived the goalkeeper into diving the wrong way. Then he shot with his left foot and scored. I can only remember the course of events forwards and am quite unable to let the ball fly from the goal to Maradona's foot or to remember how he – running backwards (but bent over forwards!), followed by the ball rebounding against his feet, side-stepping players who, reversing, slipped away from him – at last reached the place where my memory begins. The video of my memory has no 'playback'. I can, admittedly, using this metaphor, wind the cassette back to an earlier moment in the game, for instance to the 'hand of God', Maradona's 'headed' goal, but if I recall that earlier moment it is again in the form of 'play' in the forward direction. I had never realized this fact before reading Bradley: your memory can admittedly take you backwards and forwards in time, but when reproducing events you can only reconstruct the sequence of your experiences the way they happened.

You can only reverse your memory by way of a thought experiment, and even then you are testing your powers of imagination rather than your memory. No doubt you are helped by having seen films reeled backwards and know what it looks like when someone leaps out of turbulent water waving his arms, leaving a perfectly smooth surface behind him. Remembering backwards is like reversing a car: you can do it, but you realize that cars are not really built for that purpose. Living backwards is the prerogative of poems and novels. In Jan Hanlo's 'We are born', the hearse pulls the horses back by their reins to the mortuary, where the mourners retrace their steps to the gate. A few days later the deceased wakes up in the house of mourning. Once fortified and recovered he starts his work. There is so much to be done: bridges must be demolished, towns razed, coal and oil restored to the ground. The work is stimulating. Food is cooling on the stove. At the end of life school desks stand waiting for us: 'Schools make us forget all we have learned.' However in the poem people simply act and do not speak. As soon as someone begins to speak, the thought experiment of the playback of time can no longer be performed consistently. The most radical attempt to do so is Martin Amis's *Time's Arrow*, a novel that begins with the death of the main character and is then 'told backwards'. Although the dialogue runs backwards, the characters do not produce their words and sentences in reverse order. No one can understand language spoken backwards. Recounting in reverse what someone says, wrote Gerrit Krol in an essay about time, is like a compass needle you have turned the other way. 'But as soon as you let go, it leaps back to the old position. Similarly, every sentence, no matter how you twist and turn it, experiences the imperceptible but ubiquitous force of standard time, and every sentence automatically takes the direction of a story unfolding in time.' Deviations from a convention can never wholly escape the convention they are deviating from.

Bradley looked for the explanation of the forward course of recollection in the biological function of the brain. 'Life being a process of decay and of continual repair and a struggle throughout against dangers, our thoughts, if we are to live, must mainly go the way of anticipation.' Darwin had died no more than five years earlier, and the interpretation of mental functions, too, had been given a Darwinian slant. We register our perceptions and experiences with an eye to our future actions; what happened in the past only matters inasmuch as it enables us to anticipate what lies in store for us. Seen in that light, the memory is focused not on the past but on what is yet to come, and that is also why our recollections face the future. This explanation strikes me as convincing and natural; our memory is apparently designed so that it is focused towards future changes. Remembrance serves expectation.

After reading Bradley's article I realized that I did not understand his question until I had 'translated' it into a metaphor: remembering is like a film that you may well be able to reel forwards and backwards but that you can only view properly when it is played back in a forward direction. Bradley, writing in 1887, eight years before the invention of cinematography, used a classical metaphor to formulate the problem: time is like a river and the events are like objects carried past in the current. But that metaphor occasionally proved hard to use. A river taken on its own has no direction; it is only from an external point, a bank or an onlooker, that it can be told in which direction the river is flowing. We are used to thinking that the river of time moves forward, in the direction of the future. But we experience events as if they reached us from the future, backwards, in the direction of the past. In fact, Bradley concluded, the question ought to be put like this: 'Why, since events go backwards always, does our memory of them always take the other direction?'

The metaphor of the memory as a camera that takes first X and then Y and that can only reproduce the film in that order conveys a much easier and clearer idea of what Bradley wanted to say, and had he written his paper some ten years later, after the invention of cinematography, he might well have made use of the film metaphor. In 1887, the theoretical treatment of the memory was still dominated by the metaphor of the still camera. That metaphor encouraged the view that the memory was an instrument for storing exact, copy-like images, the view, that is, which continues to be popularly associated with the term 'photographic memory'. At the time, neurology considered the memory a register of immutable, permanent traces that could be 'developed' at will into a static optical picture. In the memory no less than on a sensitive photographic plate, images are fixed in both senses of the word. That is why Bradley – writing about the direction our memories take – had no use for still-photography metaphors: what does not move has no direction.

The birth of the motion picture dates back to 1895, the year when the brothers Auguste and Louis Lumière presented their cinematograph. The Lumières ran a factory manufacturing photographic plates in Lyons, and took out a whole series of photographic patents in their name. In the early nineties there were various procedures for projecting separate pictures in quick succession to suggest movement. In 1891, Edison patented a 'kinetograph' (camera) and a 'kinetoscope' (projector), but the kinetoscope could only be viewed by one person at a time and the movements were wooden. After attending a kinetoscope demonstration in Paris in 1894, the Lumières decided to develop a method for taking and projecting pictures with a better definition.

The crucial step in the invention of the moving film was the motion-picture machine designed by the Lumières. The perforated strip of celluloid was moved up one position at a time by a gripping device and the exposure reduced to a twenty-fifth of a second. During projection – for which the same apparatus was used – the picture paused in front of the projector lamp for two thirds of the time during every revolution, just long enough to project the pictures sharply on to the screen. On 28 December 1895, the Lumières gave their first public film performance in Paris. The success was immense and immediate. Two years later, the Lumières could boast a catalogue of 385 films, each about seventeen metres long and, depending on the projection speed, lasting about one minute. Their first film showed the workers leaving the factory in Lyons for their lunch break. The Lumières were able to witness a great many of the hectic developments in cinematographic technique: Louis lived until 1948 and August until 1954.

The cinematograph – born in the wake of still photography – gave rise to a new metaphor for the visual memory. During the 1902–3 academic term, Henri Bergson delivered a series of lectures on time at the Collège de France. In these lectures, Bergson asked a question underlying Bradley's. How is it possible for us to grasp the idea of movement and change if our experience actually consists of an infinite series of independent perceptions? After all, our perceptions are made up of a set of 'snapshots of reality taken by the mind', as Bergson put it. And yet our mental pictures *move* – that is the mystery. Bergson gave his lectures eight years after the Lumières, fellow townsmen, had shown their first films. He, unlike Bradley eight years before the invention of cinematograph, could use that invention to introduce a technical analogy and conceptual possibilities lacking in the still-photography metaphors. Bergson took full advantage of that fact. Suppose one wants to represent the movement of marching soldiers. An effective procedure, Bergson explained, would be 'to take a series of snapshots of the passing regiment and throw these instantaneous views on the screen, so that they replace each other very rapidly'. On each of these snapshots the regiment stands motionless. No soldier moves, since 'with immobility set beside immobility, even endlessly, we could never make movement'. To animate the pictures the apparatus must introduce movement: 'It is because the film of the cinematograph unrolls, bringing in turn the different photographs of the scene to continue each other, that each actor of the scene recovers his mobility.' The quick succession of static images produces movement, Bergson concluded: 'Such is the contrivance of the cinematograph. And such is also that of our knowledge.' The cinematograph helped to solve the paradox of movement created from immobility.

Faced with an antiquated film projector from Bergson's time, we find it difficult to see how anyone could ever have found an analogy for the human memory in this box of boards, slats, glass, lamps, chains, cogs and reels. A historian of technology might try to lessen our surprise by pointing out that the cinematograph had a stunning effect on a public being introduced to a prosthetic memory of moving pictures for the first time. Performances in cinemas – and diaries, letters and newspaper reports from the time bear this out – entranced audiences. But all this is mere reconstruction. Having grown up with the data transmitters of your own day you can perhaps try to evoke the wonderment experienced by earlier generations at photography or cinematography, but you will find it impossible actually to *experience* that sense of wonder. A hundred years after the first cinema performance, the old enchantment can no longer be recaptured. What Bradley had to say about human memory seems to apply to the historical memory as well: it can only move forwards.

### BIBLIOGRAPHY

Amis, M., *Time's Arrow*, London, 1991.
Bergson, H., *L'Evolution créatrice*, Paris, 1907. Quoted from *Creative Evolution*, translated by A. Mitchell, New York, 1911.
Bradley, F. H., 'Why do we remember forwards and not backwards?', *Mind* 12 (1887), 579–82.
Hanlo, J., *Verzamelde gedichten*, Amsterdam, 1970.
Krol, G., *Wat mooi is is moeilijk*, Amsterdam, 1991.

# 7 The absolute memories of Funes and Sherashevsky

In one of his labyrinthine stories, the Argentine short-story writer, essayist and poet Jorge Luis Borges (1900–1986) introduces his readers to one Ireneo Funes, whose name translates as 'out of the dark'. One evening in 1884, the narrator and his cousin get caught up in a storm in Uruguay. The south wind is driving along an enormous slate-coloured storm cloud that has covered the sky. Out of the darkness, a boy suddenly appears. The cousin shouts, 'What's the time, Ireneo?' Without looking at a watch or consulting the sky, Ireneo calls back, 'Four minutes till eight, young Bernardo Juan Francisco.' 'Chronometric Funes' seems to have an infallible sense of time.

When the narrator returns to Uruguay a few years later, he hears that Funes has been thrown from an unbroken horse and been left a hopeless cripple confined to a camp bed. After the fall he appears to have at his disposal two astounding gifts: infinitely detailed powers of observation and an absolute memory. Funes sees, hears and senses everything and forgets nothing. His fall has changed his memory into a perfect register. The narrator decides to call on Funes. While walking across the tiled patio to Funes's room, he hears someone reciting a Latin text. It is Ireneo Funes. The disabled boy has no Latin but has learned the text by heart while lying on his camp bed. The passages he is reciting come from Pliny's *Naturalis historia*, or more precisely from the twenty-fourth chapter of the seventh book – the part dealing with the prodigious memories of Cyrus, king of the Persians, who knew the name of every soldier in his army, of Mithridates Eupator, who spoke all the twenty-two languages of his kingdom, and of Simonides, the inventor of mnemonics. Funes is genuinely amazed that such cases are thought to be amazing: for him it is the most normal thing in the world.

The fact that Funes should have been able to recite a passage by heart about the colossal memories of great men of the past serves Borges as a mirror effect, but he also uses it to show that Funes's memory exceeded anything recorded in all the legends in history. The boy's powers of recall were absolute: 'He knew the forms of the clouds in the southern sky on the morning of April 30, 1882, and he could compare them in his memory with the veins in the marbled binding of a book he had seen only once.' He saw and remembered the tangled mane of a colt, a continually changing fire, the many faces of a dead man during a long wake. He remembered 'not only every leaf of every tree in every patch of forest, but every time he had perceived or imagined that leaf'. "'I myself, alone, have more memories'", he reported from his camp bed, "'than all mankind since the world began.'" He felt that before his fall he had been blind and deaf; that his immobility was a small price to pay for his infallible powers of observation and recall.

However, from the narrator's conversation with Funes there gradually emerges the picture of a boy handicapped not only physically but mentally as well. His absolute memory is a curse rather than a blessing. Funes keeps himself in the dark as long as possible in order to reduce the number of impressions. Only towards night does he have his camp bed moved to the window. His memory does not give him a moment's peace. He has problems in falling asleep: 'Lying on his back on his cot, in the dimness of his room, [Funes] could picture every crack in the wall, every molding of the precise houses that surrounded him.' In order to fall asleep he imagined unfamiliar black houses and concentrated on their uniform darkness. The unbearable fullness of his existence came to an end in 1889, when, not yet twenty-one years old, he died of pulmonary congestion.

The story about Funes was first published in 1942 in *La Nación*. Borges included it in his collection of short stories entitled *Ficciones* in 1944. In this rather cerebral *œuvre*, Ireneo Funes is a walking thought experiment, if one may use that phrase when writing about someone who is paralysed. For what, in fact, are the consequences of an absolute memory? What does a memory mean to someone who can make permanent use of it? The Funes story, says Bell-Villada, one of Borges's leading interpreters, is a philosophical essay on knowledge and memory, dressed up as literature. He is right. The story is Borges's answer to the question: 'Suppose someone sees everything and forgets nothing, what are his thoughts, actions and experiences like?' Writing about Funes, Borges, to use an apt metaphor of Bell-Villada's, viewed the reality of normal mental life through the prism of his fantasy. And thanks to circumstances of which Borges himself had no inkling when he wrote his story, the results of his thought experiment can be tested against a carefully recorded case study.

## S., the memory artist

In another part of the world, and in a different century, there lived a man who actually had a memory like Funes's. His name was Solomon Sherashevsky and he was a Russian Jew whose precise year of birth is not known. He is the main subject of a case study by the Russian neuropsychologist Aleksandr Lurija (1901–77), written in the summer of 1965, and published in 1968 in English translation under the title of *The Mind of a Mnemonist*. Lurija met Sherashevsky in the middle of the twenties, when Sherashevsky was approaching thirty – he could have been the reincarnation of Funes – and was working as a journalist on a local paper. His prodigious memory was subjected to experiments by Lurija at regular periods for over thirty years.

Sherashevsky's story is the experimental parallel of Borges's literary version. The parallel is based not only on the indefatigable memory that Sherashevsky and Funes shared, but also on the affinity between Borges and Lurija (who, incidentally, were unfamiliar with each other's work). Borges's account is a literary-cum-philosophical study of the nature of the human intellect. It makes an authentic, almost scientific impression. Lurija's case study, on the other hand, is an example of what he called 'romantic science', a form of science aimed not at reduction and abstract law but at the subjectivity of experience. From Borges's genre of scientific fiction and Lurija's of literary science there emerged a double portrait of an intriguing phenomenon: the memory from which nothing can escape.

The experiments began the day that Sherashevsky – referred to in the book by his initial in keeping with clinical tradition – presented himself to Lurija with a request to have his memory tested. He had been sent by his editor, who had observed that Sherashevsky took no notes even at the most detailed briefings. The young journalist himself found nothing remarkable in this and was even surprised that not everybody was able to remember the briefings. At the time, Lurija was in his early twenties. He had studied psychology in his native Kazan and had been particularly drawn to the work of Freud. Psychoanalysis linked up with what was to become an important motif of Lurija's scientific work: the part played by the emotions in human action. Lurija wrote a monograph on psychoanalysis and exchanged several letters with Freud. When psychoanalysis became discredited in the Soviet Union, *Pravda* calling it 'biologistic' and 'ideologically hostile', Lurija, too, quickly adapted himself to the altered circumstances. He moved to the University of Moscow and started what was to become a long and productive career in neuropsychology.

When Sherashevsky arrived in the psychological laboratory, he seemed diffident and absent-minded to Lurija. To oblige him, Lurija gave him some standard tests. He showed him lists of words, figures and letters of varying length, and asked him to repeat them. What started as a routine assignment quickly turned into a dazzling display: no matter how long Lurija made the list – thirty, fifty or even seventy components – Sherashevsky was able to repeat the series faultlessly, and, if asked to do so, in reverse order or starting at some arbitrary point. After the first tests, Lurija was utterly baffled: he was incapable of doing anything so simple as even to determine the capacity of his subject's memory. The problem was not that the limit was unclear – there *was* no limit.

Fresh tests a few days later established that Sherashevsky's powers of recall were not governed by normal mnemonic laws. The memory span – the number of components a subject can retrieve faultlessly after a single presentation – runs to seven or so components in most people; Sherashevsky was able to repeat series with hundreds of components. The average subject can retain words that have a meaning with considerably greater ease than groups of nonsense syllables, yet Sherashevsky was able to recall long lists of almost identical groups of nonsense syllables. Normal recall deteriorates if similar material is learned before or after the test, yet Sherashevsky dug up such material from his memory with the same accuracy. It looked as if he had absolute powers of recall, a memory that contained traces that were permanent and complete rather than temporary or fragmentary.

The tests were conducted repeatedly and in approximately the same way. Lurija would slowly read out a list of words or figures, Sherashevsky would shut his eyes or stare absently into the distance, wait until the list was finished, concentrate for another few minutes and then repeat the list in the order stipulated by Lurija. When Lurija copied a table of fifty figures on the blackboard, Sherashevsky would

$$N \cdot \sqrt{d^2 \times \frac{85}{vx}} \cdot \sqrt[3]{\frac{276^2 \cdot 86x}{n^2v \cdot \pi 264}} \; n^2b = sv \; \frac{1624}{32^2} \cdot r^2s$$

Fig. 3   The mock equation shown by Lurija to the prodigious Sherashevsky.

let his eyes travel slowly over the columns for two or three minutes before 'reading' the table off from what he described as an 'inner picture'. It made hardly any difference to the time he took whether he recalled the columns from top to bottom, or vice versa, or diagonally. Even the recall of a table several months or years later caused him no appreciable difficulties. The only difference was that he needed more time to recall the setting of the experiment: the room, Lurija's voice, and the image of himself gazing at the blackboard.

During the early years of the investigation, Sherashevsky's recollections had a spontaneous character. The tests make it clear that his memory had a visual bias. Every word automatically elicited a picture indelibly imprinted on his memory. From a conversation in 1936: "'When I hear the word *green*, a green flowerpot appears; with the word *red* I see a man in a red shirt coming toward me; as for *blue*, this means an image of someone waving a small blue flag from a window.'" Even numbers remind him of images: "'Take the number 1. This is a proud, well-built man; 2 is a high-spirited woman; 3 a gloomy person (why, I don't know); 6 a man with a swollen foot; 7 a man with a mustache; 8 a very stout woman – a sack within a sack. As for the number 87, what I see is a fat woman and man twirling his mustache.'" An extract from an introspective examination conveys an impression of how Sherashevsky impressed part of a scientific formula – in this instance a mock equation – upon his memory (see Fig. 3):

Neiman (N) came out and jabbed at the ground with his cane (•). He looked up at a tall tree which resembled the square-root sign ($\sqrt{\ }$), and thought to himself: 'No wonder the tree has withered and begun to expose its roots. After all, it was here when I built these two houses' (d² [*dom* = house]). Once again he poked with his cane (•). Then he said: 'These houses are old, I'll have to get rid of them (X) ["cross them out"]; the sale will bring in far more money.' He had originally invested 85,000 in them (85). Then I see the roof of the house detached

(——), while down below on the street I see a man playing the Termenvox (vx).

Images like these surface easily in his mind and combine into a continuous story. Lurija reports that Sherashevsky was able to repeat the formula faultlessly in 1949, fifteen years later, without any preparation.

Several years after meeting Lurija, Sherashevsky decided to turn his back on journalism and become a professional mnemonist. Between tours he gave Lurija the opportunity of observing changes in his memory at close quarters. Gradually spontaneous recall made way for a professional trick: the loci method. This technique was used by the Greeks when they had to deliver long speeches from memory. The speaker would conjure up a house or a street in his mind and, during a mental walk, place his topics along his path in symbolic visual form. During his address, he would repeat the walk and thus, at the appropriate time – in the first place, in the second place – recall each of his topics. Sherashevsky used a Moscow variant: his walk usually started in Gorky Street, beginning at Mayakovsky Square. The topics were placed in doorways and well-lit shop windows, on windowsills and low walls, in gardens and stairwells. Often, the walk would finish, somewhat ungeographically, in the small town of Torshok where he had lived as a child.

Remarkably, but quite understandably in terms of the structure of the memory, Sherashevsky's rare mistakes were the results of faulty observation rather than of a faulty memory. When he 'read' a memorized table, he made the sorts of mistakes someone might make if he read the table from a piece of paper, for instance mistaking a carelessly written 3 for an 8. The same can happen using the loci method: when Sherashevsky placed an 'image' in a dark spot or against an unsuitable background – an egg against a white wall, perhaps – he could overlook it when recalling his walk.

## Synaesthesia

Apart from his absolute memory, Sherashevsky's mental faculty showed yet another uncommon feature. Sherashevsky was synaesthetic in the extreme. The impressions of his various senses ran together. With words, he felt sensations of colour and taste and even of pain. Ever since his earliest youth, 'the words of a Hebrew prayer settled in his mind as puffs of steam or splashes'. During the tests he said to Lurija's colleague, Vygotsky, '"What a crumbly yellow voice you have."' After listening to Eisenstein, the famous Russian cinematographer, Sherashevsky once told Lurija, '"It was as though a flame with fibers protruding from it was advancing right toward me."' The sound of words conjured up taste and colour. He could not conceive how so melodious and elegant a word as *svinya* could refer to a pig. In a restaurant, he would select dishes according to the taste of the words. When an ice-cream seller asked him in a hoarse voice what flavour he wanted, he could 'see' a stream of coal and black cinders pouring from her mouth and lost his appetite.

At first sight, this synaesthesia renders Sherashevsky's memory even more puzzling. How can two deviations from the norm, each so rare in itself, occur in combination in one and the same person? Chance? Lurija shows that synaesthesia in this case is not a second mystery but rather an integral part of the explanation. We all know from personal experience that the context of what we try to remember can help us to bring the memory back. We make use of this fact when we want to remind somebody of something: surely, you remember, we were at such-and-such a place, and so-and-so was there as well. In this case the circumstances serve as association cues. Sherashevsky did not just associate the elements of the endless series of numbers and objects he had to memorize during his stage appearances automatically with a concrete visual picture, but also committed the elements to memory through their sounds, as colours and tastes. Thanks to his synaesthetic associations, he was thus put in possession of an extra set of associations. The reason why he was able to reproduce material presented to him ten or fifteen years earlier was because he could call to mind the 'taste' of the occasion. In experiments, he would concentrate for a few minutes to recall the sensory impression of the original test.

However, the synaesthetic associations also had a second function in Sherashevsky's memory. When normal subjects reproduce a list of words they have learned with the help of pictures, they will occasionally reproduce a synonym instead of the actual word. Let us say the word was 'boat': people visualize a boat, later recall the picture and think, oh, yes, a ship. For Sherashevsky that mistake was impossible. For him, the word 'boat' conjured up not only a visual image, but also a particular synaesthetic association that did not fit the word 'ship'. Synaesthesia served him as a control mechanism. In that remarkable memory, the normal psychological laws may not have prevailed, but there was no anarchy either. The deviations together formed a consistent structure, governed by laws of their own.

## The pathology of perfection

What does living with a near-absolute memory mean? From conversations and letters Lurija deduced that Sherashevsky's visual-synaesthetic approach made it easier for him to cope with certain things. Thus he had a phenomenal sense of direction: every route he had ever taken could be opened as if it were a mental map in a continually expanding topographical archive. In his autobiography, Lurija recalls that one day they were about to pay a visit to the physiologist Orbeli and that he asked Sherashevsky if he remembered the way. Sherashevsky replied: "'Come now, how could I possibly forget? After all, here's this fence. It has such a salty taste and feels so rough; furthermore, it has such a sharp, piercing sound...'" His extraordinary ability to visualize rendered some tasks obvious to him at a glance. Someone once put the riddle of the bookworm to him: "'There were two books on a shelf, each 400 pages long. A bookworm gnawed through from the first page of the first volume to the last page of the second. How many pages did he gnaw through? You would no doubt say 800 – 400 pages of the first volume and 400 of the second. But I see the answer right off! He only gnaws through the two bindings. What I see is this: the two books are standing on the shelf, the first on the left, the second to the right of it. The worm begins at the first page and keeps going to the right. But all he finds there is the binding of the first volume and that of the second. So, you see, he hasn't gnawed through anything except the two bindings.'" Where many people have to pick up two books even after this explanation to check the answer, Sherashevsky simply focused his mental eye on the two volumes.

However, this graphic precision had a snag. Sherashevsky was unable to work with concepts, such as the word 'nothing', that could not be associated with a picture. For normal people such a concept is a verbal abstraction used in logical argument. Sherashevsky's thought, by contrast, was invariably childishly concrete and visual. Nor did he have any feeling for metaphor or poetry. That may sound odd in someone for whom words conjured up concrete images and sensory associations. On closer examination it is easily explained. Metaphors can only be understood by reference to a *meaning*, but Sherashevsky merely saw pictures in the imagery. When, in a poem by Tikhonov, a peasant is said to be using a winepress to make a 'river of wine', Sherashevsky can see a red river flowing past in the distance. The meaning of the metaphor has been replaced by the picture.

Sherashevsky was even handicapped by his visual associations with his understanding of normal speech. When he listened to someone, the sounds and vivid pictures that rose up in his mind spontaneously led him away from the meaning and left him with an unlikely collection of pictures. A good example is this fragment from a conversation with Lurija: "'Take the expression *to weigh one's words*. Now how can you weigh words? When I hear the word *weigh*, I see a large scale – like the one we had in Rezhitsa in our shop, where they put bread on one side and a weight on the other. The arrow shifts to one side, then stops in the middle … But what do you have here – to *weigh one's words*!'"

Sherashevsky's mental life bordered on the pathological. His mind must have resembled the state of consciousness we sometimes experience when we fall asleep: a quick, associative series of pictures, the fleeting impressions of a chaotically edited film. On people who did not know him, just as on Lurija at first, Sherashevsky made an odd, distracted impression, as if he were not altogether in his right mind. A perfect memory is a handicap. What lends the parallel of Sherashevsky and Borges's Funes so oppressive a character is that the real man with a prodigious memory and the fictional character not only share an absolute memory but also the mental defects to go with it. 'Sherashevsky often complained that he had a poor memory for faces: "They're so changeable. A person's expression depends on his mood and the circumstances under which you happen to meet him. People's faces are constantly changing; it's the different shades of expression that confuse me and make it so hard to remember faces."' Funes had the same problems. Whenever he observed his own face in the mirror he was surprised. Where others saw constancy, he saw change. 'Funes could continually perceive the quiet advances of corruption, of tooth decay, of weariness. He saw – he *noticed* – the progress of death, of humidity.' The paradox of the lives of these two men was that their absolute memory destroyed any sense of continuity.

Sherashevsky and Funes both made a strange, absent-minded impression, burdened as they were with such exacting memories. They lacked the power of logical and abstract reasoning. 'I suspect... that he was not very good at thinking', the narrator says of Funes. 'To think is to ignore (or forget) differences, to generalize, to abstract. In the teeming world of Ireneo Funes there was nothing but a set of particulars – and they were virtually *immediate* particulars.' It irritated him that a dog he saw from the side should be indicated by the same noun as a dog he saw a minute later from the front. For Sherashevsky, too, life was one long chain of separate images; he was quite unable to discover even the simplest logical order in a series of figures or to fit words into categories. Thus Sherashevsky was quite unable to pick out the names of birds from a list of words; to do that he had first to recite the whole list to himself. Like Funes, he was 'virtually incapable of general, platonic ideas'. For both prodigious mnemonists, as Renate Lachmann observed in an essay on Borges, there applied Nietzsche's dictum in *Human, All Too Human*: 'Many do not become thinkers because their memory is too good.'

Lurija considered it his greatest achievement that he had tried to establish what influence his one extremely well-developed faculty had on Sherashevsky's personality and actions. In that respect, Lurija's experimental report and Borges's story coincide. Whether the experience of an absolute memory is viewed through the prism of literary fantasy or through that of scientific experiment, the spectrum of consequences on actions remains the same. For both, the writer and the neuropsychologist, it is an established fact that an absolute memory wreaks havoc; it turns its owner into an invalid. Lurija described Sherashevsky as a somewhat childish, rather ineffective man, who had to lock into his associations before he could answer or act. Funes suffered from the same handicap, if anything even more severely. Bell-Villada has mentioned the paradox that while Funes's powers of observation were unusually rich and varied, he was doomed to a poor and monotonous existence in the dark, his eyes shut and his mind protected against the rush of sensory impressions. In fact, the paradox runs even deeper. The faultless recording of yesterday's tree or face ensures that today's tree and face are completely new. For Funes and Sherashevsky everything was new every moment. In short they were just like someone *without* a memory.

In an interview, Borges once let slip that his story about Funes was a metaphor for insomnia, an affliction from which he suffered himself. He spoke of the 'dreadful lucidity' that can overcome you when you lie wide awake in the dark. In his poem 'Insomnia', published in 1936, six years before the Funes story, he writes of the impossibility of distracting his thoughts from his own body, his circulation, the gradual decay of his teeth, all the places he had been to, the house, the town, the muddy paths. In vain, he waits for 'the disintegration and symbols preceding sleep'. With eyes shut, he lies in bed waiting. At dawn, under a slate-coloured sky, he is still awake. Sleep is temporary oblivion and he who has to dispense with that blessing is delivered over to his memories.

The experience is familiar. During the day, under normal circumstances, the memory is a friendly aide, an intimate friend, accustomed to being taken into your confidence and doing its best to be of assistance to you. But at night, when sleep refuses to come, its treacherous character becomes apparent. While you – like Funes – lie helplessly waiting in your bed, it turns into a tyrant who keeps you from sleep with his endless gloomy stories. There is no escape. You are alone with your memory and as if paralysed stare fixedly at everything it conjures up. Images, images, images – entire days rise up sharply focused before your mind's eye, a remorseless film-like projection of everything you would sooner have forgotten. Every insomniac lives temporarily with the curse of an absolute memory. During the long, dragging hours of the night you are transformed into an Ireneo Funes, into a Solomon Sherashevsky, into a mnemonist who suddenly realizes what it means to suffer from the pathology of perfection.

BIBLIOGRAPHY

Borges wrote his story about Funes in 1942 and included it in 1944 in a collection called *Ficciones*. A translation by Andrew Hurley was published in London in 1967 under the title *Fictions*.

Bell-Villada, G. H., *Borges and His Fiction: A Guide to His Mind and Art*, Chapel Hill, 1981.

Lachmann, A., 'Gedächtnis und Weltverlust – Borges' *memorioso* – mit Anspielungen auf Lurija's *Mnemonisten*', in A. Haverkamp and R. Lachmann (eds.), *Memoria – Vergessen und Erinnern*, with the collaboration of R. Herzog, Munich, 1993, 492–519.

Lurija, A. R., *The Mind of a Mnemonist*, New York, 1968.

*The Making of Mind: A Personal Account of Soviet Psychology*, Cambridge, Mass., 1979.

Nietzsche, F., *Human, All Too Human*, Lincoln, 1984.

# 8    The advantages of a defect:
the savant syndrome

In 1887, the English psychiatrist John Langdon Down delivered a series of lectures to the London Medical Society. He listed for his colleagues the cases and pathologies he had come across during the previous thirty years as medical director of Earlswood Asylum. These lectures have become a landmark in the history of psychiatry, thanks chiefly to Down's account of an abnormal mental condition to which he himself referred as 'mongolism', but which is currently known as Down's syndrome. Far less well known is the fact that in the same lectures he introduced another classical psychiatric term: idiots savants; according to Down, these were 'children who, though of low general intelligence, possess an unusual faculty capable of considerable development'.

In his clinic, Down was able to observe such children. One mentally handicapped boy was able to recite long passages word for word that he had read just once, although there was no question whatever of his having any real understanding of what he was remembering. When he read Gibbon's *History of the Decline and Fall of the Roman Empire*, he accidentally skipped a line on the third page but reinstated it a few lines later. When he came to recite the passage from memory, he repeated the mistake: he missed a line, read on, and then read the missing line as if it had always been in that position. Another boy knew the entire Book of Psalms by heart. Yet another was able to multiply two three-figure numbers in a few seconds. Some of Down's patients had a bizarrely overdeveloped musical memory. Following a visit to the opera, one of them had perfect recall of all the arias. Finally, there was a boy who was able to tell the exact time without consulting a clock or watch. When the boy was excited, Down explained, he could not do it so well and had 'to be shaken like an old watch before he could tell the correct time'. This chronometric gift was no more inherited than other talents – Down was unable to discover any parents of idiots savants with identical gifts. Another striking observation was that during the course of his long career Down did not encounter a single female idiot savant.

The dozens of case histories of idiots savants published since Down's day have largely corroborated his findings. What has fallen by the wayside is the use of the term itself: an idiot savant is no idiot, not even in technical terms, with his IQ of between 50 and 70; nor is he a genuine savant. His gift is largely confined to repetition and imitation. Nowadays people with the savant syndrome are referred to simply as savants.

The examples Down gave fall into three categories. In the first we find those who have prodigious memories. Some savants know the entire bus timetable of a large city by heart. Other savants have an extremely good memory for historical facts or know all the birthdays and addresses of the present and former staff of the institution by heart. Down noticed that the memory of savants had a particular quality: he described it as 'sticky' with respect to concrete and simple things. It had no hold on abstractions. Savants find it easier to remember an entire timetable than instructions on how to look up a train connection. A second category of savants is made up of calculators. Most are particularly good at calendar calculations and can say in a few moments on what day of the week a certain date falls. The third category of savants is artistically gifted. As a rule their talent takes the form of being able to play musical passages by ear. They cannot read sheet music and every one of them has perfect pitch. Far less common are savants who can draw. From the age of four, Nadia, an autistic girl, was able to draw animals, preferably horses, with a gift for capturing movement that would have been exceptional even in an adult. Stephen Wiltshire, another autistic child, draws buildings and streets with an astonishing command of perspective.

According to Treffert, the American psychiatrist who, like Down, was the veteran medical director of a psychiatric institute, approximately one hundred savants have been described in the medical and psychological literature during the past century. The overrepresentation of males is six to one. Many savants are autistic or have symptoms that are usually associated with autism: echolalia ('parroting'), lack of social contact, preference for monotonous activities, and violent outbursts in response to changes in their environment. Among children diagnosed as autistic some 10 per cent have savant-like abilities. Virtually all calendar calculators are autistic. Anyone who looks into the case histories of savants and the enormous diversity of their

MONTANA STATE UNIVERSITY
Jedediah Buxton

Fig. 4 The calculating prodigy Jedediah Buxton (1702–72).

talents and feats is forced almost as a matter of course to the conclusion that the traditional division of savants into mnemonists, calculating prodigies and artistic savants is somewhat arbitrary. In future, that division may well be considered the same sort of 'silly list' as that of the 'degenerates', a term under which nineteenth-century psychiatrists lumped together epileptics, alcoholics and the mentally handicapped. It is a tripartition based on the form of the syndrome and the specific accomplishment of the savant rather than the psychological processes enabling him to develop precisely these accomplishments. In later research it could well become clear that what Down called a 'sticky memory' also covered the feats of calendar calculators, pianists and draughtsmen. It may well turn out that all savants have a hidden spatial ability. Many of the hypotheses and theories rife in the current literature apply specifically to the particular savants for whom they were developed, but render other types of savants all the more mysterious. To gain an idea of the diversity of savant abilities, it may be helpful to make the acquaintance of a few savants.

## Calculating prodigies and calendar calculators

Carl Gauss, the greatest mathematician of the nineteenth century, was a calculating prodigy in his youth, as were Leonhard Euler one century earlier and Alexander Aitken a century later. The precocious feats of these mathematicians fitted into the pattern of the talent that unfolded at a later stage of their life. The promise of youth was fulfilled by what they eventually became: masters of a talent granted to one in every few million. The gifts of Euler, Gauss and Aitken have their place on the extreme right of the normal distribution curve.

The reverse is not the case. Exceptional calculating feats are not always early indications of genius. Indeed, the opposite is often true: many youthful calculating prodigies must, except for that one gift, be placed on the extreme left of the normal distribution, that is, among the mentally handicapped.

Jedediah Buxton was born in 1702 in the village of Elmton, Derbyshire. His father was a schoolmaster and his grandfather a vicar. Jedediah never learned to read or write and became an agricultural labourer. According to a biographical sketch which appeared in *Gentleman's Magazine* in 1754, Buxton's 'life of laborious poverty [was] necessarily uniform and obscure: the history of one day would almost include the events of all. Time, with respect to Buxton, changed nothing but his age, nor did the seasons vary his employment, except that in winter he used a flail, and in summer a ling hook.' The author felt that this might very well have been the explanation for his illiteracy: 'His perpetual application to figures has prevented the smallest acquisition of any other knowledge, and his mind seems to have retained fewer ideas than that of a boy of ten years old, in the same class of life.'

The calculating ability of this simple soul was indeed astonishing. Buxton excelled above all in computing spatial relations, such as areas or volumes. Some of these calculations involved the multiplication of three numbers, each consisting of eight digits, and Buxton would come up with the twenty-seven digits of the answer, in reverse order if asked. In 1751, a correspondent from *Gentleman's Magazine* called on Buxton and set him a series of problems. Asked 'the number of times a coach wheel six yards in circumference would revolve during the 204 miles' ride from York to London', Buxton came up with the correct answer in thirteen minutes: 59,840 revolutions. Another question – 'When three barleycorns measure one inch, how many barley corns are required to reach eight miles?' – was answered in eleven minutes: 1,520,640 barleycorns. Buxton's greatest feat was squaring a sum of money running to thirty-nine (!) figures. The calculation – for the record, by heart – took him more than two months. The result appeared in a report published in 1751: a number running to seventy-eight figures. The writer added that any reader with a lot of time and curiosity to spare might well try to repeat the feat. No contemporary of his took up the challenge. Computer calculations have since shown that, except for one digit, Buxton got the sum right.

As we saw, Buxton had learned or remembered so little that he knew less than a normal ten-year-old. However, when it came to the odd subject that did interest him, his memory seemed to work extraordinarily well. Thus he kept a mental score of all the pints of beer to which he was treated. When the list was drawn up in 1753, more than sixty persons figured on it, many of them local nobility, but also such luminaries as the mayor and the vicar. The Duke of Kingston alone had been good for 2,130 pints. Apart from pints of beer, the doings of the royal family were the only thing that could distract his attention from numbers. In the spring of 1754, Buxton walked the 150 miles from his village to London in the hope of catching a glimpse of the king. Unfortunately, the king was away on holiday. But with Buxton in London, the opportunity was taken to invite him to give a demonstration of his prowess before the Royal Society. The extent to which calculation was an obsession with Buxton may be gathered from what happened after the demonstration was over. He was taken to a performance of *Richard III*. When someone asked him afterwards what he thought of the play, it appeared that he had failed to understand any of it. He did, however, know how many words the leading actor had spoken.

This suggests that Buxton had an exceptionally good memory for numbers. However, the mathematician Steven Smith argues in his standard work on the great mental calculators that proffering a superior memory as an explanation is to confuse cause and effect. It is their interest in numbers that enables these prodigies to remember them so well, not the other way round. The quality of the memory of calculating prodigies, inasmuch as we know anything about it, varies in fact from average to downright poor. The teacher of the French calculating prodigy Mondeux wrote in 1853 that his pupil was unable to learn anything other than numbers: 'Facts, dates, places, pass before his brain as before a mirror without leaving a trace.' In 1894, when Binet studied the calculating prodigy Inaudi, he discovered that his subject was unable to repeat as few as five letters, while he could, after a single presentation, reproduce every calculating problem he had been set. With calculating prodigies the ability to fix long series of figures in the mind is more the result of performing many calculations than the cause. This very fact challenges a second hypothesis, namely that such prodigies have learned multiplication tables by heart, not the tables up to 12 or 13, like most of us, but up to 100 or even 200. The memorization of all these products would make tremendous demands on the memory. For a calculating prodigy it is much easier to perform a multiplication than to remember it permanently.

The link between numbers and the memory must be sought elsewhere. For calculating prodigies numbers have properties and relationships that normal people do not appreciate. Numbers elicit associations that endow them with significance, and in that sense they have much in common with words. Prodigies see numbers in a sentential context. For Wim Klein, the longtime world champion in the extraction of square roots, the number 429 was the result of 3 times 11 times 13, and also the year (BC) of the death of Pericles. When Aitken heard the year 1961 mentioned once, he broke the number down into 37 times 53, or into the sum of the squares of 44 and 5, or into the sum of the squares of 40 and 19. These operations occurred to him spontaneously; he did not have to perform them on purpose. Thanks to such associations, numbers can also have an emotional or aesthetic significance. Thus when Shyam Marathe flew over the Grand Canyon for the first time, he said the vast expanse reminded him of the 20th power of 9.

The fact that figures and numbers are to a calculating prodigy what words and sentences are to normal people is a helpful analogy. Nobody remembers a word as a set of isolated sounds or a sentence as a chance collection of words. The meaning is added automatically there and then, just as quickly as we read or listen. *How* that happens eludes our observation. The processes enabling us to read, to speak or to listen are not accessible to introspection. That too corresponds to what happens with calculating prodigies: they can rarely tell you how they arrived at their results. True, reports based on the explanations of the way they set to work by such prodigies as Aitken and George Bidder, Jr, have been published, but they were unable to tell us a great deal about the processes *behind* their methods. Aitken even declared on one occasion that he had the impression his calculations were being done for him on a deeper level of his mind, and he himself did little more than check the answer reached subconsciously, without ever having to correct it.

With savants we do not even have that sort of report. Most mathematical savants are calendar calculators, and almost without exception they are autistic. If they are able to speak, they cannot tell you how they arrive at the right answer. Introspective accounts of their working method rarely rise above the level of 'Well, there are seven days in the week...'. However, in the past few years there have been a fair number of psychological experiments with calendar calculators and these allow of a few conclusions. A very small minority of these calculators were able to memorize data. Their repertoire covers at most about ten years. Some of them have simply learned calendars by heart; others use 'anchor days', that is, several hundred data scattered over these years and of which they know the precise day, generally days when something that was personally important happened to them. Other days they access by counting forwards or backwards from a particular anchor day. The time they take to arrive at an answer depends on how far the day in question is from the anchor day.

The vast majority of calendar calculators answer questions about future dates as quickly as questions about the past, which means that they do not rely exclusively on their memory. A plausible assumption is that they *calculate* the answer. Calendars are based on regularities that can be expressed in mathematical terms (algorithms).

An example of such an algorithm can be found in perpetual calendars of the kind included in almanacs. It is conceivable that calendar calculators have seen such algorithms or deduced them by themselves and then gone on to make use of them.

Quite a few results would, however, seem to refute this assumption. The average calendar calculator is bad at figures. He can hardly do sums with single digits and multiplication or division seems quite beyond him. Nor can he make use of existing calendar algorithms; for a start he cannot grasp the rules. The calculating hypothesis is also refuted by the fact that many calendar calculators can answer questions for which no algorithms are known, such as, 'In which months between 1960 and 1970 does the first day of the month fall on a Sunday?' But if the explanation is neither a superior memory nor an extraordinary ability to handle numbers, how then do they do it? The British psychologists Michael Howe and Julia Smith have suggested a hypothesis that provides the beginnings of an explanation. They based this hypothesis on a case study of the calendar calculator Dave, fourteen years old at the time.

Dave was a mentally handicapped boy with an IQ of about 50. He was able to draw fairly well, but his reading ability was that of a child of six or seven. During the fourteen sessions of the investigation he spoke no more than a few words. He exhibited the classical symptoms of autism: he parroted, was shy and withdrawn. He referred to himself as 'Dave' and never as 'I'. The investigators' questions seemed to draw him out of his small world for a moment, but when he had given his answer he would retreat into it again. This taciturn boy was able to answer all questions about days and dates in the period from 1900 to 2060 almost faultlessly, which excluded the possibility of his use of anchor days. The year 1900 drew a strict line, with questions about earlier dates receiving no better than random answers, although when it came to the future there was a much more gradual decrease in the number of correct answers. A possible explanation of this is that the year 1900 is an exception to the rule stating that only years divisible by four are leap years (2000 is not such an exception). Remarkably enough, many answers about dates before 1900 were out by just one day.

This might suggest that Dave mainly made use of calculation, counting forwards, and for that reason Howe and Smith first examined his counting ability. Dave seemed unable to work out such individual sums as 1,973 minus 1,908, but when they asked him, 'I was born in 1908, so how old am I in 1973?', the correct answer came in a second or two. The same happened with the question: 'If I was born in 1841, how old will I be in 2302?' This pattern recurs quite frequently with other calendar calculators as well: 'bare' sums prove insoluble, while much more complex sums presented in the terms in which the savant normally thinks are readily solved. That Dave did not make use of the usual method of calculating dates and days was established when he gave a faultless answer to the question: 'In which year did 9 October fall on a Wednesday?', since no arithmetical methods of solving such problems had ever been published.

In the course of the investigation, Howe and Smith gained the impression that Dave had stored his calendrical information in the form of visual and spatial representations that he could call up from his memory. Two of his mumbled comments, too, suggested that he was consulting an internal visual image: 'Yes, that's on the top line ...' and 'Thursday's always black ...'. These remarks appeared to refer to a kitchen calendar Dave had seen in his youth. Although tests of visual memory showed that he did not have an eidetic (popularly called 'photographic') memory, he nevertheless seemed able, with the old kitchen calendar as his basis, to construct and to 'read off' imaginary calendars for other years.

Howe and Smith framed their further questions on the basis of this hypothesis. A question such as: 'What month in 1957 starts with a Friday?' is far more difficult for someone who has to calculate the answer than for someone who has stored the relevant information in the form of a visual representation. Dave gave the right answer without hesitation. Next he was presented with a list of seven different months from different years, and asked which was the odd month out. Without hesitation he named the only month that did not start with a Friday. The mistakes in his answers also pointed in the visual direction. When he gave the wrong day for, say, 21 March 1931, then his other answers for the same month were also wrong. Clearly, he did not have the right visual image of that particular month. A final corroboration was that it took Dave a long time to discover that some dates – such as 31 September – simply did not exist. For someone working with visual representations the alternation of 30 and 31 days is of no importance; for someone who calculates dates, by contrast, the difference is crucial.

The attraction of Howe and Smith's hypothesis is that it combines the advantages of the other two hypotheses – counting and memorization. Dave seemed to count with pictures, and in data-processing terms that presents a very great simplification. Since every month starts with one of seven days, there are only seven possible configurations of days and dates. If we know the first day of a particular month, we also know the rest of the month. Moreover, the entire block is repeated in a cycle of twenty-eight years. Anyone capable of turning the information in that block into a visual image can answer difficult questions about dates in a very short time. With calculations, a few moments is an extremely short time span; for conjuring up a mental picture it is no more than a natural interval. Dave's feats begin to look a little less inexplicable with this hypothesis.

## The graphic memory of Stephen Wiltshire

Stephen Wiltshire, too, is autistic. He can barely read or write and has the intellect of a six- or seven-year-old. He leaves conversations to adults and hardly ever speaks, even to his younger sister. There is no point in talking to him unless the conversation is kept strictly within the bounds of his interest: American cars, earthquakes and the film *Rain Man*. His fascination with earthquakes hides an obsession with collapsed buildings. In his native London he can look as if mesmerized at demolition work for days on end. All he could remember in a conversation with the author of a visit to Utrecht cathedral was that the nave had been destroyed in a storm centuries before and had since been divided into two separate parts.

In addition to being autistic and mentally handicapped, Stephen is also a savant: from earliest youth he has been able to draw towns and buildings with a skill that talented artists take years to acquire. His mastery of perspective in particular is astonishing. After the BBC devoted a documentary to him in 1987, various books of his drawings were published. For *Floating Cities* he made drawings in Venice, Amsterdam, Leningrad and Moscow. According to him, Amsterdam is more beautiful than Venice: 'It has cars.'

Fig. 5   Drawing of Westerkerk, Amsterdam, by Stephen Wiltshire.

Stephen draws quickly and accurately with a natural feeling for proportion. He finished his drawing of the Westerkerk in
Amsterdam in less than two hours. He draws without having to use
construction lines – freehand, without a ruler, without using a van-
ishing point. To anyone who watches him draw, the comparison with
a 'plotter' is irresistible. There is no hesitation at all in his movements,
but also no reflection; he does not look at the paper from a distance
every so often to check the proportions and all parts of the drawing
are executed with equal speed and assurance. The hums and mutters
he produces while drawing reinforce the plotter association even further: if he did not hum something every now and then, you might
think you were sitting beside the printer of a graphic computer.

Fig. 6   Drawing of Westerkerk, Amsterdam, by an unknown artist.

Yet his drawings also reveal his limitations. What is missing in them is interpretation, atmosphere. Some buildings were drawn on a radiant spring morning, others on an autumn afternoon; yet none of that is reflected in his drawings. You see no light, no shadow, no emphasized details; you cannot tell which part of a building is in the sun or if the sun is shining; there is no background, there are no clouds. You will find no houses looking bleak and threatening in the twilight in Stephen's sketchbook. A pen drawing of the Westerkerk by an unknown master makes the difference clear: the master's work is full of atmosphere; Stephen draws pure space composed of lines and contours. If artistic talent is the ability to impose an interpretation on forms, it might have to be said that Stephen's drawings cannot really be called art. His façades coincide with their spatial structure. His drawings are purely figurative and concrete.

Someone with exceptionally good visual recall is often said to have a photographic memory, to store visual impressions as if on a light-sensitive plate, later transforming it into an internal impression. Memory psychologists identify two processes that bear a resemblance to this type of photographic recall: eidetic memory and visual memory. People with a strongly developed eidetic memory are able to retain a picture shown to them 'before their mind's eye' for a short time, at most a few minutes. The picture is more like an after-image, a visual echo, than a remembered picture. Eidetic memory tests usually take the following form: the experimenter places a small picture on an easel against a uniform background. The experimental subject inspects the picture. When the picture is removed, he is able to 'project' the image on to the background. He can 'see' the picture as part of the world outside. Once faded, the picture has disappeared for good; if questions about it are asked a day later, then the subject is unable to reproduce any more of the picture than those without an eidetic memory. With a visual memory, by contrast, the experimental subject is able to recall a fairly accurate image to mind days or even months after the display. Unlike people with an eidetic memory, the subject sees the picture 'in his head'. It is this introspective difference in particular that suggests that there is a distinction between the two memory processes.

There would be little point in asking Stephen whether he saw the pictures of the houses, bridges and churches 'inside' or 'outside' – he would not understood the question. His handicap entails a lack of aptitude for abstractions or metaphors. Experiments, too, have failed to throw light on the matter. The British psychologist Neil O'Connor conducted several memory tests with Stephen that in a sense deepened the mystery even further, for they showed that Stephen had neither type of visual memory. A case in point was a brief experiment in which Stephen was asked to look at a random collection of line drawings and small figurines. Afterwards he proved unable to reproduce them any more accurately than most people of his age group. Another indication that he lacked a natural photographic memory for visual forms appeared when somebody asked him to write the word AMSTERDAM from memory. He started out like a child who had only just learned to write: for every letter, he first drew a short line above and below and then with great difficulty, his tongue lolling from his mouth, he fitted the capital letters between the lines. Gone was the ease with which he would draw the most intricate façades and towers; the capitals stood stiffly and unevenly between the lines. Why did he have so much trouble forming letters when he could reproduce buildings so accurately from memory?

Observations of his method of drawing suggest that he applies a mixed strategy composed of encoding information, deftness and, especially, an exceptional feeling for patterns. To start with the first, one of the contributors to *Floating Cities* wrote that, with drawings that he could not finish on the spot, Stephen would sometimes make notes in a kind of secret writing at the bottom of the page and consult them as he finished the drawing. No one has been able to decipher his scribbles, but it is quite possible that he has developed a code of his own for visual forms. A second part of his strategy involves a kind of trick. Draughtsmen normally begin by drawing the contours of a building: outer wall, roof, floor. When the windows in the front of the house have to be added, certainly if there are many, a fairly complicated measuring and calculating process is employed to place the windows in their correct position. Stephen sets about it in quite a different way. He simply works from left to right: he begins by drawing one side wall and adds windows and ornaments until they are all in place, and then he puts in the other side wall. There are, of course, all sorts of problems still with the proportions, but there is never any apparent need for counting and measuring.

However, the most important aspect of Stephen's special gift seems to be his feeling for spatial relationships. He never makes mistakes with the number of windows, decorative features or doors. That is all the more surprising as he can barely count. Something other than a code has therefore to be involved. Stephen seems to have a gift that is shared by other savants, namely the ability to tell at a glance the number of elements present without having to count them. In fact, every one of us has this gift, at least to some extent. If I put down five coins, arranged like the spots on a die, everyone can tell that there are five of them without having to count. If I put down another four and then another three, also shaped like the spots on a die, then everyone will be able to draw the coins without a mistake after a single glance. No one doing that is aware he has drawn twelve elements; what he records are the patterns of five, four and three spots. Perhaps Stephen's talent is an extreme extension of this ability to recall patterns. The highly structured and symmetrical arrangement of most façades naturally aids this process.

The code, the draughtsman's tricks and the skill in handling spatial patterns are no more than part of the story. For instance, the virtuosity with which Stephen solves perspective problems remains unexplained, nor is it clear why the processing of spatial information is so much more highly developed in him than it is in others. Oliver Sacks, who accompanied Stephen to Moscow, once asked Stephen to solve a large jigsaw puzzle. He did so with extreme speed. Sacks then asked him to solve the same puzzle, but this time with the picture underneath. Stephen solved the puzzle just as quickly. He evidently saw the pieces as separate shapes, not as part of a picture. Whenever he is asked to reproduce something from a photograph or a picture postcard, so that the problem of reducing the subject from three to two dimensions has, as it were, been solved for him already, the result has an almost photographic precision. But why is his spatial talent confined to bridges, buildings and squares while the portraits he draws are so clumsy? Stephen's pathological background makes it unlikely that he should be able to transcend the limits of his gift with his drawings. That gift is the almost mechanical precision of perspective drawing. Stephen seems like someone running a graphic program that is firmly installed in his brain and incapable of further extension.

## Musical savants

The music psychologist Leon Miller has given us the case history of thirteen musical savants in his *Musical Savants* (1989). He starts with 'Blind Tom', born in 1849 on a slave plantation, who became a travelling concert pianist by the age of ten. With a vocabulary of less than a hundred words and a repertoire of thousands of concert pieces, he was the first representative of what can be identified as a pattern. It is repeated with relatively few variations. The majority of musical savants are male, in a ratio of 5:1. All of them without exception have absolute pitch. Their talent appears extremely early, sometimes before they are one year old. There are no indications of a genetic factor: most of the parents of these savants are no more musically talented than the parents of normal children. Nor do musical savants grow up in unusually musical surroundings, albeit their talent, once discovered, is usually given every chance to develop. Savants play the piano. Not the guitar, the violin or the oboe: the piano. Almost all musical savants are visually impaired. The causes may differ. Some musical savants are blind or partially sighted because their mothers contracted German measles during pregnancy. Other savants received too much oxygen after their premature birth, so that the vessels carrying blood to the retina suffered morbid growth. All musical savants have major speech defects and if any speech development does take place it is retarded. Their vocabulary remains very limited. Even when savants are able to repeat long texts or conversations word for word – 'Blind Tom' could repeat a conversation lasting a quarter of an hour verbatim – they have no idea of their meaning. Almost all savants parrot words. Their other skills are untestable or rudimentary. Abstractions, analogies and sayings are quite beyond them. The only thing that is not retarded is their memory for figures, which seems as well developed as that of their contemporaries. Perhaps this single surviving faculty is responsible for a small overlap with other categories of savants: some musical savants are also able to perform calendrical calculations.

For a long time it was believed that the talent of musical savants was based exclusively on imitation. They were thought to be able to reproduce what they heard or what was played to them. At the end of the nineteenth century, their memory was being likened to the wax cylinder of a phonograph; nowadays the metaphor is known as the 'tape recorder view of memory'. This idea is reinforced by anecdotes about savants who repeat the music they have heard note for note, including the mistakes. The speed with which savants start repeating pieces of music, too, with no pause for reflection, gives the impression of pure imitation, as if the playing back is no more than a musical variant of their echolalia. Savants are said to reproduce the bare musical structures without interpretation or emotion, and with the regularity – but also the feeling – of a metronome. More recent studies have helped to qualify that view. Leon Miller believes that the older literature reflects some embarrassment at the discrepancy between the musical talent of savants and their mental handicap. That problem is often 'solved' by taking a relative view either of the talent or else of the handicap. Experiments with savants he has conducted himself, and publications about the musical savant Paravicini, suggest that the abilities of savants involve a much greater share of normal musical talent than was generally assumed.

Derek Paravicini was born prematurely, at only twenty-five weeks, and weighed just over a pound when he was born. The oxygen that kept him alive caused irreparable damage to his retinas. His motor system, too, suffered serious dysfunction. When he was about two years old, his response to sound was found to be remarkable: whatever sounds he heard – the radio, birdsong, or the tinkling of glass and cutlery – he tried to mimic with his voice. He was able to play back the tunes he had been hearing on a miniature electric organ. One year later, his parents bought him a piano. Derek's mentor, Adam Ockelford, the music teacher at an institute for children with multiple handicaps, helped to develop his talent further. On his ninth birthday, Derek gave concerts with jazz ensembles. All the awkwardness in his movements, Ockelford wrote, vanished the moment he touched the keys. With hands that were incapable of doing up a button or a buckle, he was able to play the most intricate pieces of music.

Learning pieces of music takes time and Derek had to listen to a new piece a few times every day for some time before he could remember it. But once remembered it never vanished. The remembering of one piece was not linked to the memory of another. In a conversation with Wim Kayzer, Ockelford compared Derek's memory to a hedgehog. Every spine is completely independent of the rest. Once you know how to gain access to a particular spine, you can take out what is in it. But if you are even slightly off target, you will never grasp it. Thus Derek failed to associate 'Mood Indigo' with any other music associated with moods.

His musical talent was as isolated as the hedgehog's spines. Derek did not speak, he merely uttered sounds, and was virtually incapable of learning anything unconnected with music. Yet that single talent was not purely repetitive. Derek liked to improvise. When he accompanied someone who did not start on the correct note he was able to transpose the piece straightaway, no matter how complicated the accompaniment. He could play all the pieces in his repertoire in any key. His talent, as Ockelford stressed, was based not on instant recall but on a well-developed ability to handle musical structures.

After an experimental study of five musical savants, Miller came to a similar conclusion. He compared the performance of savants in a series of musical tests with that of five adult pianists and four children said by their teachers to be exceptionally talented. Miller studied the most divergent ingredients of musicality, such as a sense of rhythm, a memory for melodies, the ability to hear separate notes in a chord and to judge intervals by ear. Savants proved to be the exception when it came to tests involving absolute pitch – in that area they had a clear advantage. But in other tests, their performance looked very much like that of the control group. The musical understanding of savants seemed, as Miller put it, 'more literate than literal'; it had nothing of a 'tape recorder memory' about it. Like his other experimental subjects, savants proved sensitive to the implicit structures of music, such as harmony and rhythm. When it came to deviations from the musical order, for instance the presentation of disconnected, random notes, irregular intervals or unusual chords, the performance of savants resembled that of the control groups. Their hearing and memory worked as selectively as that of other musically talented subjects. The talent of musical savants, Miller concluded, resembles the intact variant of musical talent. The fact that the savant has an ability in a limited field does not mean that the ability itself is limited.

In this one important respect, musical savants are unique. Generally the abilities of savants do not overlap those of non-savants. The difference between Dave and us is not that he could do calendar calculations better than us but that we couldn't do them at all. But apart from this one factor, musical savants are just like the others. They, too, are mostly male, show forms of behaviour associated with autism and have underdeveloped linguistic abilities. This last factor in particular is considered a crucial explanation of the origin of their skill; it will be raised in the context of theories about the development of the savant syndrome.

## A failed genius?

Anyone looking at the dozens of case studies of savants is faced with a frustrating list of incomplete generalizations. By far the greatest number of savants are male, but female savants do exist. Many musical savants are blind, but some are not. The majority of calendar calculators are autistic, but some calendar calculators are not. Savant skills are almost invariably innate, but can also emerge as a result of brain trauma, such as meningitis. If therapists succeed in developing other skills, the savant talent often disappears; sometimes it does not. Nearly all savants suffer from speech impediments or cannot speak at all, but there are also savants who can master a foreign language in an extremely short time. Savants obey few rules. They may fit into stereotypes, such as the blind savant pianist or the autistic calendar calculator, but the differences between the stereotypes are great, and even within an apparently uniform category, such as that of calendar calculators, we encounter a host of diverse strategies.

In looking for an explanation of the savant syndrome it seems reasonable to distinguish between what savants are capable of doing and how it is that they can do it. The first calls for an investigation of the strategies savants use and whether these strategies are based on memory, on enumeration, or on handy rules of thumb. The second calls for a theory that explains why savants are able to make use of these strategies, while most other people cannot. At the moment, we have no grand theory explaining the hidden nexus between draughtsman savants and autistic calendar calculators, or between blind musical savants and mnemonists capable of reciting long timetables by heart. Most hypotheses have a limited range; they are focused on two or three savants in just one category, and have little if any explanatory value outside that range.

The oldest and the most romantic hypothesis by far is that savants were destined to come into the world as geniuses, but that something went wrong before or during their birth. The consequences were catastrophic: all their talents were destroyed or irreparably damaged, except for – by a bizarre accident – just one. Without the disaster they would have had a radiant intellect, turning them into brilliant mathematicians, or composers or artists of genius. Their brain was like a brightly illuminated palace in which in one room after another the lights were extinguished by some catastrophe, entire wings being dimmed until finally a light shone from just one window. The suggested causes were manifold. In the eighteenth century, people thought that if a pregnant woman had a sudden shock, the results might prove fatal to her child. In the nineteenth century fears were voiced about the mental powers of children conceived in a drunken stupor. Nowadays we believe that the absorption of toxic matter during pregnancy or lack of oxygen at birth can cause grave damage. But no matter what the cause, if the damage leaves one single talent intact, we have the pattern of the savant: an isolated gift in the midst of defects.

There is much to argue against this hypothesis, so much in fact that it can be safely ignored. The gifts of savants are rarely of the kind that goes with a brilliant mind. If chance had wiped out almost all Gauss's talents, the gift of calendar calculation would not have survived. Picasso, stripped of nearly all his gifts, would never have drawn like Stephen Wiltshire. No Derek Paravicini would have emerged from a damaged Bach. Nor do the special talents of savants develop as if they had ever been part of a general spectrum of talents. For that, they appear too early in life, often at the age of two or three, and by then have generally assumed their definite form. The gifts of savants often look static. Nadia could draw better at the age of five than the precocious Picasso could at ten, but she continued at that level while Picasso's talent went on developing. The same was true of Stephen, who started to draw as a child but never passed through the stages of the normal picture-drawing child: he did not begin by drawing heads on legs or little dolls with rakes for arms. His drawing had an adult appearance from the outset. With musical savants, too, their talent appears extremely early, well before the age when even the most precocious young geniuses begin to show their promise. What the savant can do has little of a surviving talent about it. An ordinary person, not a genius, has been lost in him.

A second hypothesis looks for the explanation in compensation. Savants without exception take very little interest in what goes on around them. Sometimes a sensory handicap excludes them at a stroke from entire fields of information; sometimes a mental disorder such as autism encloses them in a carefully confined world in which as little as possible ever changes. Savants focus their one-track minds on the development of their single talent. They are not distracted by social conventions and by the thousands of facts and faculties they involve, but reserve all their mental energy and memory for calendars, maps, timetables, records of free pints of beer and whatever else manages to attract their attention. For the rest all is practice and repetition. With a concentration that at first sight seems irreconcilable with the common idea of mental retardation, the idiot develops into a savant in his own special little groove. The savant is the product of concentration, a single-track mind and endless repetition.

Michael Howe, having studied the calendar calculator Dave, went on to apply this compensation hypothesis to the working of the memory. He found that with standard memory tests, savants have slightly higher scores than at tests for other abilities, but considerably lower scores than normal experimental subjects. How could the endless lists of marks, serial numbers, post codes, population statistics and other apparently meaningless data ever finish up in their memory? A non-savant anxious to fix something in his memory – say, a poem – relies on his familiarity with his memory. He knows what strategies to employ, he learns the poem line by line, tests himself, keeps rehearsing. But according to Howe, insight into the workings of one's own memory ('metamemory') is not a prerequisite of memorization; the crucial factor is *attention*. There is no doubt that savants take a keen interest in the material they store in their memory, that they pay extremely careful attention to it, and that they persist in doing so. The faultless storage of that material is the natural result of the attention they pay to it. Non-savants, too, who for a while take a keen interest in, say, aeroplanes, makes of car, or railway engines – and many boys never lose that interest – can easily and with pleasure store a host of the most bizarre data. Where the savant differs from them is not so much in *how* he remembers as in *what* he is determined to remember.

The question is therefore: why do savants take an interest in such uninteresting things? Now, what we find interesting depends on our other options. If we study a calendar, our thoughts quickly stray to more enthralling subjects. Some dates conjure up memories of birthdays, celebrations, anniversaries of deaths, or holidays. All these associations distract us from the bare structure of the calendar. 'Having a relatively sparsely furnished mind', Howe writes, 'may be an advantage as far as sustaining one's attention to details is concerned.' Howe has likened the savant's condition to solitary confinement, a situation in which even normal people can catch themselves developing an interest in the number of bricks in the wall.

What the concentration hypothesis leaves unexplained is the *nature* of the savant's gift. The skill of savants hides a paradoxical tension. On the one hand it is often isolated, trivial facts that are memorized so lastingly. In that respect, their memory is extremely selective; savants, as Langdon Down put it, remember the bare, superficial facts, not the links between them or the categories into which they fit. On the other hand, savants seem able to access regularities beneath the surface, be it in the order of the calendar, the harmonic structures of a piece of music or the laws of perspective. Such access seems to call for an ability that is conspicuously absent during memorization, namely abstraction. How is it possible that a musical savant has a feeling for the complex order of chords and modes, while the structures of speech remain closed to him? Why can a calendar calculator fathom the implicit rules of the calendar, but not those of simple multiplication?

## Lateralization

One hypothesis that places at least some of the individual findings into a comprehensible context has been framed by Galaburda and Geschwind, two Harvard neurologists. Between the tenth and eighteenth week of embryonic development, there is an acceleration in the formation of the brain. At the peak of that phase, the growth of the brain is explosive: about ten thousand neurons appear *every two seconds*. All these neurons are engaged in a life-and-death struggle: shortly before the child's birth, a large proportion of the neurons that failed to forge links to other neurons die off. On the basis of experiments with the brains of humans and animals, Galaburda and Geschwind postulated that the left half of the brain develops slightly more slowly than the right and is therefore more susceptible to harmful prenatal influences. One of these may well be due to the action of the male hormone testosterone, which circulates in the body during the formation of the foetal testicles. For reasons that are not yet clear, a high testosterone level has an inhibiting effect on cortical growth.

Because of the divergent rate of development of the two halves of the brain, the consequences can be more serious for the left side than they are for the right. In that case, Galaburda and Geschwind maintain, free, as yet unattached, neurons can migrate from left to right. In the most extreme case this can lead to the dominance of the right half of the brain.

In the distribution of mental functions one would then expect the eventual appearance of precisely the same pattern as is found in savants: an impairment of the functions that, in most people, are directed chiefly by the left half of the brain, such as the processing and production of speech, and a compensating shift in the direction of tasks involving spatial information, such as the memorization of maps or the memorization of patterns taken in at a glance. This hypothesis may also explain the intriguing phenomenon of the predominance of male over female savants: female foetuses have a much lower testosterone level. The fact that the same overrepresentation of males is found in such milder speech defects as dyslexia lends further support to this hypothesis. And perhaps its most important merit is that if the shift is gradual rather than a complete change of dominance, then the variety in the special gifts of savants also has an appropriate neurological background.

Leon Miller has convincingly fitted many of his findings with musical savants into the hypothesis of a cortical shift. Two of his savants showed signs of neurological defects in the left half of the brain. One was paralysed on the right side; scans of the other revealed atrophied tissue in the left of the brain. Nearly all musical savants have serious speech defects, with the result that a psychological function that is normally the more important channel of communication falls by the wayside. It also means that a potential means of blocking the development of other functions has gone. Speech and music are in some respects rival functions, with speech in a slightly predominant position: we are able to read and talk while music is playing in the background; listening to music while people are talking is much more difficult. Savants develop their ear for music at a critical period in the development of speech. The energy normal children invest in the acquisition of a vocabulary, the sensitivity to sound and pitch they must develop for this ability, the discovery of the implicit rules of word construction and sentence structure, the mastering of the subtle motor system needed for reading, speaking and writing, the recognition of letters and word pictures – all that is used by the savant for the development and refinement of his special gift. If, as is almost always the case, he has a visual handicap as well, his acoustic sensitivity may increase even more. The result is the musical equivalent of a vocabulary, a grammar and an accentless mastery of the mother tongue.

The human brain has the ability after even the most serious injury to recover some of its former balance. No ravages are too severe for the introduction of a new order. Blockages and damages lead to a network of escape routes, detours and temporary bridges. The minus of one handicap is often followed by the plus of compensation: a defect by a hidden benefit. In savants, the one gift can open a channel of communication. The mental calculations of Jedediah Buxton did not develop as an instrument for social intercourse, let alone as the quickest route to free pints of beer, but they did have precisely that effect. Savant gifts, once discovered and developed, become a means of contact, the more valuable when communication by speech is so often impossible. The drawings of Stephen Wiltshire are chinks in an autistic armour. In his institute for people with multiple handicaps, Ockelford sometimes had to deal with patients who had the same handicap as Derek Paravicini but did not have music as a means of expression. If someone like that has a little understanding and wants to share his feelings with others, the blocked path leads to disappointment, frustration and aggression. For Derek, according to Ockelford, music served exclusively as a means of communicating with his friends. 'He would never sit down and pour out his heart in a piece by Chopin or the like. Music for him is not an end in itself, but a means of reaching something.'

Inherent in the benefits of this one, narrow contact lies a danger. For daily intercourse in a world outside the family or institution, savant talents are often ineffective. To help the development of more conventional means of communication such as speech, the cultivation of the savant's gifts is in some cases stopped or discouraged. The consequences of such therapeutic interventions differ. Stephen Wiltshire has taken vocational training and now works as a *sous-chef*. His draughtsman's gifts have not suffered as a result. Young Nadia, who drew such beautiful horses, learned to speak and to count at a school for autistic children, but the spontaneous drawings of former years have almost completely gone. Nowadays she only draws occasionally on a steamed-up windowpane.

## BIBLIOGRAPHY

Anonymous, 'The life of Jedediah Buxton', *Gentleman's Magazine* 24 (1754), 251–2.

Geschwind, N., and A. M. Galaburda, 'Cerebral lateralization', *Archives of Neurology* 42 (1985), 428–59.

Howe, M. J. A., *Fragments of Genius: The Strange Feats of Idiots Savants*, London, 1989.

Howe, M. J. A., and J. Smith, 'Calendar calculating in "idiots savants": how do they do it?', *British Journal of Psychology* 79 (1988), 371–86.

Kayzer, W., *Vertrouwd en o zo vreemd*, Amsterdam, 1995.

Langdon Down, J., *On Some of the Mental Affections of Childhood and Youth*, London, 1887.

Miller, L. K., *Musical Savants: Exceptional Skill in the Mentally Retarded*, Hillsdale, NJ, 1989.

Ockelford, A., 'Derek Paravicini: a boy with extraordinary musical abilities', *Eye Contact* (1991), 8–10.

O'Connor, N., and B. Hermelin, 'Idiot savant calendrical calculators: maths or memory?', *Psychological Medicine* 14 (1984), 801–6.

'Visual and graphic abilities of the idiot savant artist', *Psychological Medicine* 17 (1987), 79–90.

Sacks, O., *An Anthropologist on Mars: Seven Paradoxical Tales*, London, 1995.

Smith, S. B., *The Great Mental Calculators*, New York, 1983.

Treffert, D. A., *Extraordinary People*, New York, 1989.

Wiltshire, S., *Floating Cities: Venice, Amsterdam, Leningrad – and Moscow*, London, 1991.

# 9  The memory of a grandmaster: a conversation with Ton Sijbrands

At 9.30 in the morning of 6 November 1999, Ton Sijbrands was sitting in the boardroom of an insurance company in Gouda in the Netherlands. On the table in front of him lay a box of Dannemann cigars, and next to it a sheet of paper with the names of twenty opponents. In another large room in a different part of the building each of these was sitting behind his own board: six first-class and fourteen strong players, for the most part members of the Gouda Damlust draughts society, ranked in the national first division. Sijbrands had just shaken each one by the hand and wished them an enjoyable game. At 9.40, he used a permanently open telephone line to send his opening move on board 1: 32-28. Precisely fifteen hours later, at 12.40 a.m., the last opponent resigned. Sijbrands had won seventeen games and conceded three draws. None of his opponents ever had a serious chance of winning.

Sijbrands, the former world champion, enhanced his own record with this score of 92.5 per cent wins. He had played his first official simultaneous blindfold game in 1982 at The Hague, with a new world record of eight out of ten. He has never surrendered his title since then. The Gouda simultaneous blindfold was an improvement of 100 per cent on his first title.

In that last simultaneous game, 1,708 moves were made. Every move is a choice out of a multiplicity of options that have to be evaluated. After the opening moves a decision tree is established, the branches of which thicken into a full crown in the middle game. Sijbrands coped with twenty such trees. During the fifteen hours of the simultaneous game, tens of thousands of positions must have run through his mind. *How did he manage to do that?* Does he have a photographic memory? Does he 'see' all the positions?

When we met for a conversation six months after the simultaneous blindfold game, that last question proved a poor opening move.

'That's the very question I was afraid of. A few days ago I said to my wife, I bet he asks what I actually see when I play a simultaneous blindfold. And I really find it almost impossible to say. What exactly appears before your mind's eye when you think of a position? It's a picture, but it isn't of anything very concrete. For instance, it isn't that I see the edge of the board, or the kind of piece being used, or the colours. I don't think what I see is all that different from what you see when you play an ordinary game and try to picture the moves to be made. Every draughts player who thinks ahead is actually playing a blindfold game. That's all I can say. I just hope you won't think our talk's a washout because of that.'

Next I tried a few outflanking movements. Do any special strategies exist perhaps to make things easier for yourself? Do you use special codes?

'In the opening phase, I do. During the late eighties, I developed a system of opening codes. Each code consists of a maximum of three figures. The most common opening, 32-28, starts with the figure 1. In a simultaneous blindfold game I use eight different openings and I link these to the different boards. On board 1, I play 32-28, on board 2, I play 33-28, and so on. In theory there are nine openings, but I never play opening 32-27 – for me that is code 9. I don't like it very much because there is a good chance that it will quickly turn into the position following openings 31-27 or 31-26. Opening 8 – 35-30 – is fairly risky, a very dangerous opening move. I do play it, but then I try to get an opponent on board 8 who allows me to get away with it. Board 9 then has opening 1 again, and so on.'

So the code brings order into the opening phase and helps you to recall all the positions one by one?

'Precisely. I would have to be mad to play the same opening over and over again. I make the games as varied as I possibly can. I like to envisage the largest possible range of games. Even so, you have to watch your step because even though you use different openings, the positions can coincide later on anyway. In this simultaneous match there were two games, on board 3 and board 19, which ran parallel for eleven moves and then I put a stop to it, because it put an extra strain on my memory.'

Which games are the hardest to remember?

'The games I'm afraid of most during simultaneous matches are the ones that have no pattern at all. A major exchange of pieces in the beginning resulting in the gain of a piece is something I have to put up with, but if you then reach a position in which white is predominantly in its own half and black mainly in its own half as well, you get an endless series of pointless developing moves without any pattern emerging. That sort of game is a real disaster. It happened to me during a blindfold simultaneous in 1993: I crowned a piece, my opponent took my king, with a crucial loss of pieces, but the game nevertheless continued for a good eight hours. It turned out to be one of the longest games in that simultaneous. At the time I remembered the entire build-up but that took a great deal of hard work. I wouldn't want to have to play eighteen games like that. For the last simultaneous I arranged with the referee that in such cases he ask the opponent nicely to stop, though he can't of course be forced to do so. My opponents kindly kept to this arrangement. I think there was even one player who gave up in a draw position.'

There would appear to be even more obstacles for a blindfold player. Every position is a spatial pattern but is also being developed. Manœuvres are in train, traps are sprung, moves are blocked. And you also have to navigate in time.

'What takes a great deal of concentration is devising a plan and, when your opponent makes the moves you have anticipated, remembering precisely what point in the planned course of the game you happen to have reached.'

When you are busy thinking you often keep moving your fingers as if you were trying out moves in the air. What are you actually doing?

'I often sit there tapping the edge of the table softly, in a kind of rhythm. Every tap stands for a black move followed by a white move and so on. It has nothing to do with the direction of the moves; it's all about the cadence of the game.'

If you think in patterns, in more or less logical developments, do blunders by your opponents have an off-putting effect on your game?

'They do in fact demand a great deal of concentration. The most difficult thing is the opponent who plays a solid game but suddenly makes an absolutely stupid move. In such cases, giving the obvious reply takes a great deal of courage; you keep thinking: perhaps I am making a mistake, this cannot possibly be right. You are terribly afraid of making a blunder yourself; you assume that your opponent must have had some reason for making such a peculiar move. You go over the whole game once more to make absolutely certain that it really is a blunder. For that reason, too, it is in my own best interest to play against top-level opponents who make logical moves.'

What do you think of the quality of your game in a blindfold simultaneous as compared with a normal game?

'I have the impression that I play a blindfold no worse than I do, for instance, a simultaneous against the clock. I think you would do better to compare it with a timed simultaneous than with a normal simultaneous game. In a blindfold simultaneous you have more time to think. In a normal simultaneous I would not have scored more points against these opponents than I have done now. I don't lose more often in a blindfold simultaneous than in a normal game; I think I've only ever lost two blindfolds in my entire life. In a blind simultaneous I have the advantage of staying in my seat. That may sound trite, but the fact that you are sitting down helps your concentration. It's hard having to assess the precise level of the game you are playing. You are up against good players and that's all to the good, since it increases your chances of coming across recognizable patterns, but of course they are not the very strongest players.'

A blindfold simultaneous like that is bound to be an enormous test of your powers of concentration. Does it become more difficult to keep your concentration as the game proceeds? Does the effort you have to put in increase or decrease?

'There's a wonderful decrease. To go on being able to cross off a name all the time helps you to persevere. Halfway through the going is often tough. You've been at it for hours then and you know it's going to go on for as many hours again. But that has little to do with the state of affairs on the board, which I can still remember perfectly well. Once an endgame comes up it really does go on getting easier. The only problem I can imagine at the end is an endgame with my having several kings and my opponent having kings as well, say a five to two endgame. That's easily won in theory, but those kings can be anywhere and that is hard to remember. Still, that's something I have never come across in any of my simultaneous blindfold games.'

Amongst chess players, the ability to play blindfold seems to depend on the overall skill of the player. Nearly all grandmasters can play blindfold, but below the grandmaster level, and certainly below the master level, almost no one is able to do it. It is therefore not a gift that develops independently but is part of the talent and routine of grandmasters. Is that true of you as well? Did you train to play blindfold? How did you discover that you were able to do it?

'One of my opponents in the Gouda blindfold simultaneous was a friend of my youth, Harry Kolk. I often used to stay over with Harry at his home, and we would play in his room until late at night. His mother would come and tell us to turn off the light. But we'd be in the middle of a game so we'd finish it by calling out our moves. I never really trained for it. When I was about sixteen I once played blindfold against ten opponents and I seemed to be able to do it. And it doesn't seem to wear off as I get older. It's just that simultaneous games always last longer, but that's because there are more players.'

Anyone watching Sijbrands playing twenty blindfold games at once must wonder if he has an exceptionally good memory.

'That's what people tend to think. I do believe that I have a good memory for things that interest me, such as literature and politics, but my memory for everyday things is awful. If someone asks if this blindfold draughts player has to take a shopping list to the greengrocer, the answer is yes. My memory is highly selective.'

That is evident. Sijbrands is also a very keen chess player and has been the champion of his chess club several times. But when it comes to blindfold chess he is out of his depth.

'I manage to see up to four moves ahead but no more. Then the pieces start to dance in front of my eyes and I get completely confused.'

With a grin: 'In short, the same reaction as with bunglers in draughts. In ordinary chess, I can't see any further than four or five moves ahead either.'

There are some colourful stories doing the rounds about the after-effects of their extreme exertions on blindfold chess players. The Argentine chess player Najdorf, who in 1945 set up a new record of forty-five games, could not fall asleep for three days and nights until, at his wit's end, he took refuge in a cinema. In Sijbrand's case, too, some games go on haunting him for days.

'In one of the games I could see in my mind's eye that a piece was in the wrong place. That became obvious a few moves later

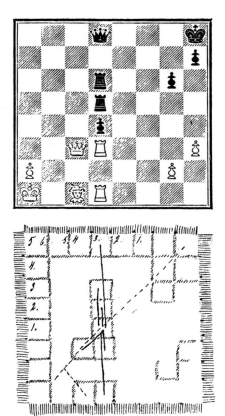

Fig. 7 Chess position and Sittenfeld's drawing of his mental picture of that position.

when my opponent opted for a draw. But the game would not let go of me. For the first twenty-four hours after the simultaneous I was convinced that that mistake had cost me a point and that I should have won easily. The next day I was in the stand at a Sparta–Ajax football match, went over the endgame once more in my mind and came to the conclusion that it would have had to end in a draw anyway.'

So you can watch a football match and go over an endgame in your mind? The fanatical Ajax supporter apologized:

'Oh well, the game wasn't really worth watching, they were giving the ball away too much. It finished 2-1, but Ajax weren't really up for it, you could tell.'

There is little literature on the subject of blindfold draughts, but much more on blindfold chess. Interest in the psychology of blindfold chess is as old as psychology itself: as early as 1894, Alfred Binet made a study of the feats of Parisian blindfold chess players. One of his conclusions applies equally well to blindfold draughts: their prowess does *not* rest on what is commonly called 'photographic memory', thanks to which the simultaneous player has a faithful visual copy that he can call to mind at will. The blindfold chess player Sittenfeld drew a sketch, at Binet's request, of 'what he saw' when he thought of a particular position, which turned out to be a fairly schematic and abstract representation, more a pattern of possible moves than a static picture.

Sijbrands can identify himself with Sittenfeld's sketch.

'What I "see" is certainly no complete and detailed picture, but rather the relevant part of the position and the pattern of the moves.'

Too concrete a picture might well turn out to be a handicap. Sijbrands points out that someone who normally sits behind a board playing draughts must, as it were, look through the pieces to 'see' the future positions. Too persistent a picture of the present position is a disadvantage. The chess grandmaster Reuben Fine once asked for an empty board during a simultaneous blindfold to be able, so to speak, to project onto it the positions he saw before his mind's eye. He never again used this stratagem – it proved an obstacle to his thought.

Binet drew his conclusions from a study of blindfold players. Experiments subsequently confirmed that they do not store positions as photographic images. A good example is the experiment described by the psychologists (and chess masters) De Groot and Gobet. In this experiment a chess master was shown two positions and asked to remember them. Then the board was removed. Next he was asked which pieces were found on which squares. In the one case, he was first asked to recall a series of squares in the second position. In the second case he was asked to recall squares from the two positions alternately. Although all the answers were correct, the second case took longer. Clearly the memorized positions did not fit into the brain like two photographs; switching from the one to the other position always took extra time. A much simpler refutation of the photographic-memory hypothesis is the fact that a random arrangement of pieces is far more difficult to remember than a logical one.

Later studies have confirmed that playing blindfold is a *spatial* rather than a *visual* achievement. In the world of draughts and chess, there are examples of blind players who have reached the master level and of grandmasters who became blind but maintained their standard of play. In his *In het oog van de meester* (In the eye of the master), the psychologist Jongman has shown that the 'picture' seen in a blindfold game is not a kind of sensory after-image but a form of revisualization. Thanks to his high standard and expertise, the grandmaster can call on all the associations and codes he needs to reconstruct a position in his memory. The essential element of blindfold play is the *pattern* of the moves. In an introspective report, Reuben Fine describes how he plays blindfold games, and in this account he devotes a great deal of space to the associations that pieces and positions call forth in him. In this area, the memory plays a key role.

With Sijbrands, too, the positions activate a whole network of memories of earlier games, classic openings, analyses of endgames, tactical manœuvres and proven traps. In his journal *Dammen* ('Draughts'), Sijbrands analyses a number of games played in a blindfold simultaneous, and here you can read such remarks as 'this position turned up previously in the Wiersma–Sijbrands game at the Suiker tournament in 1969' or 'by filling square 18 from his *left* wing, Ijssel revived the days of Koeperman and – above all – of Pieter Bergsma'. Writing about his game with Schep, Sijbrands even remarked that the play was reminiscent of the 'Sijbrands–H. Voorburg simultaneous played against the clock in 1995, which took you back so clearly to the fifteenth Deslauriers–Koeperman world championship match in 1958'. Every one of these is a reference to patterns. Positions activate a subtle network of associations in Sijbrands, all of them anchoring the board position firmly in the memory.

Jongman has called the gift of playing blindfold an 'epiphenomenon', a by-product. It is part of the grandmaster's repertoire. It develops automatically, without any special training. But as well as grandmaster skill there is another condition to be satisfied. An achievement such as Sijbrands's is only possible thanks to a life spent studying draughts. This accounts for the expertise and routine that enable him to store positions and developments in a game as units, thus preventing his memory from being overtaxed. The knowledge already present in his memory helps him to recognize the patterns in the games played during a simultaneous.

This conclusion leads to a paradox. Part of the explanation of Sijbrands's phenomenal memory is that he remembers both more and less at the same time. Less, because he does not remember a particular position as the sum of all the individual positions of the pieces, but as an overall pattern. More, because the pattern in its turn conjures up an entire network of associations with games played or studied in the past. The real mystery is how someone can play draughts so brilliantly, not that he can also do it blindfold and simultaneously against twenty opponents.

On 21 December 2002 Sijbrands set a new record. After 19 hours and 35 minutes he reached a score of 88 per cent: seventeen victories, five draws.

BIBLIOGRAPHY

Binet, A., and L. Henneguy, *La psychologie des grands calculateurs et joueurs d'échecs*, Paris, 1894.
Fine, R., 'The psychology of blindfold chess. An introspective account', *Acta Psychologica* 24 (1965), 352–70.
Groot, A. D. de, and F. Gobet, *Perception and Memory in Chess: Studies in the Heuristics of the Professional Eye*, Assen, 1996.
Jongman, R. W., *Het oog van de meester*, Assen, 1968.
Sijbrands, T., 'Goudse notities', *Dammen* 141 (2000), 15–26.
    *Wereldrecord blindsimultaan dammen*, Gouda, 2000.

# 10 Trauma and memory: the Demjanjuk case

From August 1942 to August 1943, the German extermination camp of Treblinka (Poland) employed the services of a Ukrainian whose exceptional brutality and huge stature earned him the nickname of Ivan Grozny – Ivan the Terrible. He operated the diesel engines by which the gas for the gas chambers was produced. Ivan was implicated in the murder of 850,000 Jews.

More than thirty years later, in 1975, suspicion fell for the first time on one John Demjanjuk, a worker in the Ford plant in Cleveland, Ohio. He was of Ukrainian descent and had been living in the United States since 1951. He owed his job to his mechanical skills. The name of Demjanjuk appeared on German documents confiscated by the Red Army at the end of the war, which the Soviet authorities had forwarded to several American senators. American law does not provide for the prosecution for war crimes committed in other countries. However, if it can be proved that a person lied during the immigration proceedings he can be stripped of his United States citizenship. From 1947 to 1951, Demjanjuk had been kept in a German camp for stateless persons, where he had been interrogated by members of the US immigration service about, among other things, his activities during the war. Demjanjuk had told them that from 1937 to 1943 he had been 'a farm worker in a Polish hamlet called Sobibor'. This conflicted with the German documents, which stated that a Ukrainian by the name of Ivan Demjanjuk had been trained in Trawniki camp for concentration camp duty. In a long series of legal actions, Demjanjuk objected to being stripped of his US citizenship, but in the end he was extradited to Israel. Many people will remember the television footage of a ranting Demjanjuk on the aircraft steps. The trial, which started in Jerusalem in 1987, hinged round the question of whether or not John Demjanjuk and Ivan the Terrible were one and the same person.

The Israeli prosecutors tried to link Demjanjuk to Ivan in two ways. During the preliminary investigation, a number of survivors from Treblinka – Jews who had been forced to work at the gas chambers and who escaped after an uprising on 2 August

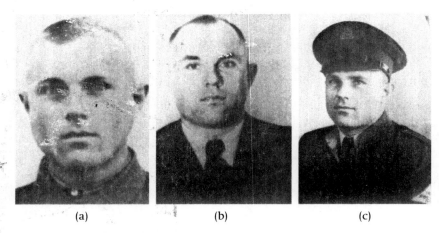

(a)          (b)          (c)

Fig. 8   Three Demjanjuks. Photograph (a) was taken in 1942 and is part of the Trawniki identity card, known as the 'Trawniki certificate'. Demjanjuk was twenty-two at the time. Photograph (b) was taken in 1951 by the US immigration department. Photograph (c) shows Demjanjuk at the age of twenty-five. This photograph was not discovered until 1987 and could therefore no longer be used for identification purposes since the other photographs had by then been widely seen around the world.

1943 – testified that they recognized Ivan on the photograph the US immigration department had taken of Demjanjuk in 1951. Secondly, there was an identity card with a photograph showing that Demjanjuk had attended a training course in Trawniki for concentration camp guards. In addition to the testimony of witnesses and the identity card, the court was presented with a poor and constantly changing alibi by Demjanjuk for the time he allegedly worked in Treblinka. In 1988 he was found guilty and sentenced to death. While he was locked up in his cell pending the outcome of his appeal, the Berlin Wall fell and documents became available from Soviet archives that gave the affair an unexpected turn.

At the Jerusalem trial, a Dutch professor of psychology, W. A. Wagenaar, was called as an expert witness for the defence. Shortly before, five survivors had testified against Demjanjuk. Their insistent and emotional testimony seemed to remove any doubts about the identity of the accused. The television pictures went round the world. The attacks on Wagenaar following his decision to appear for the defence were largely due to the feeling that there was something ignoble about questioning the testimony of old people who had so obviously summoned up all their courage for their confrontation with Demjanjuk/Ivan. The horrors of Treblinka still filled their minds – and their dreams – and any reference to the 'unreliability of eyewitnesses' seemed unbecoming. The witnesses themselves spoke of ineradicable memories and that is undoubtedly what these recollections were: some events are not merely 'remembered' but etched in the memory.

In 1988, Wagenaar published his *Identifying Ivan*. The conclusions of the book and the developments that took place after its publication make it clear that the Demjanjuk case can teach us a great deal about memory and recognition under the traumatizing circumstances that prevail in an extermination camp, and the precautions that must be taken in identification procedures.

## Treblinka

Treblinka was an extermination camp. Together with Belzec and with Sobibor, 120 miles away, it was part of 'Aktion Reinhard', the SS operation to exterminate all Polish Jews. Those sent to Treblinka were not used as slave labourers, as in Buchenwald or Dachau, but gassed. The camp was served by a special branch of the main railway line and lay hidden in a thickly wooded area. The Jewish victims, driven from ghettos in Poland and later also from Czech, Greek and Bulgarian towns, were delivered in crammed goods trains. After the appointment of Franz Stangl as camp commander the preparation for the exterminations began to take on the style of a grotesque stage play. On his orders a make-believe station was built, complete with a large clock and signs reading 'Restaurant' and 'Telegraph and Telephone Office'. Timetables on the platforms gave the arrival and departure times of trains from Vienna and Berlin. Once forced violently off the trains, the newly arrived victims – about two to three thousand at a time – were told that they had arrived in a transit camp and had to be prepared for a further train journey. First they were to go to a bathhouse, while their clothing was being disinfected. All valuables were to be handed over; they would be kept in the camp safe and returned to them after their bath. The men were separated from the women and children, who were driven to a barracks in which they were ordered to undress. The women had their heads shaved (the hair collected in concentration and extermination camps was processed into industrial felt that was used among other things for slippers for U-boat crews). All those too weak, too old or too ill to walk by themselves were taken to a 'Lazarett', a 'military hospital', on top of which fluttered a Red Cross flag. Once inside the barbed-wire fence camouflaged with pine branches, everyone was made to stand by a pit and was then shot dead with a pistol. The rest of the group were marched in a long naked procession past the sign 'Zur Badeanstalt' ('To the bathhouse') along a path called 'Himmelfahrt Strasse' ('Ascension Street'). Once the doors had been hermetically sealed, a diesel engine appropriated from a captured Russian tank was started, giving off carbon monoxide. The gas was pumped into the 'baths' through pipes mounted with showerheads. After thirty to forty minutes everyone inside was dead. German soldiers stood outside listening at the door. At their shout of 'Alles schläft' (all asleep), the door was opened. Because hundreds of people had been crammed into a small space there was room neither to fall down nor to collapse. When the door was opened, all the bodies were upright. Between arrival at the 'station' and the removal of the corpses less than two hours had elapsed.

Many of the victims must have been taken in by the masquerade. During the Nuremburg trials (1945–6) Samuel Rajzman, one of the survivors, testified that one day a train from Vienna arrived. A woman in her eighties reported to SS Deputy Camp Commander Kurt Franz with a document indicating that she was Sigmund Freud's sister. She begged him to give her an office job. Franz pretended to study the document carefully, replied that there must have been a mistake, walked with her to the timetables and said that a train would take her back to Vienna in about two hours' time. If she would just leave her things and go to the bathhouse, her documents and a train ticket to Vienna would be waiting for her.

The camp was manned by twenty to thirty SS-men. Kurt Franz, who had been brought in from Belzec, was responsible for the day-to-day running of the place. He was feared for the totally capricious way in which he ill-treated people and summarily executed them. On his tours of inspection, Franz was accompanied by his dog Barry, trained to attack people in the abdomen. Ukrainians were employed as camp guards. These men were originally prisoners of war but had gained their liberty by training as *SS-Wachmänner* (SS guards). In Treblinka there were about a hundred of them. The work associated with the extermination of Jews was fobbed off on to a *Sonderkommando* (special commando) of Jewish convicts. These 'working Jews' had to sort the clothing, shave the women, empty and clean the gas chambers, pull gold teeth and bury the bodies. At the beginning the turnover in these men was great. During the Eichmann trial (1961) survivors reported that most of the *Sonderkommando* could not stand it for more than a few days and would ask at morning roll call to be shot. Elijahu Rosenberg, who also testified at the Demjanjuk trial, said in 1961 that after their first long day of removing corpses, men hanged themselves by their belts in the barracks, helping one another to kick the chairs from under them. Later on, Stangl introduced a form of division of labour and a relatively permanent group of 'working Jews' stayed alive.

Early in the spring of 1943 Himmler paid a visit to the camp. He gave orders to burn the bodies, even those that had already been buried. The mass graves were emptied with a dragline excavator, and the corpses cremated on a gridiron constructed of rails. By summer the pits were practically empty, and the 'working Jews' noticed that fewer and fewer victims were being brought in. They concluded that the camp was about to be shut down and that they themselves would finish up in the gas chambers. They decided on an uprising, and at midday on 2 August 1943 they broke into the arms store with a duplicate key. But even as the arms were being handed out, the German guards got wind of the revolt and the plan to occupy the camp had to be abandoned. Some seven hundred prisoners then tried to break out of the camp. Most of them were shot from the watchtowers, but some twenty men were able to escape into the surrounding woods and to survive long enough to see the liberation. Several of them wrote accounts or memoirs about their stay in Treblinka. That of Yankel Wiernik, a Jewish carpenter from Warsaw, appeared as early as 1945; later Richard Glazar from Prague also recorded a version. Most of the witnesses in the Demjanjuk case came from the group that managed to escape on 2 August.

During the abortive revolt, most of the buildings – all built of wood except for the gas chambers – went up in flames. The remaining prisoners had to dismantle the camp and eradicate all traces of the exterminations. Then they were shot. The Germans ploughed up the ground, planted lupins, built a farm on the site and handed it over to a Ukrainian peasant family.

## The identification of Demjanjuk

Demjanjuk was born in 1920 in a small village in the Kiev district. After the First World War, the Ukraine was incorporated into the Soviet Union. During the early thirties – when Demjanjuk was about twelve years old – Stalin's agricultural policy caused a man-made famine that claimed millions of lives in a country previously known as 'the breadbasket of Europe'. When the Germans invaded the Soviet Union, Demjanjuk – by then a nineteen-year-old tractor driver on a kolkhoz – was drafted into the Red Army. His loyalty to the Soviet Union was not particularly great, but in the army he at least had the prospect of being fed. In May 1942, he was taken prisoner in the Crimea. The camp in Chelm, Poland, in which he finished up was not much more than a field surrounded by barbed wire. Prisoners slept in holes in ground they had dug themselves, and these filled with rainwater in the autumn. Few rations were issued. Eating grass, cannibalism, pollution, death on a massive scale – Demjanjuk rediscovered in this camp what he had experienced in the thirties at home.

In the spring of 1942, the German army began to recruit volunteers for 'security units' in the camps. These units were earmarked for the hunting of Jews and for guarding concentration and extermination camps. Many Ukrainians considered Stalin's regime a conspiracy of Jewish Bolsheviks, which helped to reinforce their anti-semitism and made them ideal as henchmen of the Germans. A special *SS-Wachmann* training camp was opened in a deserted sugar factory in Trawniki in Poland. In July 1942, Demjanjuk volunteered for work in Trawniki.

Up to this point there was no difference between the prosecution and the defence as to Demjanjuk's war activities, not even after the discovery of new documents in the former Soviet Union. Remarkably – in view of the subsequent trial – the earliest documents stated that Demjanjuk had worked in Sobibor, not in Treblinka.

Fig. 9 The page from the album with photographs of Demjanjuk
(*bottom left*) and Federenko (*bottom right*).

For war crimes in Treblinka, attention was focused above all on another Ukrainian, Fjodor Federenko. Both names appeared on a list of Ukrainians living in the United States and suspected of war crimes. At the beginning of 1976, the US immigration service asked a special police section in Israel to look for witnesses who had been in Sobibor or Treblinka. The Israeli Unit for the Investigation of Nazi Crimes (INC) was the successor to 'Bureau 06', set up to prepare the case against Eichmann. The INC was provided with seventeen photographs of Ukrainian suspects. The investigation fell to the then seventy-year-old Mrs Miriam Radiwker. She placed an advertisement in the papers announcing that an investigation was being carried out into the 'Ukrainians Ivan Demjanjuk and Fjodor Federenko', and appealed to survivors of Sobibor and Treblinka to come forward. With this announcement, she thus let slip the names of the suspects before the actual identification process began. The seventeen photographs in the possession of the INC had been stuck to pages of stiff card and could not be shown individually. There were no distractors, or 'red herrings' – all the photographs were portraits of suspects.

With the first witnesses, Turowski and Goldfarb, the investigation concentrated on Federenko. At that time there was no reason to suppose that they – as survivors of Treblinka – would have known Demjanjuk. Turowski had worked as a mechanic in the Treblinka machine workshop. He stated, hesitantly at first but then with increasing assurance, that he recognized Federenko. Demjanjuk's photograph, next to that of Federenko, was in view the whole time but Turowski made no mention of him. Goldfarb did not recognize Federenko, but declared that the man in photograph 16 seemed familiar to him. He mentioned neither the name Demjanjuk nor the name Ivan. There are strong suspicions that the link between these two names was (inadvertently) suggested by Mrs Radiwker. Unfortunately she had the habit of writing her reports of the identification procedure after the event and then in summary form, and during the trial in Jerusalem – by which time she was eighty-one years old – the precise course of events could no longer be reconstructed.

The next day Turowski was questioned again. This time he declared that he knew both the names Demjanjuk and Ivan. Moreover, he recognized Ivan 'immediately and with absolute certainty' in photograph 16. The question naturally arises whether he actually

Fig. 10   The Trawniki series. Demjanjuk is second from left, bottom row.

recognized Ivan or the photograph he had seen the day before next to that of Federenko.

Another problem is the relative importance of positive and negative identifications. One of the Treblinka survivors, Shlomo Helman, had helped to build the gas chambers and had been in the camp until the uprising. He had worked side by side with Ivan for many months. He estimated that Ivan had been about thirty years old. The name Demjanjuk meant nothing to him, just as little as did the man in photograph 16. Federenko in photograph 17, by contrast, looked familiar to him. Another witness, Elijahu Rosenberg, saw a striking resemblance between photograph 16 and the 'Ukrainian Ivan, who worked in Camp 2 and was called Ivan Grozny [Ivan the Terrible]' – the same shape of head, round and balding, with a thick neck and heavy chin. But Rosenberg also said, 'I cannot identify him with absolute certainty.' Moreover he was not struck by anything special when identifying Federenko, though Demjanjuk's photograph appeared next to Federenko's.

The testimony against Federenko, in short, was more convincing from the outset than that against Demjanjuk. It also sealed his fate. In 1979, Federenko confessed during a trial in the United States that he had been an *SS-Wachmann* in Treblinka. He was extradited to the Soviet Union, where he was put on trial in the summer of 1986 and shortly afterwards executed by firing squad.

In 1979, the Soviet Union released fresh evidence. Captured German documents included an identity card with a photograph issued to Ivan Demjanjuk – the so-called 'Trawniki certificate'. The photograph was ostensibly taken in 1942. The identity card also bore Demjanjuk's service (identification) number: 1393. It was dated 27 March 1943 and stated that he was stationed in Sobibor. At the same time, the Soviet Union also handed over a report on an interrogation of Ignat Danielchenko, a fellow guard in Trawniki, who declared that he had worked with Demjanjuk in Sobibor and later in the Flossenbürg and Regensburg concentration camps. The American investigators – the Demjanjuk trial was still conducted exclusively in the United States – did not manage to question Danielchenko in person and had to make do with a transcript of his sworn statement. The investigators added the unexpectedly provided portrait to a series of eight photographs, and asked the Israeli examiners to show this 'Trawniki series' to witnesses. Identifications of Demjanjuk in the midst of seven 'extras' would indeed have been more convincing, but the problem this time was that nearly all the witnesses were familiar with the 1951 photograph. The US immigration service itself missed a unique chance of confronting a witness with the Trawniki photograph before he had seen the 1951 photograph. Witness Chil Meir Rajchman was first shown a series with the 1951 photograph and then presented with the Trawniki series. On that occasion he identified the 1951 photograph but not the Trawniki photograph. One year later, however, at the Cleveland trial, he did identify the Trawniki photograph.

The American judge found that that there was now sufficient evidence to show that Demjanjuk had lied to the immigration service in 1951. Regardless of whether he had worked in Sobibor or in Treblinka, he had in any case not been a farm worker, nor could any confirmation be found for other versions of his alibi. In 1981, Demjanjuk was stripped of his American citizenship.

During the trial in Jerusalem, by contrast, the question of where precisely Demjanjuk had been stationed was of crucial importance. The witnesses and the documents differed on that point. The Trawniki certificate gave the lie to Demjanjuk's alibi, and placed him in Sobibor.

The testimony of Treblinka survivors was inconsistent. Some identified him positively. A German nurse who had worked in Treblinka also declared that she could recognize him on the photograph. Of the few survivors from Sobibor, by contrast, not a single one recognized him. During the trial it also emerged that some thirty witnesses had tried to identify Demjanjuk and that negative identifications – which were the majority – had not been made available to the defence. Moreover, the former deputy camp commander, Kurt Franz, who was serving a life sentence in Düsseldorf, was unable to identify him in 1979. For the sake of consistency it was proposed that Demjanjuk had worked in Sobibor first and then in Treblinka, or even that he had commuted between the two. The possibility was also left open that the German administration had been slapdash in the matter.

In Jerusalem Wagenaar concentrated his expert testimony on the identification process during the preliminary investigation. According to the explanation he gave later in *Identifying Ivan*, fifty rules and regulations have to be satisfied in a proper identification procedure. Forty-two of these rules were relevant to the identification of Ivan, but no fewer than thirty-seven, he wrote, were broken by the investigators. There was no clear report of the facts: no written record, no tape recording, no report of the instructions, no verbatim shorthand report of the proceedings. There were no safeguards against leading the witness ('Just take another good look') or against directing the attention of witnesses to one particular photograph. The series of portraits on the album page contained no photographs of innocent persons so that there was no chance of 'wrong' answers. The photographs were a varied assortment: even though it had long been clear that a man with a round head and a thick neck was being sought there was only one photograph that satisfied those conditions, that of Demjanjuk. Negative identifications were not carefully taken into account. It was left to the investigators to interpret such answers as 'This face reminds me of...' as positive or negative identification. Photographs were repeatedly shown to the witnesses in a second attempt, although that increased the chances of their recognizing the photograph they had seen before and not the wanted person. There were no precautions to prevent witnesses from influencing one another. Witnesses who had spoken to one another about the identification were not excluded from the procedure. The investigators told the witnesses who they were looking for. Afterwards the witnesses were told whether or not the identification had been a 'success', so that during possible contacts between witnesses there really was something they could pass on. Wagenaar took a very poor view of the whole approach: 'I will not say that the investigative procedure was a farce, but a total farce could have violated only a few more rules.'

At a time when pictures of Demjanjuk had already appeared dozens of times in the press, there took place what for the world was the most striking part of the identification procedure. During the trial in Jerusalem five Treblinka survivors testified that they were absolutely certain that the man now facing them in the dock was Ivan the Terrible.

In April 1988 the court found that the witnesses, combined with the discrediting of his alibi, had proved beyond reasonable doubt that Ivan the Terrible and John Demjanjuk were one and the same person. Demjanjuk was sentenced to death. Just like Eichmann on 31 May 1962, he was to be hanged. While waiting for the result of the appeal that he lodged straightaway, Demjanjuk disappeared again into his cell.

## Trauma and memory

The psychoanalyst Bruno Bettelheim (1903–90) spent a year imprisoned in Buchenwald and Dachau even before the war. After his release in 1939, he emigrated to the United States, where he wrote his recollections of his life in the camps. He laid his notes to one side for three years to put sufficient distance between him and the events and then, in 1943, he published a psychological analysis of human behaviour under the extreme conditions prevailing in a concentration camp. For him, the observation of his own reactions and that of his fellow prisoners and the SS-men who guarded them was a means of keeping his mental balance, as he explained in the introduction, a form of protection against the disintegration of his personality.

In the camp, there were no means of taking notes. Everything had to be remembered. But Bettelheim observed that he was 'seriously hampered by extreme malnutrition and other factors that deteriorate the memory; most important of these was the ever present sense of "what's the use, you'll never leave the camp alive," which was daily re-enforced by the death of fellow prisoners'. He only managed to memorize things by repeating them time and again to himself and going over them again while at work. After his emigration, when he felt safe at last, much of what seemed to have been forgotten came back to him. Even so, concentration camp life clearly had a detrimental effect on the memory: what had been automatic and natural in the past, now called for a deliberate effort.

In fact, the problem was deeper still. Even the observation of things around him had lost its natural character under these conditions. The first prerequisite of getting out of the camp alive was to be inconspicuous. Anyone who drew the guards' attention to himself for whatever reason was risking his own life. The injunction not to be conspicuous under any circumstances was followed by a second injunction: *Thou shalt not look.* A prisoner who was seen watching an SS-man ill-treating a fellow prisoner was flirting with death. Even the passive observance of the injunction to see nothing was not enough, Bettelheim wrote; it was much safer actively to demonstrate that you had not noticed anything. He gave the example of an SS-man thrashing a prisoner.

> But in the midst of it he might call out a friendly 'well done' to a passing work column who, having stumbled upon the scene, would fall into a gallop, heads averted, so as to pass by as fast as possible without 'noticing'. Obviously their sudden break into running and their averted heads showed clearly that they had 'noticed'; but that did not matter as long as they also showed so clearly that they had accepted the command not to know what they were not supposed to know.

The situation had a perverse logic: to know what you may not see you have to look, and in order to know what you must pretend you must know what you actually saw. According to Bettelheim, noticing nothing and knowing nothing were part and parcel of the SS scheme of breaking the prisoners' will. To know only what another allows one to know is the condition of the infant. To see for yourself and to act accordingly is the beginning of an independent life. Not noticing when it is of the utmost importance to take careful note is destructive of one's personality.

There was yet another reason why people tried 'not to notice'. Anyone who saw a prisoner being beaten up and was so carried away by his emotions as to come to the victim's aid was asking to be killed.

> Knowing that such an emotional reaction was tantamount to suicide, and being unable at times not to react emotionally when observing what went on, left only one way out: not to observe, so as not to react. So both powers, those of observation and of reaction, had to be blocked out voluntarily as an act of preservation. But if one gives up observing, reacting, and taking action, one gives up living one's own life. And that is exactly what the SS wanted to happen.

Other concentration and extermination camp survivors have also mentioned the problems with what in normal life are such matter-of-course functions as observing and remembering. In *Sun Turned to Darkness* (1998) David Patterson writes that the memory was one of the many things eradicated or destroyed: a great many people who had been to a concentration camp complained of having a poor memory. Recalling her stay in Auschwitz, Fania Fénelon wrote that she found it increasingly difficult to tell children stories and that the children failed to realize that her memory was deteriorating. Olga Lengyel, another Auschwitz survivor, became aware of her own mental decline and that of others chiefly through the deterioration of memory. The constant mortal danger, the state of alertness to the ever-present threat, the exhaustion, as well as the lack of nourishment and vitamin B with its consequent dulling effect, acted on the ability to remember and caused large gaps in the memory.

The prisoners' powers of recognition were also adversely affected. Elie Cohen, a medical practitioner from Aduard in Groningen Province, was deported to Auschwitz and given the task of examining prisoners. He was able to save some temporarily from the gas chamber by certifying that they were ill. In 1971, he published his recollections of the war years under the title of *De Afgrond* (The abyss). He writes that in Auschwitz, a man came up to him in the hall and said:

> 'Elie, you've got to save me! They're taking me to the *Durch-fallstation* [diarrhoea ward] and that means the gas chamber.

You've got to save me.' I said, 'And who on earth are you?'
'I'm Jo Wolf from Folkingestraat.' He'd lived four houses down
from me, and we knew each other extremely well. You couldn't
recognize people any more. I should be quite unable to testify
at a trial of SS-men. If they were to ask me, 'Point out anyone
you recognize' – I wouldn't be able to, I wouldn't recognize
anybody. Everything is so terribly changed. Just as the Jews
changed so quickly in that particular camp because of their
physical condition, so I wouldn't be able to recognize these
SS-men any more either.

What can a psychologist, trained in the experimental traditions of
his trade, accustomed to clearly defined stimuli and control groups,
say about remembering, recognizing and identifying under such extreme circumstances? The honest answer must be: next to nothing.
Psychology does not conduct systematic research into the reliability
of the memory under the traumatic circumstances of an extermination camp. But what few data have been gathered in situations that
involve at least some elements of life-threatening circumstances suggest that even very intense and emotional memories can be liable to
distortion. A well-documented demonstration of that fact is the investigation by Wagenaar and Groeneweg of the testimony of witnesses
in the De Rijke case.

Marinus de Rijke worked between 1942 and 1943 as *Oberkapo*
(chief overseer) in Kamp Erika, in Ommen in the Overijssel Province.
This was a prison camp for Dutch offenders, but the regime there
was reminiscent of German concentration camps: privileged prisoners were given the task of disciplining their fellow inmates. Some of
the prisoners were fatally beaten up. De Rijke was one of the most
vicious of the guards. In 1943, when the Dutch authorities discovered what was going on, the camp was closed. During the war years
the prisoners lived under extremely harsh conditions. One group of
a thousand prisoners was transferred to Germany to do hard labour,
of which no more than four hundred returned alive to Kamp Erika,
too sick and exhausted to do any work. Of these four hundred, many
died in the camp. From 1943 to 1948, the police took statements
from the survivors. At the time De Rijke escaped trial but in 1984
it was decided to prosecute him after all. Following an appeal in a

television programme about him various witnesses came forward, but the judge decided in the end that the charges of ill-treatment had been nullified by the statute of limitations. During the trial fifteen witnesses who had testified during the forties were re-examined, which enabled Wagenaar and Groeneweg to compare the testimony forty years on with the court records taken directly after the events. The discrepancies cast doubt on the reliability of memories after so long an interval.

There were records of the dates on which the offenders were detained in the camp. In the examination during the forties no more than two of the eleven witnesses remembered a date that differed by more than a month from the actual admission date. Forty years later that ratio had increased to eleven out of nineteen. Various witnesses were more than six months out, which meant that they remembered their arrival in quite the wrong season. People who had been ill-treated by De Rijke – and in that sense had been directly involved with him – did not seem to recognize him any better in a photograph than people who had not been ill-treated by him. Twenty witnesses declared that De Rijke wore a uniform in the camp; twenty-eight said that he had been in civilian clothes. Eleven witnesses declared that he whipped prisoners; an equal number that he never used a whip or other devices. Of the former prisoners who had not watched the De Rijke television programme beforehand, only 58 per cent recognized him in a photograph taken during the camp days. Recollections of events that might be supposed to have been etched into the memory also turned out to be inaccurate. Thus witness V. had seen De Rijke and another guard batter a fellow prisoner to death; by 1984 he had forgotten the names of both guards and confused the culprit and the victim in another ill-treatment case. Witness Van der M. had been so badly treated by De Rijke that he could not walk for several days; all he remembered in 1984 was that he was given a blow now and then. Witness Van de W. had also been ill-treated, but remembered De Rijke as 'De Bruin' and had forgotten his maltreatment. Witness S. declared in 1943 that De Rijke and another guard had drowned a prisoner in a cistern; in 1984 he had not only forgotten the incident, but also denied that he had ever made such a claim.

Although many recollections seemed to be accurate and might therefore have been stored intact in the memory for more than forty years, there is an obvious problem here: there is no criterion for deciding which declaration must be accepted as true. A similar problem cropped up in the Demjanjuk case. One of the prosecution witnesses, Elijahu Rosenberg, issued a statement in Vienna in 1947 while on his way to Israel. He declared that Ivan had been killed during the uprising in 1943. Several prisoners had rushed the barracks and had killed the Ukrainian guards asleep there with spades (because of the extreme heat early morning shifts had been introduced). During the trial in Jerusalem he explained that the interviewers in Vienna had misunderstood him: he had meant that others had *told* him that Ivan had been killed. But not much later a statement signed by Rosenberg himself in 1944 resurfaced in which he had declared that he had seen Ivan's death for himself. Whom are we to believe: the Rosenberg of 1944, that of 1947 or the one of 1987?

There are further reasons for putting the infallibility of traumatic memories in the right perspective. In 1978 Frank Walus was charged with war crimes in the small Polish town of Czestochowa. Walus was alleged to have been a member of the SS and the Gestapo. After the war, he settled in America, adopting the name of Wallace. He was identified by no fewer than eleven eyewitnesses. One of them, David Gelbhauer, had been forced to work in the Gestapo headquarters in Czestochowa and had seen Walus almost every day for more than three years. Gelbhauer had witnessed torture, maltreatment and murder. Another witness declared that Frank Walus had broken into their house and had beaten up his father. Neighbours had told him that the man was called Walus Frank. After yet another series of statements by witnesses, all equally positive, Walus was stripped of his US citizenship. At an appeal, Red Cross documents provided Walus with a watertight alibi by proving irrefutably that he had been about fifteen years old at the time and working on a Bavarian farm. Contemporary photographs showed him in the company of farmers. Wallace was acquitted and had his citizenship restored.

Anyone bearing in mind Wagenaar's long list of rules and regulations is bound to ask himself how it relates to recall and recognition under the conditions in which inmates lived in Treblinka. Do these extreme circumstances not call for a special approach? Can someone who spent a long time in a life-threatening situation – and a very long time ago, at that – be subjected to the procedure used in the identification of pickpockets and bag snatchers? Such questions arise almost as a matter of course, but it is equally certain that they are the wrong questions.

So many years later, it is no longer the actual suspect whom the witnesses are asked to identify. He can no longer be produced at an identification parade as the man he was forty or fifty years ago. Something has replaced him. The war criminal of yesterday and the suspect of today are separated by a new layer, mainly of paper: identity cards, certificates, photographs, entries in registers, initials in a record. In trials such as Demjanjuk's, each of them is produced as exhibit number so-and-so in a dossier running to many thousands of pages. The new layer connects even as it separates. The documents must help to bridge the distance in time; they have to prove that the man now in the dock is the same man who once committed war crimes. But the same documents also cause a kind of eclipse. The eyewitnesses' memories of the man in the past are of relevance – *legal* relevance – only inasmuch as they can be linked to the suspect by documents. Everything they suffered and experienced at his hands in the past, all they saw, heard, feared about him, comes down to answers to questions emanating from the paper layer: is this his photograph, is that his handwriting, did he wear that particular uniform?

The questions from that paper layer and the way in which they are put have their own logic. The rules and regulations of identification, however formalistic, are aimed at the removal of any doubt. Every mistake in the procedure, every lapse, can harm the defence *as well as* the prosecution. If Demjanjuk was really Ivan the Terrible, then the mistakes helped to render the proof of that fact less convincing than it could have been. Clear identification criteria are needed not only to protect the suspect, but also to lend substance and authority to the evidence. Conversely, an improper identification procedure can lead to the conviction of an innocent person. That did not happen in the Demjanjuk case. During the hearing of his appeal a most dramatic consequence came to light.

## Alibi: Sobibor

The weakest part of Demjanjuk's defence was his alibi. It changed many times and no corroboration could be adduced for any new – or old – version. Originally, Demjanjuk declared that he had worked on a farm in Sobibor. Later he said that he had failed to tell the American immigration service in 1951 that he had served in the Red Army and had been taken prisoner by the Germans. Nor was that all: during the last phase of the war he allegedly joined a Ukrainian army unit and a few months later he enlisted in an anti-communist division under the command of General Vlasov. He was trying to prevent extradition to the Soviet Union at any cost, knowing that Stalin made short shrift of men who had served in foreign armies. That was why he had claimed that he was a farmer. But why in Sobibor of all places? When he filled in the form at the time, Demjanjuk explained that he had asked somebody standing beside a map of Poland to name a place, and that place had happened to be Sobibor. But Sobibor was no more than the junction of two railway lines, too insignificant to appear on any map. One would have had to be very near Sobibor, the Israeli court found, to have known of its existence.

Another problem with Demjanjuk's alibi was a detail that cropped up in the statement of *SS-Wachmann* Danielchenko. All members of the SS and of the Waffen-SS had their blood group tattooed under their left armpit. Danielchenko testified that he and Demjanjuk had been given just such tattoos while serving in Flossenbürg, a Bavarian concentration camp. Demjanjuk had a scar in the area. He explained that the tattoo that had been there had been Ukrainian, not German, and that he had removed it himself with a gouge when he joined Vlasov's division. At no time during the many years of his trials was Demjanjuk able to come up with a convincing alibi. Only during his appeal did it become clear why no such alibi could have been expected from him.

The fall of the Berlin Wall and developments in the Soviet Union allowed the prosecution as well as the defence to undertake archive research. Before then, the only material available to them had been screened by the KGB. The prosecution discovered a list of the names of men who had been transferred from Trawniki to Sobibor. The list included Demjanjuk's name, complete with date and place of birth and his number: 1393. On another document, dated 1 October 1943, Demjanjuk and Danielchenko were listed as being stationed in Flossenbürg. In Vilnius, Lithuania, a petition dated in January 1943 was discovered demanding that Demjanjuk be given twenty-five lashes for leaving Majdanek camp without permission: he had gone out to fetch onions and salt from a neighbouring village. In addition, a deposition by Danielchenko, taken as early as 1949, turned up, in which he referred to Demjanjuk as a guard who assisted so efficiently in the exterminations that he was allowed on several occasions to help with the transportation of Jews from their ghettos to the camp. In addition to these documents from Ukrainian and Lithuanian archives, other documents were discovered in Coblenz, stating that Demjanjuk and Danielchenko had been stationed in Flossenbürg in 1944. According to an armory ledger they had each been issued with a Mauser and a bayonet.

But if Demjanjuk was not the Ivan of Treblinka, then who was?

In 1988, a CBS documentary team set out to discover whether there were people still alive in the surroundings of Treblinka who had known Ivan the Terrible. In a small village about half a mile from the camp they were referred to Maria Dudek, who had worked as a prostitute during the war and whose clients had included some guards. She had known Ivan the Terrible well, she declared; for a whole year he had been a regular client. He had talked to her about his work in the camp. Asked whether she knew his real name, she said without hesitation, 'Ivan Marchenko.' Ashamed of her past as a prostitute, Dudek, then about seventy years old, refused to testify before the camera. When Yoram Sheftel, Demjanjuk's defence lawyer, got hold of a transcript of the 'Sixty Minutes' documentary, he decided to pay a visit to Dudek himself. He showed her a series of photographs, including one of Demjanjuk, and asked if she recognized Marchenko amongst them. She said that she could not. Sheftel pointed to the photograph of Demjanjuk and asked if he was Ivan Marchenko. Again she said no. Unfortunately for Sheftel she refused to go to Jerusalem to testify there, but since the name of Marchenko had cropped up it was possible to make a direct search of the archives.

The discoveries followed in quick succession. A Ukrainian state archive yielded a collection of confessions by *Wachmänner* who had served in Treblinka and who had been arrested by the Red Army after the war. More than twenty of them named Ivan Marchenko as the man who had operated the diesel engine. A Trawniki identity card of Marchenko was also discovered and some witnesses recognized him on the photograph. They put his age at the time at about thirty. Marchenko's assistant at the gas chamber was identified as Nicolai Shalayev. After his arrest in 1950, he had stated at his own trial that, together with Marchenko, he had been transferred to Trieste following the closure of the camp, which was borne out by declarations of SS officers in the sixties. Aleksandra Kirpa, a Ukrainian woman who had served forced labour in Treblinka, testified as early as 1951 to the Soviet authorities that she and Marchenko had lived in the camp 'as husband and wife' and that he had told her exactly what his duties at the gas chamber were.

The new documents appearing in so many places bearing one another out finally brought order into the chaos of testimonies, declarations and identity cards. There had indeed been an Ivan the Terrible (something that had never been in doubt), but his name had been Ivan Marchenko and not Ivan Demjanjuk. Now it also became clear why Demjanjuk lacked a credible alibi. Any doubt that as a volunteer in the service of the Germans he had played an active part in the destruction of the Jewish community had been removed. But the certainty that he had committed war crimes in Sobibor was bought at a high price. The same evidence acquitted him of the charge of having committed such crimes in Treblinka.

Seven years after the beginning of the trial in Jerusalem and five years after having sentenced Demjanjuk to death, the judges now faced an impossible dilemma. The death sentence could not be carried out: Demjanjuk was not guilty of the crime with which he had been charged. But he was not innocent either: he had committed crimes in Sobibor for which he would undoubtedly have been sentenced to death had he been accused of them. After long deliberations the three judges reached the unanimous verdict that he be pronounced not guilty of the original charge. Demjanjuk was a free man again.

Were the witnesses who identified Demjanjuk as Ivan the Terrible mendacious? Not mendacious; they simply made a mistake.

Perhaps not all of them; perhaps no more than one. The real fault lay with the fact that the identification procedure was so organized that the individual mistakes spread and multiplied, with dire consequences for the evidence. The best service one could have rendered the witnesses was a procedure involving the utmost precision, care, strictness, secrecy and observation of all the other rules. Under no circumstances should the witnesses have been subjected to an identification procedure that had as little to do with a genuine identification as the 'station' in Treblinka had with a genuine railway station.

## Postscript

*Franz Stangl* (born 1908) had been camp commandant of Sobibor before he came to Treblinka. He was the brain behind the reorganization that turned Treblinka into an efficient extermination machine. After the war, Stangl was arrested but in 1948 he escaped from his Austrian prison. With the help of the Vatican, he was able to flee to Syria. Later, he emigrated to Brazil, where he found work as a motor mechanic in a Volkswagen factory in São Paulo. After a tip from a former Gestapo officer, Simon Wiesenthal was able to trace him and have him extradited to the German Federal Republic. On 22 December 1970, Stangl received a life sentence for the murder of at least 400,000 Jews in Treblinka. In the spring of 1971, the British journalist Gitta Sereny held a series of interviews with him. He told her that he was still proud of having once been the 'youngest master weaver in Austria'; those years had been his 'happiest times'. The day after his last meeting with Sereny, Stangl died of a heart attack.

*Kurt Franz* (born 1914) resumed his old trade of cook after the war and settled in Düsseldorf under his own name. Upon his arrest in 1959, a photograph album was confiscated. It contained snapshots taken in Treblinka that were pasted in under the heading of 'Happy Days'. In 1965 Franz was found guilty of complicity in the death of 'at least 300,000 persons' and in addition of thirty-five murders and one attempted murder. His punishment was carefully chosen: thirty-five life sentences plus eight years. The announcement of his release for health reasons coincided more or less with the acquittal of Demjanjuk. Franz died in 1998.

(a)             (b)             (c)

Fig. 11    (a) Franz Stangl. (b) Kurt Franz. (c) Ivan Marchenko.

*Ivan Marchenko* (born 1911) was the real Ivan the Terrible. Nicolai Shalayev, his assistant at the gas chamber, was executed in 1952. Shalayev declared in 1950 that he met Marchenko for the last time in the spring of 1945, when he saw him coming out of a brothel in Fiume. Marchenko told Shalayev that he had joined the Yugoslav partisans and that he was presently on leave. He had met a girl with whom he wanted to start a new life. From that moment, all traces of him were lost. In the sixties, the Soviet Union put a host of Ukrainian *Wachmänner* on trial; almost without exception they were sentenced to death. Marchenko was not amongst them. As late as 1962, the Soviet authorities were still looking for him. His daughters in the Soviet Union did not learn until as late as the beginning of the 1990s about the wartime activities of their missing father.

*Ivan/John Demjanjuk* (born 1920) was deported from Israel on 22 September 1993 and put on an El Al flight to New York. In the United States the reasons for his original extradition were revoked. He now lives a life of retirement in his old home in Cleveland, Ohio.

BIBLIOGRAPHY

Arad, Y., *Belzec, Sobibor, Treblinka: The Operation Reinhard Death Camps*, Bloomington, 1987.

Bettelheim, B., 'Individual and mass behavior in extreme situations', *Journal of Abnormal and Social Psychology* 38 (1943), 417–52.

*The Informed Heart*, Glencoe, 1960.

Cohen, E. A., *De afgrond: een egodocument*, Amsterdam and Brussels, 1971.

Glazar, R., *Die Falle mit dem grünen Zaun: Überleben in Treblinka*, Frankfurt am Main, 1992.

de Mildt, D., *In the Name of the People: Perpetrators of Genocide in the Reflection of their Post-war Prosecution in West Germany. The 'Euthanasia' and 'Aktion Reinhard' Trial Cases*, The Hague, 1996.

Patterson, D., *Sun Turned to Darkness: Memory and Recovery in the Holocaust Memoir*, Syracuse, 1998.

Sereny, G., *Into that Darkness: An Examination of Conscience*, London, 1974.

Sheftel, Y., *Defending 'Ivan the Terrible': The Conspiracy to Convict John Demjanjuk*, Washington, DC, 1996.

Steiner, J.-F., *Treblinka*, Paris, 1996.

Wagenaar, W. A., *Identifying Ivan: A Case Study in Legal Psychology*, New York, 1988.

Wagenaar, W. A., and J. Groeneweg, 'The memory of concentration camp survivors', *Applied Cognitive Psychology* 4 (1990), 77–87.

Wiernik, Y., *A Year in Treblinka*, New York, 1945.

# 11 Richard and Anna Wagner: forty-five years of married life

Our memory does not really handle the daily round well. It is hard put to reconstruct unremarkable happenings, or the way voices used to sound, how things used to feel, how rooms smelled, the way food tasted. Or what your loved ones used to look like. Your parents in former days, your children when they were younger, your wife, husband, friends – by remaining close to you and changing imperceptibly and slowly, they have managed to expunge their past appearance from your memory. Even the transformation of your own looks eludes you: the face you see in the mirror today blurs the face you wore yesterday, let alone a month or a year ago.

If our appearance were a book, and if our memory were a bibliophile, then our memory would place each new edition next to the carefully preserved previous editions. We would be able to look at an early edition at our discretion and compare it with a later one and so tell what had been removed, added, scrapped, revised or corrected. Instead our memory is a tool designed for evolutionarily useful purposes, and that does not involve the collection of old editions. After all, if we cannot see our children as they used to look ten or twenty years ago, then there is no point in recalling their former appearance – so away with it!

We must forgive our memory for yet another reason. It finds it easier to determine what has changed than to tell what has stayed the same. The people we have around us every day change as quickly or slowly as everyone else, but thanks to our daily contacts with them their changes are played out on a scale that makes them seem to stand still. It is unfair to blame our memory for throwing away editions when, on the face of it, the latest imprint differs in no way from the preceding one.

The confrontation with what you used to look like is provoked in our time – and in our part of the world – by photographs rather than by recollections. Photography has altered our relationship to our memories of past appearances. Before the middle of the nineteenth century, the problem of trying to remember somebody and being

Fig. 12   Richard and Anna Wagner, Christmas Eve 1900.

unable to tell whether you recall his face or his photograph did not
exist. This uncertainty follows on from the certainty a photograph
proffers, the knowledge that once, then, on that particular occasion,
he had looked like that: that glance, that hairstyle, those features.
These days we have something like a photographic biography of nearly
everyone, from their birth to the present day or their death – a visual
record that may not document every phase of life with equal intensity,
but nevertheless comprises the entire life and records the changes
that pass too slowly for our memory to notice.

From the first year of their marriage in 1900, the Berlin couple Anna and Richard Wagner took photographs of themselves on
Christmas Eve and sent the photographs to their friends as Christmas

Fig. 13   Richard and Anna Wagner, Christmas Eve 1915.

cards. The series continued until 1942, three years before Anna's death. Only a few years are missing. A female friend of the Wagners kept all the photographs. Almost a half a century later they were discovered in an attic in the former East Berlin and were published. At a cursory glance, all the photographs are of the same thing. The couple themselves, a table with a display of Christmas presents, a Christmas tree, an interior that changes little. Each of the photographs has been taken on the same day of the year. But against the unvarying background, you notice the changing seasons in a human life all the more clearly. You see how gradual the changes are, though they can also be abrupt, like the first true day of spring every year or the morning when winter seems to have arrived. By moving

Fig. 14   Richard and Anna Wagner, Christmas Eve 1917.

forward exactly one year with each click of the self-timer, the Wagners demonstrate clearly that the aging process does not follow the
even rhythm of the calendar.

Richard Wagner, born in 1873, was a passionate amateur pho-
tographer by the time he married Anna, regularly buying the latest
cameras, even if they cost him a month's salary or more. The Christmas photographs are stereoscopic shots. The Wagners – Anna was a
year younger than her husband – were a middle-class couple. Richard
had a job as a secretary for the railways, and finally worked his way
up to inspector. At first they lived in Essen, but in 1911 they moved to
Salzburger Strasse in Berlin, where they rented a new two-and-a-half
room apartment. They stayed there for the rest of their lives. Nothing

Fig. 15   Richard and Anna Wagner, Christmas Eve 1927.

is known of their political views, although the portrait of Wilhelm II that continued to hang over the sofa long after the Kaiser had taken refuge in Doorn in the Netherlands suggests that they were of a conservative bent.

Richard did not have to serve in the German army in either of the two world wars – by 1914, he was forty-one and too old for military service. The Wagners had no children.

On the first photograph, taken in 1900, Richard and Anna look younger than their actual ages of twenty-seven and twenty-six respectively. Anna is playing with Mietz (Pussy), their cat, Richard is adding a festive touch to the Christmas tree; the scene almost gives the impression that they were playing at father and mother. On the table, the still life of Christmas presents that was to hold so prominent a place in all the photographs is shown for the first time. Anna gave Richard the album that lay before him on the table; it could hold two hundred picture postcards. Many of the belongings in their room would still be present on photographs taken dozens of years later. The tablecloth, the busts on the wall, the carpet, the chairs, the knick-knacks – the Wagners belonged to the generation in which the wedding gifts lasted throughout the marriage.

Fifteen years later the external circumstances have changed drastically. On a map of Europe, which was also shown on the 1914 photograph, the successful advance of German troops is recorded. Although many provisions now needed coupons, as did clothing, paraffin and coal, the Wagners were still able to provide a well-stocked Christmas table, with a cake, apples, sausages and drinks. With the somewhat curious sense of humour that crops up now and then in other photographs as well they have hung a small card with the inscription 'Famine' close to the basket of eggs and the platter of sausages.

Two years later in 1917 the deprivations of the war have hit even the Wagners' living room. The reason why they are wearing winter coats has been written underneath: 'coal shortage'. The map with German troop movements has gone. No candles have been lit on the Christmas tree. Richard is wearing the slippers that were among the Christmas presents a year earlier. Grey streaks in his hair appear for the first time. The Christmas presents are dominated by a 'hay box' with which food could be prepared with a minimum of fuel.

In 1927, halfway between the two world wars, the Wagners were manifestly doing well. Both of them were in their fifties by then, Richard with a middle-age spread and a cigar, but also with spectacles and greying hair, Anna behind a table on which stand elegant shoes, wine, fruit and an engraved crystal glass. In the tree, electric candles shine for the first time. But the most important item is displayed right in the front: a 'Progress' electric vacuum cleaner. It was neither the first nor the last electrical aid to appear in Anna's household: the year before she had been given an electric iron. Later she also received a massager and a hairdryer, which, according to the instructions, could be adapted with the help of various attachments to setting the hair and also as a bed warmer.

Fig. 16   Richard and Anna Wagner, Christmas Eve 1935.

On the 1935 and 1937 photographs there are more appliances: in 1935 an electric heater, in 1937 a Volksempfänger wireless set. The speed with which Anna seems to be aging is even more striking: within two years she has changed from a lively woman into someone who looks older than her sixty-three years. Grey-haired, visibly thinner and watched by what appears to be an anxious husband, she is shown sitting behind an open sewing box.

In subsequent years the still lifes on the table grow more and more frugal. In 1940 the Wagners are again sitting by the Christmas tree in their winter coats. The last photograph of them together was taken in 1942. On the table there is a bottle with a small amount left in it; there is little food on display. For Richard there are still a few

Fig. 17   Richard and Anna Wagner, Christmas Eve 1937.

cigars. The electric candles on the Christmas tree are switched off; real candles were so scarce that women used leftover stubs in aspirin bottles as candles. On 24 June 1945, Richard took the last photograph of Anna, then seventy-one. The war had just finished, but for her it had lasted too long; the food shortage has left visible traces on her. She weighed just eighty pounds in her clothes ('gross weight' as Richard put it with his curious sense of humour). She died on 23 August, from 'serious emaciation' according to the cemetery register. Richard died a few weeks before Christmas 1950. He was seventy-seven.

Every age has its own ideas about the passage through the stages of a human life. These are expressed in symbols, metaphors, sayings and allegories. In the medieval imagination life was often

Fig. 18   Anna Wagner, June 1945.

considered a journey or a pilgrimage; books told what could befall a man between departure and arrival. Sometimes the journey was shown in pictures: in a corner of a panel we see a child that in ever-older versions of itself roams over the entire painting. Another favourite was the 'staircase of life', where the small child who clambers up on to the first step on the left hand side steps off again on the right as an old man. The number of steps differed, as did the stages into which a human life used to be divided: there could be seven but also as many as ten. These stages could be linked to the division of time itself. On Titian's *Allegory of Time Governed by Prudence*, painted between 1560 and 1570, three faces appear under the text 'From past experience the present steps circumspectly, lest it mar the future.' An old man and a boy, both shown in profile, look at the past and the future, while a man in the middle of his life looks the spectator in the face. On some clocks on the façades of cathedrals or town halls the stages of life are shown passing by in the form of mechanical figures, the child in the morning, the old man in the evening. A quadripartite division might link human life with the change of the seasons, the birthdays of the young being counted in springs and that of the old in winters.

We know nothing about the Wagners' motive for taking their photographs every year. Perhaps it simply seemed a good idea in 1900, and continued to be so in 1901 and the years that followed. Nor do we know how they themselves viewed the photographs once the series had started. Did they perhaps place the photographs into the stereoscopic viewer now and then and observe their own aging process, the minor changes in their room, the almost annual reappearance of new gloves? It seems unlikely that they ever planned to create a photographic memory of their own lives when they started in 1900. It is a memory that preserves all the previous editions and records of the deceptively slow changes that no one notices in himself and in others. For the modern spectator who can page through the whole series and in perhaps an hour watch forty-five years pass by in review, this photographic memory has become an unintended work of art. It reveals something of what past generations expressed by pilgrimages, stages of life and seasons, all the more tellingly because the photographs do not portray a medieval Everyman, but people just like ourselves.

BIBLIOGRAPHY

The series of photographs of the Wagners is to be found in the Heimatmuseum Charlottenburg, in Berlin. The complete series has been published in B. Jochens (ed.), *Deutsche Weihnacht: ein Familienalbum 1900–1945*, Berlin 1996. All the data about the life of the Wagners have been taken from that publication.

'In oval mirrors we drive around': on experiencing a sense of déjà vu

> In oval mirrors we drive around;
> see in ourselves our own background
> and know it too could once be found.
>
> GERRIT ACHTERBERG, 'Déjà-vu', 1952

*David Copperfield* is a tale of two loves. When young David goes to school in Canterbury, he is taken into the hospitable home of Mr Wickfield, a lawyer running a rich gentleman's estate. There he meets Wickfield's daughter Agnes, who is about the same age as himself and who captivates him with her lovely face and composed manner. He quietly observes the tact with which Agnes treats her father who, after his wife's death, has started to drink more than is good for him. Unfortunately she cannot prevent his practice from going into a steep decline, and Uriah Heep, Wickfield's crafty clerk, is able to force her father to make him a partner. When David continues his education in London, he often seeks Agnes's advice, revelling in her wisdom and affection.

In London David is articled to Mr Spenlow. At a dinner he is introduced to Spenlow's daughter Dora. It is love at first sight: he loses his heart and perhaps a little of his good sense as well. Dora is in many respects the very opposite of Agnes. She is a 'child wife', playful and flighty, but also capricious and easily upset. Against his great-aunt's advice he marries Dora. The marriage is idyllic in the beginning, but it gradually becomes clear that David cannot really count on her support. Eventually, she dies after giving birth to a stillborn child. The young widower goes abroad for three years.

On his return, he seeks out Agnes. His great-aunt had given him to understand that Agnes was engaged to another man, but that proves not to be the case. David realizes that he has loved Agnes all these years. In a frank and tearful scene, they confess their love for each other. Within fourteen days they are married.

Dickens indicates how overwhelming David's feelings for Agnes were by twice in succession having him experience what most people encounter no more than a few times in their entire lives. The first of these experiences takes place in Mr Wickfield's chambers. David is left alone with the fawning and cunning Uriah Heep who brings the conversation round to Agnes. To his dismay David is told that Heep has admired Agnes silently for many years. "'Oh, Master Copperfield, with what a pure affection do I love the ground my Agnes walks on!'" David tries to hide his revulsion: 'He seemed to swell and grow before my eyes; the room seemed full of the echoes of his voice; and the strange feeling (to which, perhaps, no one is quite a stranger) that all this had occurred before, at some indefinite time, and that I knew what he was going to say next, took possession of me.' The second experience involves David's friend, the eloquent Mister Micawber, who starts talking, in all innocence, about Dora and Agnes: "'If you had not assured us, my dear Copperfield, on the occasion of that agreeable afternoon we had the happiness of passing with you, that D. was your favourite letter,... I should unquestionably have supposed that A. had been so.'" David muses: 'We have all some experience of a feeling, that comes over us occasionally, of what we are saying and doing having been said and done before, in a remote time – of our having been surrounded, dim ages ago, by the same faces, objects, and circumstances – of our knowing perfectly what will be said next, as if we suddenly remembered it! I never had this mysterious impression more strongly in my life, than before he uttered those words.'

To say that David had experienced a déjà vu would be an anachronism – the term had not yet been coined by 1850, when Dickens wrote *David Copperfield*. But the experience itself is timeless: Saint Augustine wrote as early as the fifth century about *falsae memoriae* and tells us how the Pythagoreans, a thousand years earlier still, had looked upon it as proof of the transmigration of souls. That all of us have experienced a déjà vu, as Dickens suggests, is however untrue. In reply to questionnaires, between one third and one half of the respondents declared that they had never had one. But those who have had one know that Dickens's description is accurate. A sense of déjà vu has a sudden beginning. The feeling of recognition appears from one moment to the next, without development or transition. From that moment on, everything feels as if you had experienced it before, the things around you, the sounds, the faces, the conversation; even your own thoughts are something you seem to have had before. It is as if you had relived a fragment of your life, though you cannot tell when it happened the first time.

It all seems so familiar that you feel sure you can tell what is going to happen next. But that knowledge is passive; it strongly resembles the feeling that you can foresee what is going to happen next in a book that you reread after a long time – only when you actually reach the passage in question do you recognize it completely. A word on the tip of your tongue has the same quality: you cannot say it, but later recognize it at once as the word you were looking for. Or you return to a house you used to know and say to yourself, 'Behind this door there used to be, uh, let's see, yes, of course! A cupboard.'

The impression that you know what is about to happen goes hand in hand with a sinking feeling, often referred to as *un sentiment pénible* in French accounts of déjà vu. The vague threat it poses is halfway between slight amazement and downright panic, and it is hard to tell if it is part of the déjà vu experience or caused by it. After all, a déjà vu lifts you unexpectedly out of the even track of your normal associations and this brief dislocation can seem alarming.

A sense of déjà vu is almost invariably felt to be fleeting. It is quickly dispelled, sometimes by virtue of the surprise at the experience itself. What William James wrote about introspection – that it is like quickly turning on a light to see what the dark looks like – also applies to the observation of your own déjà vu: it is as if the sudden concentration on its strange character is enough to put a stop to it. Most experiences of déjà vu last no more than a few moments; after that the feeling that you are witnessing the repetition of a familiar scene ceases. The confusion at what you have just experienced may linger a while, but normal life soon resumes its course. The mysterious replication of what you see, hear and think has vanished.

For what Dickens left unnamed but what is nowadays called a déjà vu, some twenty different names came into use in the second half of the nineteenth century. In French literature, the experience was linked to an aberration of the memory, as reflected in such terms as *fausse mémoire*, *paramnésie* and *fausse reconnaissance*. German physicians and psychiatrists seemed struck above all by the duplicating effect of a déjà vu, expressed by such terms as *Emfindungsspiegelung*, *Doppelwahrnehmung* and *Doppelvorstellung*. The philosopher-psychologist

Ebbinghaus tried – in vain – to introduce the term *Bewusstsein des Schondagewesenseins* (awareness of having been there before). After 1896, the scientific community adopted the view of the French physician Arnaud, who declared in a lecture to the Parisian Société Médico-Psychologique that a technical term must not anticipate the explanation and that a neutral term was therefore preferable. His suggestion, 'déjà vu', found general acceptance, although the term *fausse reconnaissance* continued for a long time to offer resistance to this quiet reform.

The educated nineteenth-century citizen could find references to feelings of déjà vu in the most diverse places: in books on the memory, in psychiatric case histories, in neurological journals and medical textbooks, but also in poems and novels. Contributions to the scientific literature came chiefly from physicians and psychiatrists. Their explanations had a clinical bias, based as they were on the experiences of patients. The evidence was often confined to the few cases encountered in the doctor's practice or in a mental institution. In 1898, Eugène Bernard-Leroy – trained as a physician in the Salpêtrière, Paris – tried to systematize the research. He collected all the case histories he could find and compiled a questionnaire that he sent out to a thousand acquaintances, colleagues and the readers of a number of professional journals. Some of the questions were designed to link a sense of déjà vu to sex, age or the quality of the memory. Other questions asked about the estimated duration, the accompanying feelings and the accuracy of the sense of being able to predict what would happen in the next few moments. Sixty-seven forms were sent back to him, close on fifty of which he quoted in full in his published dissertation, *L'Illusion de fausse reconnaissance*. The relatively small number of responses did not lend itself to statistical analysis. Instead, Bernard-Leroy confined himself to a summary survey of 'tendencies'. Feelings of déjà vu were said to occur relatively often during adolescence. He could find no evidence for the link with epilepsy, exhaustion and tension suggested by earlier authors, nor find any correlation with sex, race or social status. The results of the thousandfold questionnaires that had been sent out provided few new insights. As for the origin of experiences of déjà vu, even Bernard-Leroy believed that we remained entirely in the dark on the subject.

Not that there was a lack of explanations – far from it.

## 'Has this been thus before?'

In 1844, the English physician A. L. Wigan described an experience of déjà vu as a 'sentiment of pre-existence', and many poets and authors have hinted that this is the true explanation of the phenomenon. A few years before he wrote *David Copperfield*, Charles Dickens travelled in Italy, and in his account of the journey he tells us that, one evening, he let the horses have a rest and went for a walk. After a while he came to a spot that looked very familiar. 'If I had been murdered there, in some former life, I could not have seemed to remember the place more thoroughly, or with a more emphatic chilling of the blood.'

In 'Sudden Light', written in 1854, the poet Dante Gabriel Rossetti described how, standing beside his ladylove one evening and watching a swallow skim past, he had an overwhelming feeling that in a former life he had stood beside her in just that way:

> You have been mine before, –
>> How long ago I may not know:
> But just when at that swallow's soar
>> Your neck turned so,
> Some veil did fall, – I knew it all of yore.
>> Has this been thus before?

For Rossetti this was a comforting thought: time would restore their love as well as their life.

The idea that 'this has been thus before' may explain the sensation of déjà vu has several variations. The first is that a déjà vu marks an intersection with a former life. You walk about unsuspectingly in some town which you are visiting for the first time, turn a corner and suddenly you are standing before a house you know so well that you must have been there in some previous life. According to this explanation, your memory contains latent recollections of that former life, which, thanks to the sudden coincidence with the present experience, begin to resonate and hence produce a sense of repeating the past. The déjà vu is bound up with the single moment at which the two lives intersect. This hypothesis fits how a déjà vu feels. But there is also much to argue against it. With resonating 'old' memories you would expect the déjà vu to take a more gradual course, not to have a sudden beginning and end. Moreover, you would expect the sense of recognition to increase as the correspondence between the present and the former life becomes greater. By walking towards the seemingly familiar house you ought to be able to intensify or prolong the déjà vu. Neither seems to be the case; a déjà vu has an all-or-nothing character and is too fleeting to hold on to. The former-life hypothesis is also gainsaid by the fact not only that a déjà vu makes a particular scene – that house – seem familiar, but that the people round you, the time of day, the weather, even your mood and thoughts have a vaguely familiar character.

The impression of coming face to face with a perfect duplicate has sometimes been seen as proof of the much more radical hypothesis that our life is repeated endlessly and in exactly the same form. In normal, everyday life we are not aware of this fact, but every now and then, in a moment of 'sudden light', we recognize the repetition in our present-day life. A déjà vu is the crack in time that suddenly grants us a glimpse of the eternal return of our own existence. 'Some veil did fall' – for a short moment all is clear. But the exact repetition raises an awkward question. Why do we not see our entire life as a protracted déjà vu? Would a déjà vu not have to be the rule, and ordinary, unduplicated life the exception? Another ticklish question is whether a déjà vu is part of the repetition of former lives. If the déjà vu is a novel event, then present-day life can no longer be considered an exact repetition. And if feelings of déjà vu occurred in former lives in the same places, we are still left without an explanation. It is a hypothesis that conjures up a dizzying illusion of infinity – the explanation repeats the mystery ad infinitum.

Perhaps it is best to leave the last word about this 'sentiment of pre-existence' to Wigan, who, after all, started the whole thing. He himself sought the explanation in a brief brain disorder, a hypothesis to which we shall be returning. He would have nothing to do with such explanations as reincarnation or eternal repetition. In his account of what a déjà vu feels like he made a casual but conclusive remark: 'The postures, the expression of countenance, the gestures, the tone of voice – all seem to be *remembered*, and to be now attracting attention for the second time. *Never* is it supposed to be the third time.'

## 'The dream images of our sleep'

In Sir Walter Scott's historical novel *Guy Mannering* (1815), Bertram returns to Ellangowan Castle, the centuries-old seat of his ancestors. It has become a stately ruin. He wanders from one apartment to another, noting the signs of recent habitation – empty bottles, half-gnawed bones – and as he leaves the building turns to admire the massive towers flanking the gateway with the ancient family's carved stone escutcheon above.

Although he cannot recall ever having lived in Ellangowan – he was abducted at the age of five – the scene suddenly looks familiar to him. 'How often do we find ourselves in society which we have never met before, and yet feel impressed with a mysterious and ill-defined consciousness, that neither the scene, the speakers, nor the subject are entirely new; nay, feel as if we could anticipate that part of the conversation which had not yet taken place!' He even comes up with a possible explanation: 'Is it the visions of our sleep that float confusedly in our memory, and are recalled by the appearance of such real objects as in any respect correspond to the phantoms they presented to our imagination?'

That explanation is part of a whole family of hypotheses. What they all have in common is that they consider a déjà vu as a memory, not of a former life, but of something that used, in one way or another, to be present in our mind. Perhaps our mind, as Walter Scott suggested, contains memories of dreams; perhaps there is a part of the mind that is not accessible to our consciousness in normal life, but reveals itself when we experience something resembling one of our dreams. If people do indeed dream every night, then, as the English psychologist James Sully wrote in *Illusions* (1881), some of those dreams have to come out sooner or later. As soon as the similarity is strong enough, our current experience activates associations with what we have been dreaming and we have the impression of being on familiar ground. Dream and life go hand in hand for a while. Isn't it a romantic idea, Sully continued, that fragments of our waking life often crop up in our dreams, and that, conversely, dreams sometimes penetrate our waking life and reveal something of their bizarre beauty?

For Sully, a déjà vu was the negative of what Freud would later call a day residue. And much as a day residue is fitted into the dream and is no more in it than a fleeting fragment, so a dream stored away for years in the memory can cause a fleeting duplication of an event in our everyday life. The 'when' of the dream can no longer be recovered, which explains why a déjà vu feels as if it had occurred in some vague past. A déjà vu is not an intersection between the present and the past, rather is it a brief form of parallelism with a vague trace in the memory.

For many psychologists, including some of Sully's contemporaries, even the latent-memory hypothesis of dreams was too sweeping. Why not suppose that a déjà vu happens when something resembles what we have actually experienced in the past? That a déjà vu is precisely what its name implies, namely seeing something we have seen before? William James found all the mystery and speculation surrounding a sense of déjà vu exaggerated; he had repeatedly managed to trace back the familiarity of his own feelings of déjà vu to genuine memories. At first, we only see the similarities to the previous situation, he explained, so that a vague feeling of repeating a 'previous' experience arises. But if we concentrate, we can also see an increasing number of differences between the two – the original recollection becomes fuller and the feeling of familiarity begins to recede. Many authors have adopted this explanation. If someone visits Lyons for the first time and has a déjà vu while looking at an equestrian statue, the explanation might well be that he actually saw a similar statue in the past – a replica in a museum or an illustration in an art book. Even if he fails to remember when that might have been, the partial similarity can convey a sense of repetition – which, in a certain sense, it actually is.

The hypothesis that a déjà vu is the result of a partial similarity to an earlier experience also has a psychoanalytical variant. In 1930, the Swiss clergyman and psychoanalyst Oskar Pfister discussed the experience of a young officer during the First World War. A grenade had killed all his comrades in the trench, while he himself had been flung to the ground. He was convinced that he had been fatally wounded. He remembered that immediately after the blast he felt as if he were falling a long way, with an associated déjà vu: 'I had fallen like that once before.' He told Pfister that he believed the déjà vu took him back to the time when, aged nine years old and unable to swim, he had jumped into the water and only just managed to save himself. Pfister's interpretation went along Freudian lines: the unconscious must have had a hand in the construction of the déjà vu. It had sought a parallel, with lightning speed, in the man's memory, and thanks to a transparent analogy – you were in danger then and survived and this time, too, you will escape with your life – provided solace at a moment of fatal danger. The déjà vu is part of an arsenal of defence mechanisms on which we can call; it duplicates the mortal threat in order to remind us that the first time round the threat did not turn out to be fatal.

Like William James, Pfister thus believed that feelings of déjà vu could be traced back to something actually present in the memory, the difference being that James held that they arose more or less accidentally while Pfister believed that they had a *function*. Its similarity to a previous experience is not the cause of a déjà vu but rather its active component. The fact that the second interpretation does not call for a training analysis was demonstrated by Kees van Kooten in his 'Mijn Tour de France' (My Tour de France), the account of his adventures as a racing cyclist. Jammed brakes caused him to fly over the handlebars: 'While I was still in the air, I had a déjà vu (I've been through this once before, and it must have ended all right or else I wouldn't be having this déjà vu), and as my head and right shoulder crashed on to the scalding hot road surface, I watched the Dutch car sweep past my still-bouncing bike and disappear from sight.' The flying combination of analyst and analysand did indeed survive the spill.

However, the hypothesis that a déjà vu is based on the activation of something present in our minds has an even more adventurous variant. In *Vallende ouders* (Falling parents) by A. F. T. van der Heijden, Albert Egberts and his close friend Thjum break into an empty hotel at the dead of night. On the landing they have a simultaneous déjà vu. They clutch each other's shoulders in fright:

> 'Wait a second, wait a second . . . standing here like this with a flight of stairs going down and a flight of stairs going up . . . and after that a couple of boys go looking through a cupboard, pull the drawers open . . . it's all so familiar.'
> 'But when . . . when?'

'Yes, yes, carry on talking: I know exactly, and I mean *exactly*, what you're going to say next.'

'Go on, then, tell me...what am I going to say next?'

'"Go on then, tell me..." That's it – the very words. The moment you said them I remembered them. "What am I going to say next" – when did you say those words before?'

Even a sudden action by Thjum, shutting and locking a door, cannot put an end to the sense of déjà vu. Only when they have stumbled on to the roof does the spell come to an end. On the roof, the two friends philosophize a bit longer about whether déjà vu experiences provide proof of the eternal recurrence of all things. Thjum does not believe that they do and goes on to frame the following hypothesis: 'You know they always say that at the point of death we see our life pass "like a film" – and why not? – before our mind's eye? To me, feelings of déjà vu are like trailers, fragmentary previews of the film. Like a foretaste.' According to him, a déjà vu ought really to be called a *prévu*.

Thjum's explanation fits organically into Van der Heijden's *œuvre*. While he speeds up time in *Het leven uit een dag* and slows it down in other parts of his trilogy by having the time axis spread out sideways, into 'life in the broad', Thjum's *prévu* represents yet another manipulation of time, namely reversal: familiarity is based on the future, on the recognition of what still lies ahead. But the *prévu* raises the same illusory question as the hypothesis that life is repeated endlessly in identical form: is the present-day déjà vu included in the future 'film of life'? If it is not, then it would not be a realistic film (and what are the grounds of recognition in that case?); but if it is, then the déjà vu would have to be explained all over again. With his enigmatic memories of the future, Thjum's *prévu* actually invites us to exchange one mystery for two.

## Double images

In 1817, Princess Charlotte of England died. Her unexpected death in childbirth plunged the country into deep mourning, for she had been greatly loved. The young physician Arthur Ladbroke Wigan had connections at court and at his own request was taken on to the staff of the Lord Chamberlain, in charge of the funeral in St George's Chapel in Windsor. Having had no rest during the night preceding the burial, Wigan's mind, as he wrote later, had been 'put into a state of hysterical irritability'. That condition was further aggravated by distress, exhaustion and hunger – owing to the general confusion, no food was available in Windsor from early in the morning to the interment at precisely twelve o'clock at night. During the ceremony Wigan stood beside the coffin for four hours without a break and felt that he might faint at any moment. After Mozart's 'Miserere' had been played, the music stopped and complete silence filled the chapel. Slowly the coffin began to be lowered, so slowly in fact that Wigan could detect movement only by comparing the edge of the coffin with a shining object further away.

> I had fallen into a sort of torpid reverie, when I was recalled to consciousness by a paroxysm of violent grief on the part of the bereaved husband, as his eye suddenly caught the coffin sinking into its black grave, formed by the inverted covering of the altar. In an instant I felt not merely an *impression*, but a *conviction* that I had seen the whole scene before on some former occasion, and had heard even the very words addressed to myself by Sir George Naylor.

According to Wigan, his strange experience beside Princess Charlotte's bier fitted perfectly into his theory about the operation of the brain. That theory had been maturing in his mind for over a quarter of a century, developing from conjecture into a firm conviction. It was not until 1844, at the age of sixty and shortly after retiring from general practice, that he combined all his observations and case studies in a neurological monograph, entitled *The Duality of the Mind*. We falsely conceive of our brain, he contended, as consisting of two halves. The term 'hemispheres' is misleading, for even the two halves together constitute less than half a sphere. In reality we carry *two* brains under our skulls, two separate organs, much as we have two eyes. Each of the two brains leads an independent conscious life, with its own thoughts, perceptions and emotions, although one half is generally dominant and the other subsidiary. The corpus callosum, the band of fibres connecting the two hemispheres at the base of the brain, is a barrier rather than a bridge. The fact that neurological

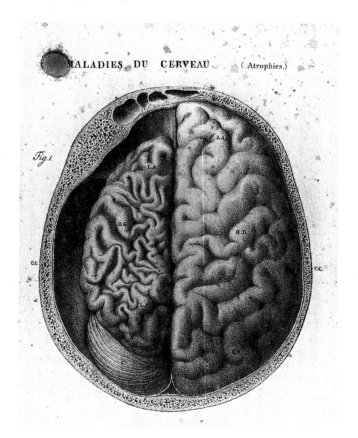

Fig. 19   Engraving of an atrophied and of an intact half of the brain.

records mention dozens of people losing a complete half of their brain through illness or injury, yet remaining the same person, proves conclusively that each of the two hemispheres can sustain our mental powers. Wigan gratefully acknowledged the contribution of Cruveilhier, the famous Parisian pathologist and anatomist. In his *Anatomie pathologique du corps humain*, published in 1835, Cruveilhier had included prints of brains, one hemisphere of which had shrivelled to half its normal size, the intact half proving adequate for living a normal life.

If both organs are focused on the same subject, the result is keen concentration. Conversely, the double construction enables us to allow one organ to rest while the other is active. In cases of exhaustion only one organ will be active. Here, according to Wigan, lay the explanation of what had happened to him in St George's Chapel. The moment immediately before his déjà vu, only one of the cerebral hemispheres was apparently active, so that at the time no more than a relatively weak sensory image was present. When, at the next moment, thanks to the unexpected cry of distress, the second hemisphere, too, was brought into play, the same scene suddenly yielded a much clearer picture. His consciousness interpreted that picture as the present and the almost identical but vague picture as an indefinite past. No wonder then that *everything* seems so familiar in a déjà vu: in reality there are no more than a few moments between the appearance of the two pictures. No wonder also that a déjà vu feels like a *second* time round – we happen to have two brains and not three.

Wigan's theory was reframed in slightly more picturesque form by later authors. The two hemispheres were said to be switched on in turn. Under normal circumstances, the alternation between left and right is carefully co-ordinated so that our sense experience is treated as a continuous whole. But if one cerebral hemisphere comes into play while the other is not yet switched off, a sort of 'double image' appears: in the present-day picture, the dying image of the other hemisphere continues to blink, so that it seems as if we are experiencing something for the second time. This hypothesis is Wigan's no longer. The analogy with double vision was not introduced until 1868, by Jensen, the German neurologist. According to him, each hemisphere processes its own stream of images, our consciousness joining these streams so seamlessly that they seem to be just one. If the fusion fails to come about, for whatever reason, a double image arises and is mistaken for a repetition.

Even in Bernard-Leroy's day, the theories of Wigan and Jensen were considered outdated. There was no neurological proof that either hemisphere could be temporarily 'switched off' or that our brain processes everything twice, on the right and the left side respectively. But the idea of a temporary double image remained highly attractive even in the absence of neuro-anatomical corroboration. Might a déjà vu not spring, the German psychiatrist Anjel wondered in 1878, from an extremely brief malfunction in our processing of sense stimuli? Perception demands that we fit our sense perceptions into a coherent picture. Under normal circumstances, the two phases – Anjel called them perception and apperception – fit so closely

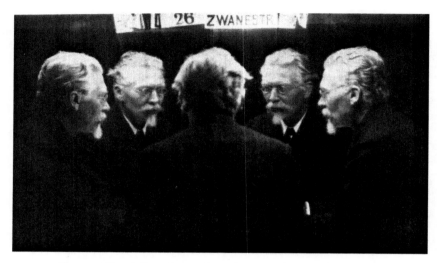

Fig. 20  The philosopher and psychologist Gerard Heymans (1857–1930). Date of photograph unknown.

together that we fail to see them as two separate steps. But if there should be a lag between these two steps, then our sense perceptions tend to become blurred at the point where they have to be joined into a single perception. As a result, we have the illusion that what we are seeing now occurred in precisely the same manner in some distant past.

The hypothesis of the double image also comes in various forms. Frederic Myers, the English pioneer of parapsychological research, posited in 1875 that the human intellect contained, in addition to the normal conscious self, a 'subliminal self', an unconscious part sensitive to stimuli that are too brief or too weak to rise above the threshold of perception, and that therefore go unnoticed by the conscious self. Myers compared subliminal perception to a camera; it not only has a greater sensitivity than the conscious self but also operates more quickly. As a result, something can reach our mind that we do not consciously perceive until a moment later. This throws our sense of time out of gear: the conscious self looks through the eyes, the subliminal self through the camera, provoking the illusion that we are seeing something from the past *as well as* something from the present. Myers called this experience 'promnesia' – pre-memory.

In all these hypotheses a déjà vu results from the comparison of two images, one sharp and the other so vague that it is mistaken for a distant memory. The images are not merely visual but constitute the sum of all our sense impressions at that moment, including smells, sounds, or sensations of cold, heat and hunger. The fact that a déjà vu feels like a precise repetition is, according to this explanation, exactly what you would expect; in reality, of course, there is hardly any interval between the two images. The sense of complete coincidence – you are in precisely the same mood, you think the same and you feel the same – reflects this small time difference. However, there is also an objection to the hypothesis of the double image, based on introspective experiences with which everyone is familiar. In everyday life it happens quite regularly that something only filters through to us the second time round. We are in the middle of reading, somebody asks us something and as we look up – 'what did you say?' – we can still 'hear' the question and we reply to it. Or we let our eyes roam vaguely over a crowded outdoor café and only realize a moment later that we spotted an acquaintance. In these cases, now often referred to as double takes, there is a delayed assimilation of something already present as a sense impression. Yet nothing like a déjà vu happens; there is no sense of repetition, no placing of an event into an indefinite past, no sense of knowing in advance what will happen the next moment.

## Déjà vu and depersonalization

No matter whether they come from literature, neurology, psychiatry or psychoanalysis, the theories mentioned above have one thing in common: they are not based on a large store of case histories. Most of them have been presented by authors who simply lacked the data needed to link experiences of déjà vu to comparable psychological phenomena, to differences between subjects or to variations in the surrounding circumstances. Why does one person experience a déjà vu while another does not? Are there special circumstances that encourage a sense of déjà vu: travel perhaps, or fatigue, drink, lack of sleep? Research into these questions did not start until the Dutch philosopher and psychologist Gerard Heymans launched two enquiries in 1904 and 1906 into the possible links between déjà vu experiences and another equally fleeting psychological phenomenon, namely depersonalization.

Depersonalization, according to Heymans, is the 'sudden, generally quickly passing condition in which everything we perceive strikes us as being strange, new and dream-like rather than real; when the people to whom we speak give the impression of being machines, when even our own voice sounds as strange in our ears as that of somebody else, and when we have the feeling that we are not acting or speaking ourselves, but are observing our actions and words as passive spectators'. The results of his enquiries bore out Heymans's theory that feelings both of déjà vu and of depersonalization are based on memory illusions of a very specific kind. Later research has corroborated this conclusion in various respects.

In his questionnaires, Heymans asked about daily rhythms (are you an early bird or a night owl?), work rhythms, emotional stability, introvert or extrovert disposition, absent-mindedness, the quality of the visual memory and possible talent for mathematics or languages. A special question bore on 'word alienation', the sensation that a familiar word suddenly seems to be 'odd, strange, a complex of meaningless sounds or letters'. The participants were asked to record the time when this phenomenon appeared, state whether they were in their normal surroundings, whether they were alone or in company, talking or listening, tired or tense, whether they had been making great physical or mental efforts, had been eating or had drunk more than usual, and so on. To gather enough comparative material, Heymans asked his students to answer the questions about their personality and intellectual inclinations even when in the period under consideration they had had *no* experiences of déjà vu or depersonalization. He took his account of how a déjà vu felt from David Copperfield's musings when Micawber began to talk about Dora and Agnes.

Heymans sent his questionnaires to two age groups among his psychology students. Through the kind offices of fellow professors from Heidelberg, Bonn and Berlin he was able to send out a German questionnaire as well. Heymans finished up with more than 130 completed forms. With an unerring statistical eye, he identified three qualities that were more common among 'positive' participants (respondents who had had déjà vu or depersonalization experiences) than among 'negative' participants. These qualities were: greater sensitivity, marked mood changes and irregular work rhythms. The same qualities also went hand in hand with the more frequent occurrence of word alienation. In the greatest number of cases, experiences of déjà vu and depersonalization had occurred in the evening or at night, generally in the company of others, while the participant himself was not speaking and often in a state of fatigue, after boring or desultory studies or after drinking – in short, Heymans wrote, in a state of flagging concentration and reduced mental energy.

Heymans pointed out that déjà vu experiences occur in the same participants as also experience depersonalization and word alienation. Moreover, the fact that these three phenomena are facilitated by the same circumstances suggests that they are related. As a result, hypotheses that merely explain déjà vu become improbable. After all, explanations in terms of partial correspondence between current and earlier experiences, of 'double perceptions' or of the delayed processing of perceptions, fail to explain why those concerned also have a greater chance of experiencing depersonalization and word alienation – the false sense of familiarity that is wrongly *present* in déjà vu experiences, is wrongly *absent* from word alienation and depersonalization.

According to Heymans's own hypothesis, the apparently so different phenomena of déjà vu, depersonalization and word alienation are expressions of one and the same process. The starting point of the hypothesis is that the familiar feeling of a perception is due to associations between that perception and earlier experiences. These associations help to date experiences in the past: the vaguer and weaker the associations, the greater the apparent time interval between the current and the remembered experience. Because of a temporary decrease in psychic energy or reduced concentration, the associations that under normal circumstances feel familiar to us can be lacking or weakened. According to that hypothesis, word alienation is due to a lack of associative links between a word and semantic memory, as a result of which the word is experienced as no more than a sound. Depersonalization is said to be the consequence of the complete absence of associations, so that not only the words but *all* aspects of the situation lose their familiarity. A déjà vu, finally, is said to arise when the associations are not completely absent, but are weak and small in number. The consciousness then has the illusion that the current experience is a memory of an event from a distant past.

Heymans went on to define the link between a déjà vu and psychic energy on the basis of personal experiences. Even when the level of concentration is normal or high, but the amount of psychic energy available for the processing of the current perception is small, it is possible for déjà vu experiences to appear. Take the case of a man due to deliver an after-dinner speech, who is engaged in conversation shortly beforehand. Since most of his psychic energy is invested in the speech, the conversation will be bound up with weak associations. A fellow professor told Heymans that he sometimes has a déjà vu when he is about to enter a crowded room: with his hand on the doorknob, he suddenly has the feeling that he has been there once before. Even close attention directed at matters outside the current perception can apparently facilitate déjà vu experiences.

In Heymans's theory, word alienation, déjà vu and depersonalization cover a sliding scale. In the weakest form, only the link between the word and its meaning has disappeared, and the word suddenly becomes a strange isolated sound in our heads. In the case of depersonalization, all the associations with the familiar have vanished so that everything seems strange and new. A déjà vu occupies a halfway position; it is familiar and new all at once. Which of the three forms appears depends on the degree of psychic energy available. On the basis of that theory, Heymans claimed, it is possible to make two predictions. The first is that, if depersonalization is a more extreme case of the same process that causes feelings of déjà vu, then the latter would have to be more common than the former. The enquiry showed that this was indeed the case. The second prediction concerns the psychological profile of people who have such experiences. If depersonalization is the most extreme variant, the profile of participants reporting depersonalization must be present in a more clearly defined form than in participants experiencing déjà vu only. Heymans found that the second prediction was not borne out by the results of the 1904 enquiry, but was strongly so by the 1906 enquiry. Participants familiar with both depersonalization and déjà vus from their own experience did indeed differ from participants who had experienced déjà vus alone.

Why should research done almost a century ago continue to hold our interest? Heymans's two enquiries were most elegant even when judged by current standards. To this day, they remain the only studies carried out prospectively: the circumstances did not have to be described by recourse to distant memories. Heymans's predictions lent themselves to empirical verification. Moreover, his explanation was decidedly less speculative than many of the hypotheses about déjà vus described in the literature: no latent memories of past lives, no eternal recurrence, and no 'this has been thus before'. These merits persuaded the psychiatrist Herman Sno and myself to analyse Heymans's material anew. Nowadays we can use statistical instruments to obtain more information from the same data. The precise results of this re-analysis are reported elsewhere; here I shall confine myself to the main conclusions. On repeating the tests, significant correlations were found in the replies to all questions, except those concerning the affinity with exact studies. The correlation of déjà vu with depersonalization, too, proved to be significant. Of Heymans's two predictions, the first was corroborated by the re-analysis. Heymans's second prediction was less successful: on re-analysis only the difference in word alienation proved significant. Participants reporting déjà vus or depersonalization or both differ strikingly from 'negative' participants, but there are no differences *within* the group of 'positive' participants.

## Déjà vu, schizophrenia and epilepsy

Heymans was not a neurologist. The students he questioned did not suffer from psychiatric disorders. But among the mentally healthy participants, the emotionally labile subjects had a déjà vu most frequently, and the circumstances in which their déjà vus appeared suggest a mental breakdown, however transitory. As a result of the discovery of a link with depersonalization, déjà vus have increasingly been relegated to pathology and mental disorder, and that is where they have remained since. Practically all the studies of déjà vu of the past thirty to forty years have been made by psychiatrists and neurologists professionally focused on links with clinical phenomena or organic disorders. In 1969, the psychiatrist Harper found the same correlation between déjà vu and depersonalization in a non-psychiatric population as Heymans had done before him. Moreover, in a study of depersonalization involving almost nine hundred students, a link with déjà vu was discovered in 1972. The same affinity with modern research can also be found in Heymans's finding that déjà vus are largely associated with certain personality traits. Richardson and Winokur established in 1968 that in a group of psychiatric patients déjà vus are found more frequently in emotionally labile persons and in adolescents with adaptation disorders.

However, for a long time déjà vus have also been linked to much more serious disorders than depersonalization. In certain forms of schizophrenia they can continue for such a long time that they assume a chronic character. They are then absorbed in so comprehensive a system of delusions that the patient thinks he is living a double life, or that he is living the same life twice over. This is a strange pathology – the patient has become his own *doppelgänger* and interprets everything he experiences or thinks as a duplicate of another life, lived elsewhere or earlier. Unlike an 'ordinary' déjà vu, this psychotic variant has a slow beginning, but once present it is almost impossible to dispel. In the same article in which he introduced the term déjà vu in 1896, Arnaud described the case of Louis. This thirty-four-year-old officer had contracted malaria while serving in Tonkin. The violent bouts of fever affected his memory: he not only forgot many incidents in his past, but was unable to retain his present-day experiences. He would repeat the same question five or six times within a few minutes. About eighteen months later, at the beginning of 1893, the first déjà vu symptoms appeared. He claimed to have read several articles in the newspaper beforehand; he even recognized them so clearly that he thought he must have written them himself. At first the confusion was confined to what he was actually reading. But a few months later he attended his brother's wedding and it seemed to him that he had witnessed the whole ceremony, down to the last detail, once before. Louis wondered why they had to go through the whole thing all over again. Thereafter he went downhill very fast and began to suffer from persecution mania. In the summer of 1894, his father was able to persuade him to enter the Vanves mental institution, where he was put under the care of Arnaud. Louis let it be known very quickly that he recognized everything: the courtyard, the rooms, the corridors, even the staff. 'I was here this time last year as well.' His inner life, too, was one long series of identical repetitions.

His first meeting with Arnaud was bizarre. Louis introduced himself formally to Arnaud, they exchanged courtesies, but suddenly the expression on Louis's face changed. 'Now I recognize you, doctor! It was you who admitted me last year, at this same time, in this same room. You asked me the same questions and I gave you the same answers. That's perfectly obvious to me now. You pretend to be surprised, but you can stop this right now.' Arnaud protested but Louis stuck to his story. Six months later Louis claimed that he had not experienced two minutes that differed from his earlier stay. He relived every event not only in the institution but also in public life: the death of Visconte de Lesseps, the Madagascar expedition, the death of Pasteur, the train disaster in the Gare Montparnasse. In a letter to his brother, he wrote that he would not be sending condolences to a friend of the family since her little daughter could not possibly have died a second time.

A case history like Louis's is not unique. Twenty years earlier, the German neurologist Pick had described a similar case: a young man suffering from persecution mania, who, once admitted to hospital, wrote in his diary that he had been convinced since the second day that he had been through it all before, as if, as he put it, he were living a 'double life'. The Swiss psychiatrist Forel reported the case of a young trader suffering from persecution mania who had declared soon after his admission that he had been there the year before. Much more recently, in 1992, Sno and several colleagues described the case of a nineteen-year-old girl who had been admitted to the psychiatric department of the Amsterdam Medical Centre as a schizophrenic. She too suffered from delusions; she was convinced that she was the reincarnation of Marilyn Monroe, all of whose films and photographs looked familiar to her. She told her psychiatrist that she recognized her fellow patients, the ward and the staff, so that she must have been there before.

Arnaud's officer, Pick and Forel's young men and the schizophrenic girl in Sno's department all shared, apart from their permanent state of déjà vu – or rather as a result of it – yet another quirk. The officer stayed in the clinic in 1894 but dated his letters 1895. Forel's young trader consistently wrote 1880 instead of 1879. Sno's schizophrenic girl explained her 'memories' by the fact that she was living one year later than the calendar suggested. When the officer's attention was drawn to the year's difference, his explanation was perfectly logical: if the newspapers he had read 'last year' were dated 1894 then it had to be 1895 now. His fellow patients in 1897 and 1992 used the same reasoning. The shift of one year – and not of two or three – is a touching illustration of the precarious balance between 'method' and 'madness' in a psychiatric disorder. If the déjà vu continues for so long and consistently that the patient can no longer remember the beginning, he is also unable to check his experiences against reality. For the officer, the clear recognition of time and place – this ward in Vanves, this summer – could only have been explained by a previous stay in Vanves, and moreover during the nearest summer, that of the previous year. Consistency is the last thing a disordered mind wants to surrender.

Déjà vus as symptoms of schizophrenia seem to spring from a disorder in the patient's sense of time. Even with an 'ordinary' déjà vu there is a brief moment of disorientation, but one that is immediately corrected. The sense of 'that's something I've experienced before' changes with lightning speed to 'I am experiencing something that *feels* as if I had experienced it before.' The awareness that one is having an illusion restores contact with reality. There is yet another type of déjà vu. This type is not as stubborn as the schizophrenic variety, but decidedly less fleeting than the déjà vus most people know from their own experience. They are connected with epilepsy and were described at length during the last quarter of the nineteenth century by the English neurologist John Hughlings Jackson.

Sometimes an epileptic seizure is heralded by an 'aura' – the patient hears strange noises or has a strange taste in his mouth; he can also have the sensation of being lifted up unexpectedly or of seeing familiar shapes stretched into bizarre dimensions. In a specific form of epilepsy, namely temporal epilepsy, the aura is sometimes accompanied by an experience that Hughlings Jackson, following his patients' description, called a 'dreamy state'. Shortly before the seizure, the normal sense of time seems to vanish, the patient has the feeling that he is outside reality, he sometimes has vivid hallucinations, or everything he experiences seems highly familiar. Hughlings Jackson called such a feeling 'reminiscence' and his account makes it clear that he was referring to what we nowadays call déjà vu. On the basis of autopsies – and there were few other means of localization in his day – Hughlings Jackson suspected that the 'dreamy state' resulted from a lesion or disorder in the temporal lobe.

Not until half a century later did a means of producing such phenomena experimentally become available. In the 1930s, the Canadian neurologist Wilder Penfield was treating serious cases of epilepsy with a new surgical technique. Under a local anaesthetic, he removed a disc from the skull, made a quick incision in the cerebral membranes and exposed the surface of the brain. The brain itself is insensitive. While the patient remained conscious, Penfield systematically probed the cortex with an electrode, in the hope of finding the area that, on stimulation, would produce an epileptic fit. In this way, he was able to detect and remove the epileptic focus. The reactions and perceptions of the patients varied when different areas were being stimulated. Some of the reactions were predictable, for instance the raising of the right arm after stimulation of the left motor projection area, or seeing flashes of light following stimulation of the visual cortex. However, the same weak electrical shocks to specific areas of the temporal lobe produced sensations connected with time perception and the memory. Some patients either had the sudden feeling that they had been in that situation before or else from one moment to the next found the situation completely unfamiliar (*jamais vu*). Others felt vaguely uneasy, as if some disaster were threatening, or were, just as inexplicably, filled with a sense of happiness. Stimulation of neighbouring parts of the temporal lobe caused hallucinations, dreamlike images and flashbacks, often of everyday events and situations. It would thus seem that Penfield was able with his electrode to evoke the 'dreamy state' Hughlings Jackson had observed in his patients with temporal epilepsy.

In 1994, *Brain*, the same journal to which Hughlings Jackson had contributed so many of his findings a century earlier, published the report of a long series of EEG measurements of sixteen epileptic patients who felt a 'dreamy state' during their aura. The experiments were carried out at the Hôpital Sainte-Anne in Paris. The results helped to determine, much more closely than Hughlings Jackson or Penfield had been able to do, the neurological co-ordinates of the cerebral areas involved in the 'dreamy state'. The object of the research, incidentally, was purely clinical, the findings about déjà vu being in effect a by-product. In these patients, epilepsy could not be treated with drugs. The measurements were primarily intended to discover the focus of the attacks and to remove it later by surgery. To that end some ten electrodes were applied to the brain under light anaesthesia and left there for over five hours. After the anaesthetic had worn off, the investigators sent a weak current through the various electrodes for one millisecond. The voltage was increased for just as long as it took to produce an epileptic seizure and the location of the focus had been found. Throughout the experiment the patient was questioned about his experiences, so that afterwards subjective findings could, as it were, be projected on to the EEG traces from the various brain areas.

The electrical stimulation elicited the entire spectrum of experiences Hughlings Jackson had classified as the 'dreamy state'. Patients saw with hallucinatory clarity images of familiar scenes, such as old neighbourhoods or friends from their past, their present-day experience feeling as if it were a dream; sometimes very old memories of domestic scenes seemed to be coming back, for instance their mother pottering about in the kitchen. For others, the images of persons were so true to life that they started to talk to them. Sometimes the current experience – sitting backwards with a tangle of electrodes sticking out of their skull – felt so familiar that the patients believed they had been through it all before. Conversely, the situation could strike them as being completely unfamiliar, as if they had been caught up in a dream. Sometimes stimulation with one and the same electrode would alternately elicit a déjà vu on one occasion and a feeling of unfamiliarity on another. With almost everybody the sensations felt during stimulation went hand in hand with a vague, undirected anxiety, even when the memories or the hallucinations seemed familiar. The 'dreamy state' always appeared during the initial phase of a seizure, generally in the first ten seconds.

When the EEG measurements were compared to the patients' subjective experiences, it appeared that the 'dreamy state' went hand in hand with stimulation of two brain centres, the amygdala and the hippocampus. Both are part of the limbic system, a phylogenetically old part of the brain. It lies deep inside the brain, close to the brainstem, and has direct links with the part of the brain responsible for vigilance and control of the emotions. Stimulation of the amygdala can, as earlier research had already established, cause feelings of anxiety or, on the contrary, of relaxation, depending on the patient's situation. The hippocampus is essential for the functioning of the memory. Damage to it, as in Korsakoff's syndrome or as the result of a lesion, causes serious impairment of memory. Bilateral destruction of the hippocampus leads to an irrevocable end of the capacity to store memories. The amygdala and the hippocampus both have a close network of connections with those parts of the temporal lobe that integrate sensory information.

According to the best information available at present, epileptic déjà vus arise in a neuronal circuit in which the amygdala, the hippocampus and parts of the temporal lobe are simultaneously active. The temporal lobe processes current experiences and passes the results to the hippocampus. But the simultaneous activation of the hippocampus, be it by stimulation with an electrode or through an epileptic seizure, interprets the incoming new information as a memory. The 'when' of that memory is missing – it is not, after all, a real memory – but the sum total of the experiences being processed at that moment conveys a sense of familiarity that happens to be associated with the hippocampus. The activation of the amygdala, finally, causes the feeling that doom is about to strike. A slightly different distribution of activities over the temporal lobe, hippocampus and amygdala can, by contrast, strip the current situation of any association with a familiar situation, even if that situation happened a few moments earlier, so that the patient believes that everything he is currently experiencing is totally new. However far apart these two experiences – the new that feels familiar and the familiar that seems new – may be introspectively, neurologically they are so closely related that even repeated stimulation of the same spot can elicit one experience on one, and the other on a different, occasion.

A sceptical question that might eventually be asked is what these findings about déjà vus under pathological conditions really tell us about the déjà vus experienced by so many normal people. Schizophrenia and epilepsy are fortunately rare afflictions, and even déjà vus occur rarely in them, the great majority of schizophrenic and epileptic patients having no more déjà vus than anyone chosen at random. The relationship to pathology is asymmetrical: in a small number of patients they constitute a part of the clinical picture; conversely they are no indication of pathological states. The déjà vu category does not figure in the diagnostic manuals of psychiatrists. One may accordingly ask oneself what eliciting déjà vus with electrodes can tell us about ordinary, spontaneously occurring déjà vus. After all, outside neurological clinics, no one runs about with electrodes in his head. Questions like that are justified, but fail to appreciate the solid gains that have been made. Pathological conditions often magnify phenomena that are too fleeting or too nugatory to lend themselves to close observation under normal circumstances. The fact that some déjà vus can be elicited experimentally allows neurologists to localize their anatomical origins. In neuropsychology, the answer to 'where' may well be the beginning of the answer to 'how' and 'why'.

In this special case of a neuronal circuit consisting of three cerebral structures that, depending on their contribution, can elicit feelings of strangeness, familiarity and fear, we have an elegant parallel with findings in a completely different field (and made at a different time). In 1904, Heymans established that déjà vus and depersonalizations were subjectively opposite processes, even though they happened to one and the same person and under the same conditions. That, according to him, indicated a hidden connection – the same process had to underlie both experiences. The experiments conducted almost a century later in the clinic of the Hôpital Sainte-Anne suggest that this was indeed the case.

## Oval mirrors

Déjà vus involve three illusions. They feel like memories but are nothing of the kind; they make you think that you know what is about to happen when you cannot really predict it; and they conjure up vague anxieties for which there seems to be no good reason. This triple deception, however slight and ethereal, has a confusing effect. It causes you to pause for a few moments in what, under normal circumstances, is a flowing stream of associations. The replication of an experience that seems both new and familiar immediately elicits a second replication, introspective in kind, namely the surprised observation of your own experience. All déjà vus share this mirror effect. For the rest there are differences. Déjà vu experiences are generally fleeting, but they also occur in chronic form. They can appear spontaneously, but may also be elicited by electrical stimulation. While one déjà vu is routinely identified as a passing illusion, another becomes part of a system of schizophrenic delusions. Déjà vus often arise without a demonstrable neuronal disorder, but they can also announce an epileptic seizure. It seems improbable that one explanation applies to all these variations. Herman Sno, currently the most productive writer on déjà vu, has stated that the findings of various investigators quite often contradict one another. One establishes a link with neurotic complaints, while another does not, or speaks of a negative correlation. Age, intelligence, socio-economic status, foreign travel, psychiatric disorders, brain lesions, ethnic background – each has been examined but no simple correlation with déjà vus has been found. The frequency of déjà vu varies with the category under investigation. There is no consensus on the question of whether the difference between 'ordinary' and chronic déjà vus is one of degree or kind. A slightly clearer pattern is found under circumstances that seem to facilitate a déjà vu: fatigue, stress, exhaustion, traumas, illness, alcohol and pregnancy. These are also the conditions under which depersonalization can appear, the only mental phenomenon in fact that has a clear relation with déjà vus.

However, the conclusion that all explanations are equally probable is too bleak. That someone can have a déjà vu the moment he takes out his mobile phone is hard to attribute to some resonance with an earlier life. If déjà vus are due to some correspondence with earlier experiences, dreamed, imagined or really lived, then it becomes all the more puzzling why they appear in circumstances that play into the hands of the opposite – a complete lack of recognition. Heymans's hypothesis of 1904, that a convincing theory must account for both phenomena, still applies. According to the hypothesis of accordance with earlier experience, déjà vus would have to be more common than they actually are and then chiefly in everyday, oft-repeated situations, not during travel or rare moments of exhaustion and tension. The same applies to the hypothesis of the 'double image', of twice-processed perception. In conditions under which we really do process the same thing twice over, as in the reading of a passage we have read mechanically immediately beforehand without taking it in, nothing like a déjà vu takes place. Heymans's hypothesis that in a déjà vu the current perception is supplied with too weak or too few associations in the wake of a temporary lapse of concentration so that it comes to resemble a vague memory has good credentials even today. Such lapses can be due to most divergent causes: alcohol, a temporary shortage of oxygen during pregnancy, a traumatic event, the tension preceding a public appearance, or exhaustion. It explains why a déjà vu is a rare experience and can easily turn into a depersonalization.

The Parisian localization experiments with epileptics provide an experimental grip on what used to be considered mainly as subjective experiences. If electrically induced déjà vus are the artificial equivalent of a disorder that, in a much milder form, may occasionally arise spontaneously, the importance of these experiments goes much further than answering the question 'where?' That a neurological mechanism has now been specified capable of producing precisely the three illusory elements of a déjà vu – familiarity, strangeness, unease – but also the strange effect of a depersonalization, is a good example of unexpected convergence. If findings assembled with such divergent instruments as questionnaires and electrodes suddenly point in the same direction, we gain something like aesthetic satisfaction. However, this investigation is unlikely to be the last word on the causes of déjà vus, perhaps not even the beginning of the last word. But, as Churchill put it in another context, it may well prove to be the end of the beginning.

In the spring of 1949, the Dutch poet Gerrit Achterberg, accompanied by his wife Cathrien and by Chetty and Jim ter Kuile, travelled by car to France. Achterberg wanted to visit the house in which the poet and essayist Hendrik Marsman had spent his last few months. The preparations had not gone off without difficulty. Following his shooting of his lover in 1937, Achterberg was still being detained under the hospital order imposed on him, which had been repeatedly extended for one or two years at a time. He had to report every journey beforehand to his psychiatrist and did not have the free use of a passport. Ter Kuile was able to use his Hague connections to lift this last restriction. In April, the group left in Ter Kuile's Ford for the south of France. Achterberg carried a notebook in which, as Chetty ter Kuile told Achterberg's biographer Wim Hazeu, he recorded everything that happened on the way, down to the kilometre readings. The collection *Autodroom* (Auto dream, 1954) ought really to have been dedicated to Ter Kuile, Achterberg declared later – poems such as 'Rivièra', 'Souvenir' and 'George de loup' were all based on what they saw and experienced together in France. From the first line of the opening poem in *Autodroom*, Achterberg played with shifts in space and time, with maps and Baedekers, distances and borders, climbs and descents, halts and the overtaking of other cars. The strange trance-like sense that a long car drive can evoke and that makes one's experience of time slide and shift is captured in the eighth poem of the cycle:

DÉJÀ VU

The smoothly lying water, sunken low
in all the hollows it is filling now
along the street's white castles in a row,
glistens as in a dream. The car moves on.

Straight from a book is what I see.
Fantasy-borne reality,
Changed into déjà vu for me.
You cannot evade the now; it has to be.

In oval mirrors we drive around;
see in ourselves our own background
and know it too could once be found.

The same road verges come and go.
The heart is filled, as long ago,
The amalgam binding all the souls we know.

Anyone going by the title alone might well have fitted 'Déjà vu' into Achterberg's psychiatric poems, such as 'Rorschach', 'Depersonalization' and 'Hallucination'. Achterberg was kept for close on a year in 1943 in the Rhijngeest sanatorium at Oegstgeest, where he had access to the psychiatric library. He showed great interest in psychiatry – which was reciprocated – and read books on art and psychopathology. While there, he may also have read the explanations of déjà vu experiences mentioned in the literature. In the quatrains of the sonnet, several of these explanations occur side by side: the reliving of a dream; the recognition of a passage you have read; experiencing something you used to fantasize about. But in the tercets, Achterberg seems to be seeking an image for the riddle, not the solution. The mirror provides an association fitting a déjà vu with its repetition and duplication. In the case of the rear-view mirror, we obtain the paradoxical image in which 'verges come and go' while you yourself are still. Framed in an oval, you see yourself, sitting still, hurtling through the landscape at great speed. Chetty ter Kuile remembered how Achterberg, on the road, 'delivered a whole disquisition about the Ford's rear-view mirror as an object in which you could see what was past. Things were past yet still visible – that was the spirit in which he spoke.'

## BIBLIOGRAPHY

Achterberg, G.,*Verzamelde gedichten*, Amsterdam, 1963.

Anjel, J., 'Beitrag zum Capittel über Erinnerungstäuschungen', *Archiv für Psychiatrie* 8 (1877), 57–64.

Arnaud, F. L., 'Un cas d'illusion de "déjà vu" ou "fausse mémoire"', *Annales Médico-Psychologiques* 3 (1896), 8th series, 455–70.

Bancaud, J., F. Brunet-Bourgin, P. Chauvel and E. Halgren, 'Anatomical origin of *déjà vu* and "vivid memories" in human temporal lobe epilepsy', *Brain* 117 (1994), 71–90.

Bergson, H., 'Le souvenir du present et la fausse reconnaissance', *Revue Philosophique* 66 (1908), 561–93.

Bernard-Leroy, E., *L'illusion de fausse reconnaissance*, Paris, 1898.

Berrios, G. E., 'Déjà vu in France during the 19th century: a conceptual history', *Comprehensive Psychiatry* 36 (1955), 123–9.

Brauer, R., M. Harrow and G. J. Tucker, 'Depersonalization phenomena in psychiatric patients', *British Journal of Psychiatry* 117 (1970), 509–15.

Dickens, C., *David Copperfield*, London, 1850.

*Pictures from Italy*, London, 1913.

Forel, A., *Das Gedächtnis und seine Abnormitäten*, Zurich, 1885.

Harper, M. A., 'Déjà vu and depersonalization in normal subjects', *Australian and New Zealand Journal of Psychiatry* 3 (1969), 67–74.

Hazeu, W., *Gerrit Achterberg: Een biografie*, Amsterdam, 1988.

Heijden, A. F. T. van der, *Vallende ouders*, Amsterdam, 1983.

Heymans, G., 'Eine Enquête über Depersonalisation und "Fausse Reconnaissance"', *Zeitschrift für Psychologie* 36 (1904), 321–43.

'Weitere Daten über Depersonalisation und "Fausse Reconnaissance"', *Zeitschrift für Psychologie* 43 (1906), 1–17.

Jackson, J. H., 'On a particular variety of epilepsy "intellectural aura", one case with symptoms of organic brain disease', *Brain* 11 (1888), 179–207.

James, W., *Principles of Psychology*, New York, 1890.

Jensen, J., 'Über Doppelwahrnehmungen in der gesunden wie in der kranken Psyche', *Allgemeine Zeitschrift für Psychiatrie und Nervenkrankheiten* (Suppl. Issue) 25 (1868), 48–64.

Kooten, K. van, *Meer modernismen*, Amsterdam, 1986.

Myers, D. H., and G. Grant, 'A study of depersonalization in students', *British Journal of Psychiatry* 121 (1972), 59–65.

Myers, F. W. H., 'The subliminal self', *Proceedings of the Society for Psychical Research* 11 (1895), 334–593.

Neppe, V. M., *The Psychology of Déjà Vu: Have I Been Here Before?*, Johannesburg, 1983.

Pfister, O., 'Schockdenken und Schockphantasien bei höchster Todesgefahr', *Internationale Zeitschrift für Psychoanalyse* 16, 3–4 (1930), 430–55.

Pick, A., 'Zur Casuistik der Erinnerungstäuschungen', *Archiv für Psychiatrie* 6 (1876), 568–74.

Richardson, T. F., and G. Winokur, 'Déjà vu in psychiatric and neurosurgical patients', *Journal of Nervous and Mental Disease* 146 (1968), 161–4.

Scott, W., *Guy Mannering*, London, 1815.

Sno, H. N., *The Déjà Vu Experience: A Psychiatric Perspective*, Amsterdam, 1993.

Sno, H. N. and D. Draaisma, 'An early Dutch study of déjà vu experiences', *Psychological Medicine* 23 (1993), 17–26.

Sno, H. N., and D. H. Linszen, 'The déjà vu experience: remembrance of things past?', *American Journal of Psychiatry* 147 (1990), 1,587–95.

Sno, H. N., D. H. Linszen and F. E. R. E. R. de Jonghe, 'Déjà vu experiences and reduplicative paramnesia', *British Journal of Psychiatry* 160 (1992), 565–8.

'Een zonderlinge zweming...Over déjà vu ervaringen in de belletrie', *Tijdschrift voor Psychiatrie* 4 (1992), 243–54.

Sully, J., *Illusion: A Psychological Study*, London 1881.

Wigan, A. L., *The Duality of the Mind*, London, 1844.

# 13    Reminiscences

The eighty years of the life of Willem van den Hull, reduced to about as many words, go as follows. He was born in 1778 in Haarlem, the son of a postman. With the financial support of some well-to-do Haarlem citizens he trained as a schoolmaster and later became the owner of an independent boarding school. He did so well that he was able to found a 'French school' in Haarlem's grandest building, where many members of the Amsterdam aristocracy had their sons educated. He remained single and with his spinster sister brought up his nephew Hubert as his own son. Van den Hull died in 1858.

That we know so much more about his life than these simple facts is thanks to his voluminous autobiography. Van den Hull began work on it in 1841. At the time he was sixty-three, had retired as head of his boarding school and had all the leisure he needed to chronicle his life. In little more than a year, he had described his life up to the age of thirty-seven. When he was sixty-five he wrote a second instalment devoted to his life until 1854. He lived for another four years, but left no further autobiographical records. The full text runs to precisely eight hundred numbered pages in unbound sections, with some four hundred words to each page, written in a neat school master's hand.

The text was probably not meant for publication. Van den Hull wrote for his adopted son and the rest of his family, and therefore devoted the first chapter to a detailed family history. Perhaps, like the people who nowadays flock to the Public Record Office in the name of genealogical research, he felt the need to locate his life within a bloodline of ancestors and descendants; perhaps he felt his life deserved to be recorded in detail. What is certain is that he felt the urge to set a few things straight. And it is also clear that he thought he was living in special times. As early as 1831, he had published a book whose full title translates into English as *On the Concerns of a Sexagenarian in the Year 1831; or a Sketch of the Most Remarkable Phenomena Characterizing This Age Above All Others*. It is a survey of what the half-century before 1831 had produced in new developments, inventions and discoveries, a period in which, according to Van den Hull, more had happened than during the preceding three centuries.

In writing his autobiography, Van den Hull is believed to have used the diaries he used to keep (and that, alas, have been lost), so that he was able to put precise dates to many events in his life. However the style is not that of a diarist. Van den Hull follows narrative threads, allows themes to be developed and ties up loose ends. Moreover, his is a candid account, even touching in places. He feels free to write about mishaps and setbacks, moments of humiliation, shame, regret and remorse. Van den Hull was a sensitive, easily hurt man, who missed the marital relationship he so passionately desired. You are unlikely to finish his memoirs without having conceived an affection for him.

All writers of autobiography draw upon their memory, though not all to the same extent. Some autobiographies are partly documented with the use of external material: minutes, reports, letters, memoranda and addresses. Like Churchill's memoirs they may be recorded with the help of secretaries. Yet no secretary could have made a significant contribution to Van den Hull's autobiography; he really did describe his life on the basis of strictly personal recollections. As a result, the characteristics of an autobiographical memory are brought out all the more sharply. The autobiography tells us little about the first three or four years of his life, lists his first memories and then follows the life course through youth, adulthood and old age. It is also without doubt the autobiography of an elderly author, reflecting a peculiarity of autobiographical memory associated with advanced age and only recently investigated more closely through experimental studies.

## The reminiscence effect

As early as 1879 Francis Galton noticed that many of his associations went back to his youth, a much larger number in fact than were linked to his recent years. The method he used is the crux of what is now known as the 'Galton cuing technique': a list of words aimed at retrieving memories. The words are chosen so that they can be linked to every period of life. A word like 'exam' is thus unsuitable, since when you are forty the chances that you have recently sat an

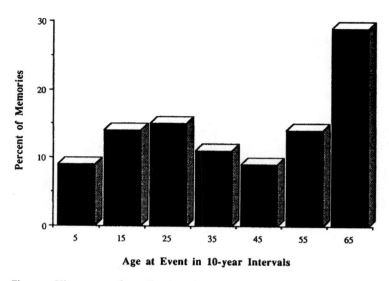

Fig. 21   Histogram of recollections by subjects aged seventy on average in response to cue words. About half the recollections referred to the preceding year and have not been included here, since otherwise the pattern of the rest of the recollections could not have been clearly represented. From right to left, the normal forgetting curve drops steeply the further back an event has occurred. However, whereas a normal forgetting curve decreases evenly after that, the curve depicted shows an increase between the ages of fifteen and twenty-five: the reminiscence bump.

examination are smaller than they were in your early twenties. Such words as 'moving house' or 'falling downstairs' by contrast, are eminently suitable. The experimental subject is asked for a recollection he associates with the cue word. Next, an attempt is made to date the recollection as accurately as possible. Broadly speaking, the greatest number of memories seems to be evoked by recent events: the last house move, the last time you fell downstairs. In a histogram in which the verticals express the percentage of recollections and the horizontals the age, the bars rise as we go to the right, with the highest bar just before the investigation. That is, in fact, the normal forgetting curve, which applies equally to many other forms of recall, declining steeply at first and then levelling off. However, the same experiment, using older subjects, gives rise to a remarkable phenomenon. In the area that levels off in persons of middle age the bars begin to rise with older people. To the left of the time axis there appears a bulge that develops into what is called the reminiscence bump. The precise position of the bump varies slightly from one study to the next, but there is an unmistakable concentration of memories from a period covering some ten years and of which the twentieth year of life constitutes the centre. The bump increases further in size when the experimental subject is not asked to respond to cue words but to describe three or four of his most vivid recollections. In that case, the bar is shortest for the most recent past and there is a solid peak at the age of fifteen. The reminiscence effect appears in experimental subjects from about the age of sixty and grows more prominent with the years.

When Willem van den Hull began to write his autobiography at the age of sixty-three he was, in fact, performing an informal experiment with just one experimental subject. Without cue words or set schemes, paging through his own diaries and repeatedly following his own associations, he simply wrote down what he remembered. He used a chronological approach. Sometimes he got ahead of his story; sometimes he had something to add that had happened earlier, but by and large he followed the course of his life. This approach makes it possible to calculate how many pages Van den Hull devoted to each year of his life. For the period from his fourth to his thirteenth birthday, the average number is close on fourteen. The chapter covering the period from his thirteenth to his twenty-first birthday comprises more than fifteen pages a year, and the next chapter, to his twenty-seventh birthday, a little more again. But then the number of pages for each year of his life begins to fall off. This happens at an even but fast rate: less than ten pages for the period between his twenty-seventh and thirty-seventh birthdays, fewer than six pages for the next five years, and then a drop to fewer than four pages for every year between the ages of fifty-four and seventy-two. The reason why, during the last four years of his life, up to the age of seventy-six, he reached an average of five pages a year, the number thus growing again slightly, was that he gave a detailed account of what he had been writing during that period, including his treatise, the title of which translates as *Conjecture about the Nature and Purpose of Saturn's Ring*.

Writing the eight hundred pages of his memoirs, Van den Hull thus demonstrated a powerful reminiscence effect. A histogram of the number of pages produced every year would by and large resemble the histogram of the septuagenarians who spontaneously report their vivid memories. The same bump on the left, the same quick decline towards middle age, the same dearth of memories of the last few years. It is a pattern that excites our curiosity. What is the cause of the accumulation of memories round the age of twenty? Is the memory simply in better condition at that time? Does someone that age have more memorable experiences? Or do we see our youth more sharply in old age because so much from the intervening years has gone? Each of these questions invites us to examine Van den Hull's autobiography more closely, to look at what he says he remembers clearly, at what incidents are vividly brought home, what events are first described in detail only to disappear from the chronicle later, to look, in short, at what kind of memories make up the reminiscence bump, what precedes and what follows it.

## 'It seems to me I can hear it still'

Of his own history, Van den Hull wrote, 'I should almost have been able to write [it] without any help from at least the age of four onwards, since Nature has bestowed an excellent memory (except for remembering names) upon me.' And if there was anything he had forgotten, his sister Elisabeth ('a living chronicle'), blessed with an equally good memory, would help him out. However, all information about the first four years of his life was at second hand. He was born in the early morning of 16 September 1778. It was an eventful year, according to Van den Hull, who liked to see things in a wider context, for it was also the year in which Linnaeus, Rousseau and Voltaire died. Moreover a remarkable incident had occurred in Haarlem: a Mr Van Ee, a prosperous shopkeeper, had been standing at the entrance to the Grote Kerk talking to an acquaintance when a stone fell off the top of the church and crashed through Mr Van Ee's hat, wig and skull. The shopkeeper dropped dead. A few years later, when one of his relatives was buried in the family grave, 'people were eager to take another look at the unhappy Van Ee's skull, and found the piece of the brainpan sunk deep inside the head, where the stone had dispatched it.'

What Willem remembered of his first years were mere snatches. He would, for instance, greet his mother as politely as possible in the mornings: 'Good morning, Mama; how are you today? – Very well, Willem, she would reply, and how are you? Very well, too, Mama, I would say then, imagining myself far superior to my brother and sister in manners.' He also recalled that Marten, the milkman, would always give him some fresh milk in a little cup, at least if his shoes were clean. 'There you are, two details, wellnigh too childish to repeat, but far from irrelevant to one's upbringing.' The memory of the hustle and bustle opposite their house is somewhat clearer; an institution was being built there with money left by the recently deceased Teyler van der Hulst. Willem also remembered his illnesses and minor accidents: the time when he had German measles, and later the smallpox from which he 'came away as unharmed as if they had used the cowpox vaccine (then still unknown) on me'; the times when he had boiling water poured over his foot, was pecked on his hand by a cockerel, slipped painfully off a footstove.

Nowadays our earliest memories are often linked to the birth of a brother or sister. In Van den Hull's youth, one was just as likely to remember a death in the family. A younger brother of Willem's died before his first birthday and his older brother Pieter died when he was seven. At the time, Willem was not yet four. Pieter had gone to stay with his grandparents. On the journey home, the barge on which he and their father were travelling was hit by a violent storm on Haarlem Lake. The skipper was only just able to bring the boat safely into the mouth of the River Spaarne. It was probably then that Pieter caught a cold, for he coughed ever since. The coughing fits became so uncontrollable one day that his mother put him into her own bed to help him recover. A few hours later he was overtaken by yet another coughing fit. His mother lifted him onto her lap to calm him down: 'But in vain: the coughing continued. My worried mother looked compassionately into her little boy's eyes: she saw that his eyes had clouded over and screamed: Oh my God, my child is dying! And indeed he gave his last gasp in her arms.' Willem was more affected by his parents' grief than by his brother's death. His memories of the event are fragmentary but the fragments are still etched on his mind. 'I cannot remember very much of the whole tragic episode other than that my brother was lying in his coffin waiting to be buried and that my parents, my eldest sister and I were kneeling round the body while my father prayed most movingly and my mother wept bitterly!'

What Van den Hull remembered of the days that followed was above all his own confusion. He kept asking where Pieter was now and whether he was unhappy; he did not understand many of the answers, could not grasp how his brother could be lying in a grave even while being in Heaven, and finally put together his own versions of it all. It was customary in Haarlem to keep the shutters closed if a dead person was in the house. They did this when Pieter died too, and every time Willem passed a shuttered house he would wonder where his brother might be now. There was a large former tollhouse beside the Spaarne that was uninhabited and whose windows were always shut. Perhaps, Willem mused, it contained a 'great number of dead people' and the windows were kept carefully shut to make sure they did not escape. Perhaps his brother was there as well. How upset he must be that he would always have to stay in that dismal darkness! Willem felt so much pity for his brother that he dreamt one night that he went to the house, opened the front door and entered a dark room in which the only light came from a small sunbeam stealing in through a chink in the window.

> The room was now filled from top to bottom with little children who, as soon as they noticed me, put their pretty heads together and, struck dumb, stared at me. However, they manifested themselves to me not as having hands and feet, but simply as lovely heads that, like so many apparitions, kept flitting through one another without cease, while a shimmer of light illuminated just those on whom the sunbeam fell. What saddened me, however, was that I could not discover my brother amongst them, and that of them all, as they flitted about with their eyes kept firmly fixed upon me, none would reply to my question of where my brother was. The only sound I could hear in that dark room was a gentle hum, caused by the ceaseless flitting of the apparitions, something I cannot liken better than to the whine of a flying mosquito.
> 
> How clearly that vision from my childhood still stands before my mind's eye, how distinctly I can still see the multitude of apparitions, and amongst them above all one that gazed at me for a particularly long time and on whose face I could discern happiness in plenty. Whenever, even today in

my loneliness, I hear the whine of a mosquito, I recall that dream, and feel something of the same emotion it caused me so shortly after my brother's death.

Much of what Van den Hull has to say about his early youth consists of 'first time experiences'. He was first allowed to join his father on a visit to his grandparents in Maartensdijk in 1785. The journey took so long, with the travelling on canal barges and the hours of walking, that it was an adventure in itself. He also remembered the first time he put on skates: one night his father poured a dozen buckets of water into the alleyway, and the next morning there was a frozen sheet of water. He witnessed the appearance of the first 'joujoux de Normandie' (yoyos). He also seems to have retained clear memories of his first days at school. Between the ages of four and seven he attended no fewer than four different schools until he was finally taught his ABC properly at the last. He writes a detailed account of his first day at three of the four schools: what his teacher looked like, the way he was dressed, the other children and the classroom. His fourth school was the Municipal School B, on the Spaarne. 'On my first day at that school', Van den Hull wrote, 'I took the measure of Master Piets and his housekeeper so carefully, albeit quite involuntarily, that the features of them both are etched ineradicably on my imagination.' Although Master Piets died only a few months later, 'I recall his narrow, fine features, his light brown, recently trimmed shock of hair, and the school gown hugging his body, just as clearly now as when he stood before me a half a century ago.'

In writing his autobiography, Van den Hull also makes it clear to the reader that a first time can never be repeated. In the summer of 1787, when he was almost nine, he was allowed once more to join his father on a visit to Maartensdijk. They took the night barge from Amsterdam to Utrecht. Towards daybreak, when everyone was still asleep, he got up quietly and climbed up on to the seat in order to look out.

> I shall never forget that early morning, never the impression that moment made on my youthful feelings, perhaps because I had never before beheld nature immersed in such stillness and calm, never before the first dawning of the most glorious break of day. Everything lay in the deepest tranquillity at the

exceptionally handsome country estates along the river; there was not a living soul to be seen; the cattle lay fast asleep in the fields; distant objects were still indistinguishable; a lone nocturnal bird flew across our bow; there was no wind; the water rippling before our barge (it seems to me I can hear it still) and the rattle now and then of the towline passing over the winches were the only sounds I could hear.

The memory of this journey was so vivid that half a century later, once again in the summer, Van den Hull took the same night barge to Utrecht to find out if 'this time, too, I would revive the same sensations as I had in my youth'. To that end, he stayed awake, climbed up to the upper deck at two o'clock in the morning and tried to see everything he had seen fifty years before. The experiment was a miserable failure. Much had remained the same, but it no longer had the power to move the now close on sixty-year-old Van den Hull. Instead he was beset with gloomy thoughts. Where were all his travelling companions of yore? The skipper at the helm, the manservant, the driver of the barge horse, the rich families asleep in their country houses, and also his own father: 'Alas, they are no longer; they are lying in their graves, stiff, perhaps decayed! Then still so full of strength and life, now, old and young alike, all of them in the same state of decomposition!' Only the cathedral spire towards which he was gliding in the light of dawn still stood in the same place and would, Van den Hull mused, be standing there still when he himself had followed his beloved forebears.

What begins to emerge as a central theme early in the autobiography is the attention Van den Hull pays to his eagerness to learn as a child. He records the knowledge he acquired (or failed to acquire) in every school he attended, what prizes he won, how his own achievements differed from those of the other children, what textbooks he was given or bought for himself. In that sense his are indeed the memoirs of a schoolmaster and not of, say, a businessman or a clergyman. In later years, he gives an equally detailed account of what he learned during his career as assistant to Master Schouten ('double-entry bookkeeping and spherical trigonometry'), of his activities as assistant master and of the various positions he held as a teacher in boarding schools. Another theme is his single-minded determination to improve his social standing by moving in circles just above his own – the well-to-do bourgeoisie. Throughout his autobiography, we find him paying great attention to the clothes appropriate to his aspirations, to the conventions he had to observe, the talents that were particularly suited to his career, the friendships that could stand him in good stead. Much of what he experienced as a child, as a young man and as an adult pointed the way to the social position he was ultimately to attain. Conversely, it is that position that gives these memories their significance: Van den Hull saw himself as a man who had become what he had dreamed of in his youth.

## 'As if it had happened yesterday'

That ambition also had its drawbacks. Van den Hull, as he himself wrote, had been 'very touchy about being humiliated, wronged or misunderstood' since early youth. This is indeed one of the most salient aspects of his autobiography. Every time when – looking back – he remembers something that upset him, he gives a detailed account of it. In later years his touchiness seems to be linked to his humble origins. He describes various incidents in which he thinks he was not treated with the respect he had earned with so much effort. But even as a child he found it hard to dismiss affronts. Later, when, together with his friend Dictus, he became assistant master at Master Schouten's school, he expected the harsh regime of corporal punishment – the cat, the strap, a length of rope – to be applied to the pupils, but certainly not to the assistants. He was wrong: 'I remember only too well how, shortly after my appointment to that post, he dealt me a few heavy blows with the strap one morning in front of all the children.' Schouten did not need much prompting either; 'a single line written poorly' was reason enough. One day Van den Hull was summoned to Schouten's room following a minor breach of the rules. To protect himself, he had stuffed an exercise book into his trousers. That stratagem was discovered and Schouten clearly found the whole thing so amusing that he told his maid, Krijntje, all about it. Then the real humiliation began; later that day Krijntje asked him teasingly what he kept in his trousers. 'This joking about a punishment that had affected me so painfully and humiliatingly hit me so hard at that moment that the spot where Krijntje stood, the manner in which she put that question to me, the place where Dictus was sitting, and where I myself was, is still as clear in my mind as if it had happened yesterday.' Photography had not yet been invented, let alone the flashbulb, but the scene has all the characteristics of a flashbulb memory.

Equally vivid is the memory of what befell him when he had a teaching post in Groningen and was planning to travel back there on the tow barge after having spent his leave in Haarlem. He had reached Stroobos when he discovered that he did not have enough money on him. The shortfall was four cents, not a large amount but also not a sum at which Groningers would shrug their shoulders. He decided to continue to Vierverlaten and to walk the rest of the way. While he was standing on the pier in Stroobos with the other passengers, ready to step into the barge, he heard the skipper call out something that sounded like, 'All of you folk for Groningen?' but no one replied and Van den Hull boarded the barge like the rest. Half an hour later, the captain came round to collect the fare. Van den Hull asked how much it was to Vierverlaten. An embarrassing wrangle ensued:

> I don't take fares to Vierverlaten, he replied, you'll have to pay to Groningen. I am not going to Groningen, I explained, I have to get out at Vierverlaten. You can do that, boy, he said in a disdainful tone, but you'll pay me as far as Groningen, that's my fare and that's why I called out in Stroobos, All of you folk for Groningen? It was then you should have said I'm going to Vierverlaten, but now you'll have to pay me in full . . . Since it was quite impossible for me to do that, I had to refuse him outright and in a manner that made it clear that I should hold him to account in Groningen. But no matter what I said or threatened, he sneered and swore that I would not leave the barge until, in accordance with the law, I had paid my full fare, and with that, refusing to take my money, he returned to the pilot's seat, calling me every name under the sun again – chiefly, a stuck-up young scrounger.

In the hope of extricating himself from this ticklish situation he took a fellow traveller into his confidence and asked him if he would be kind enough to lend him four cents. But the man, suspicious, turned him down, so that his disgrace was doubled for nothing. Anxiously he watched Vierverlaten come up, where to his relief – 'God has seen my predicament' – he spotted a friend's sister on the quay. She was more than pleased to advance him the extra fare and Van den Hull was able to proceed to Groningen.

The causes may have differed but each time his sense of humiliation was equally intense. One sunny afternoon, Van den Hull was walking past a house in Haarlem where he spotted a few nursery governesses and their girlfriends sitting by an open window. Politely, he raised his hat. 'But instead of acknowledging my greeting, or at least allowing me to pass unnoticed, I suddenly heard all these prim young girls breaking into peals of laughter, so that the whole street resounded with it. To make sure that it was all on account of my person, I walked past once more an hour later, again raised my hat politely, and this time the group burst if anything into even louder laughter. This encounter took place on 3 May 1817.' On another occasion he accompanied one of his young pupils, Jonkheer Collot d'Escury, on a trip to his parental home in The Hague. They travelled comfortably in the hired deckhouse of a tow barge, but on arrival at Jonkheer's home, the young man stepped straight inside, leaving Van den Hull on the doorstep, where he remained waiting until a surprised lackey came to tell him that everything was all right and shut the door behind him. 'The distinguished position I had held on the Hague tow barge thus forsook me on the Collot d'Escury family's doormat.' Not much later, he was taking offence on another doormat, this time that of the minister of the Walloon congregation, who did not ask the maid to show Van den Hull in, 'as is customary with well-bred people', but came to the door, did not return his bow and allowed him to depart after having heard his message. The minister's maid slammed the door shut behind him 'as if I were a tramp'. She, too, was someone he had not forgotten forty years later: 'Oh, how indelibly the impertinent face of that maid is etched in my soul!'

Getting no further than the doormat was a fate that would befall him a few times more. In a metaphorical sense it also marked his standing with the Haarlem elite. The bitterness he felt in his old age was due to the fact that he, who lived in the grandest house in Haarlem, was not asked to join societies and associations, public committees and councils. In this, Van den Hull saw the hand of

Josué Teissèdre l'Ange, the very same minister who had treated him so shabbily at the door. His name cropped up for the first time when the autobiography had progressed to the year 1800, and was only to disappear from it again when Van den Hull was able to report the clergyman's death in 1853. He never felt so deeply and persistently humiliated by anyone as by the Reverend l'Ange.

Their first contact followed Van den Hull's appointment as precentor in the Walloon congregation. Even during the trial reading there was an exchange of words about correct pronunciation. Van den Hull had been taught French in Groningen by a born French-man but in Haarlem he encountered a pronunciation that, perhaps as the consequence of 'Franco-Swiss tutors and governesses', struck him as being quite wrong. He refused to conform and the differ-ence between the French emanating from the pulpit and Van den Hull's reading from the lectern was obvious to all. The difference turned into open conflict and finally into a feud. It was due to l'Ange, Van den Hull felt certain, that he lost the private lessons he had been giving to various families, and that he would 'never again be able to earn a single cent from the so numerous offspring of Messrs Enschedé, Guepin, etc., with whom Mr l'Ange rubbed shoulders'. It was also at the instigation of l'Ange, he suspected, that he was dropped from the orchestra of the Instructive Entertainment Dramatic Society in the most humiliating way: during an interval he was dismissed 'in front of the staff and everyone else sitting there'. To these incidents must be added a dispute about his salary. While l'Ange, according to Van den Hull, made plenty of time to prepare the children of the well-to-do for their confirmation (and was rewarded by their parents with 'loads of mantel clocks'), he left the teaching of orphans and destitute children to Van den Hull. In 1806 it all culminated in a bit-ter row about the examination for which Van den Hull had to coach his pupils. The church council, incited by l'Ange, suspended him from the post of precentor and teacher.

Van den Hull's response in his autobiography to this episode was out of all proportion. The incident still galled him in 1842 just as much as it had in 1806. It was as if he had suddenly opened an old file and, with growing agitation, had started to read one document after another. He also reprinted actual letters at length, presented extracts, pointed out errors and inconsistencies in the accusations against him and here and there harangued the reader or addressed l'Ange. In paragraph after paragraph, he ended every sentence with an exclamation mark. Every account of a discourteous encounter seemed to call up another. L'Ange has a long record of misdeeds in these memoirs; no lapse is too petty to be ignored, no breach too old to be forgotten. In this one chapter, the narrative structure so typical of the rest of the autobiography is completely missing. Van den Hull pleads, refutes and accuses, and while writing it all down he relives everything once again, as with the Krijntje incident which still rankled 'as if it had happened yesterday'. The fact that shortly after his suspension and dismissal he was asked to give private lessons that brought in much more money than the pittance he had earned in the Walloon church continued to be cause for deep satisfaction more than thirty-five years later. 'While I am writing these lines, the memory of that godsend still causes tears of gratitude to escape from my eyes.' The dozens of pages Van den Hull devoted to l'Ange, not as a continuous story but in the form of a detailed charge sheet, underline the exceptional place these humiliations held in the memory – or rather, could not be condensed like the rest. They retain their original impact, but also their colour, taste and acuity. In old age, they still seem to have the vividness that one would rather reserve for other memories.

## 'In the whole wide world I saw no one but Lina'

In 1811, the Reverend l'Ange accepted a post in Amsterdam. He disappeared from Haarlem but not from Van den Hull's life. For years, Van den Hull continued to feel thwarted by him, or if not by the man himself then by one of his numerous friends and relations. By degrees, the story of his own rise in the face of so much obstruction assumes a triumphant character. In 1803, he opened his own boarding school, renting a house for the purpose in Oude Gracht. For his father he bought some land, 'measuring 140 Rhenish roods', half orchard and half kitchen garden. Thanks to the quickly growing number of pupils, he had to move to larger premises in 1809 and again in 1814. Affairs went so well that he finally cast his eyes over a splendid house in St Jansstraat. The prospect of being able to buy the house, he wrote, made him drunk with happiness: 'At night, after ten o'clock, I would slip a good twenty-five times out of my house, in the dark, to walk round my future home, and to count the footsteps I needed to do that: the house was 110 of my footsteps deep and with the gardens 135 footsteps wide, undoubtedly the most commodious property in Haarlem.' With loans from his pupils' parents and from several Haarlem patrons, he was able to buy the place for 10,000 guilders.

In 1820 Van den Hull moved into this elegant house. His parents moved in with him and spent a carefree old age there. Two unmarried sisters helped to keep house for the pupils. He had devoted assistant masters. His name was made. The most distinguished families in the Netherlands sent their sons to Haarlem. For him these were blessed and prosperous years. And yet he was never as unhappy as he was in that house: 'All the trials and tribulations of the first forty years of my life in no way compare with the mortal anguish that tortured me for eleven long years like a constantly gnawing worm.' That worm was unrequited love, the most dreadful state in which a man can find himself, Van den Hull wrote, and which can only be understood by those who have experienced it themselves, though he thought their number could not be very great, 'because such violent emotions undermine the sufferers' lives, death snatching them away quickly, or turning them into madmen, and some in their desperation even cut their own lives short'.

Having moved house, Van den Hull's mind turned to marriage. He was now forty-two, was comfortably off and longed to have a family of his own. One of his pupils had a sister. Van den Hull had never seen her, but from what her brother told him, he gathered that she would make a suitable wife. On top of that, she was heir to a large fortune. During the summer holidays of 1821, he called on her. He did not think her very beautiful, but sweet and friendly enough, and left again without disclosing the purpose of his visit. To avoid an overhasty decision he determined not to write to her until a Saturday in the following month of August. The day arrived and he was on the point of starting his letter when he decided to do some shopping in town first. On his way back home he encountered a young lady in Nieuwe Gracht, 'on whom I fixed my gaze and who, as she approached me, began more and more to blush, while I myself was affected without being able to account for this sudden feeling: I greeted her, our eyes met and her look pierced me to the marrow. Bless my soul, I said

Fig. 22   Rear of Willem van den Hull's 'French School' in St Jansstraat, Haarlem. Drawing by Gerrit Scholten, 1822.

to myself, what an enchantingly beautiful girl! Oh, if only she could become my wife!'

He was badly stricken. On Jan's Bridge he turned round and saw her stepping into the Reverend Serrurier's house. That evening he asked one of his pupils, a nephew of the reverend gentleman, to enquire discreetly from the servants who the 'heavenly girl' might be. It appeared she was the Honourable Miss Roelina (Lina) de Vos van Steenwijk tot den Havixhorst, and that she was staying with Mevrouw Camerling. This news made him feel ill at ease. He was a commoner, a former assistant teacher, while she came from one of the noblest families in the land; the gap between them was 'one of the most immeasurable you could conceive'. On top of that he was more than forty and she, he guessed, eighteen at most. But their encounter, and on this day of all days, was surely a sign from God. Next morning he saw her again – in the Walloon church. He sat in his usual place; Lina joined her girlfriends, who, it so happened, were sitting right next to him, with between them 'a space of no more than three feet'. He glanced at her out of the corner of his eye, and from the 'irregular swelling of her bosom', concluded that she was as moved as he was, even more so in fact, and that his love for her had kindled love for him in her.

More encouragement there was none, nor did he need it. He bribed a groom, who whispered to him that Lina would be leaving Haarlem the following Sunday for an address in Amsterdam. Van den Hull reserved a carriage for the same time, packed his linen, took some money and hoped that he would be able to persuade Lina to change her carriage for his and to marry him clandestinely. It was a bold plan, but he was no longer open to reason, as he conceded in retrospect: 'In the whole wide world I saw no one but Lina; she alone was always in my mind, and my prayer to God was nothing less than a desperate cry.' When the Sunday of her departure came round, he first attended a church service at which she, too, was present. Yet during the service it became obvious to Van den Hull that he would have to abandon his plan. For the subject of the Reverend Serrurier's sermon was the commandment 'Honour thy father and thy mother.' Van den Hull sat as if turned to stone in his pew. The sermon was so apposite 'that had somebody whispered to the minister, "There are two lovers in your congregation who are bent on a reckless plan – speak to them!" he would have been unable to find a more suitable text to keep them from their foolhardy plan'. He cancelled the carriage.

The fact that Van den Hull mentioned *two* lovers in the Walloon church demonstrates clearly his conviction that Lina returned his love. But he did not dare to approach her or even to write to her; the chance was far too great that she, uplifted by the Reverend Serrurier's sermon, would do nothing to go against her parents' will, let alone enter into a marriage with an unacceptable suitor. He saw no way of giving voice to his feelings. He could not take his own parents or sisters into his confidence, nor his assistant teachers; he had to cope with it all in silence and loneliness. His only relief, albeit temporary, was addressing long poems to Lina. He never sent them. She was not out of his thoughts for a single moment: hardly had he woken in the morning 'when the most terrible fears gripped me, and I also fell asleep groaning, as it were'. In this way a full year passed by.

The next summer, when she came back to stay with her friends again, he saw her walking by but once more dared not approach her. Again she left. This time she travelled back to Zwolle by barge, he was told, and in a poem he accompanied her in his thoughts on her return journey. Two of the twenty verses will suffice to convey a flavour of his efforts:

> Bon voyage, my pretty maid,
> Bon voyage as North you go:
> Oh, could I but be by your side;
> Alas, for that my rank's too low.
>
> If you, with my sweet maid on board,
> Sail past another ship close by,
> Then every sailor there will shout:
> The fairest maid sails on the Ij!

'And so I entered upon yet another year of suffering' – and another and yet another were to follow. Not even his parents' wedding anniversary could shift his thoughts from his unattainable love. In 1827, six years after he first saw Lina, nothing in his feelings had changed, nor for that matter in his prospects. His despair became even greater when he learned that the day after her arrival for her annual stay in Haarlem she had been coughing up blood. Van den Hull was beside himself – perhaps she was at death's door ('brought about by her endless suffering for my sake?'). He fasted for three days, entreated and prayed, walked past her house, and imagined her wrestling with death in a dimly lit room ('Will she be dying with my name on her lips?'), and then saw her a few days later walking about in the town in perfect health. He was grateful that his prayers had been answered so speedily, but also in despair because once again she would be leaving without his having met her. Another year passed, and the year after that, 'amidst thousands of tears and sighs'.

During the night of 26 July 1830 he dreamt that he was taking a walk over the ramparts of Haarlem and that he sat down at one of the loveliest spots to enjoy the view over the dunes. From out of nowhere there appeared a man, 'a person of exalted rank', who without saying a word, even of greeting, sat down beside him, began to lean against him and finally pushed him from the spot. Indignantly,

Van den Hull reclaimed his place, saying he had been there first. To his astonishment the stranger was suddenly transformed into a man of the utmost courtesy who apologized, said that he had not realized that he had been sitting there for so long, quickly stood up and left. When Van den Hull woke up, the dream was still clear in his mind, though he had no idea of its meaning. That very morning one of his pupils paid him a visit and told him that the Honourable Lady de Vos had been staying in Haarlem, but had left again. He added in one and the same breath that she had become engaged to Esquire van der Wyck from Assen.

> I do not have to tell the reader what I then felt! Or irk him with an account of my emotions! How that news cut me to the quick! How the sweat of despair streamed from my face! How hard I found it to pull myself together in front of my mother and my sisters! How, as soon I had shown the boy out, I fled to my room, locked the door behind me, fell on to my knees and my face and bellowed at the Lord in despair: 'Lord, is that the reward for my trust in You?'

When he came to himself, he remembered the dream he had had during the night. Suddenly everything fell into place. The spot with the lovely view was Lina's heart. The noble promenader who had forced him from his place was his rival. But when the intruder had learned that the other man had the first claim, he had humbly apologized and left. In other words, Van den Hull was still hopeful: perhaps God would still drive Van der Wyck out of Lina's heart and prevent the impending marriage. Thus he continued to teeter between hope and fear for a whole year until, 'with the greatest anguish', he caught sight of their marriage announcement in the *Haarlemmer Courant* of 30 April 1831. Only then did he know with certainty that Lina would never be his. He cursed the day he had seen her walking in the Nieuwe Gracht.

For those in love and unsure whether their feelings are requited, everything the other does or fails to do is filled with significance. For a long time there is no such thing as an idle gesture or a casual remark, since everything the other says and how she says it and at what moment she says it can hold a cue and must therefore be meticulously examined and tested. All the cues taken together finally come to-gether to form a conviction: yes, she too is in love; or no, she is not. But there are also feelings of infatuation so intense that the con-viction lends the cues their meaning. These are the cases in which someone is literally in love enough for two and everything the other says or does contributes to the irrefutable proof of mutual love. Of course, it may eventually turn out that the lover has been mistaken. He has failed to read the signs correctly. He has seen none but himself in the other. The moment he realizes what the true feelings of the other have been all along, something is triggered in his memory that causes him a few painful weeks or months. All the recollections stored with the warm glow of love emerge again, as if they had been chased from the memory. They have to be reassessed one by one: 'Thus, when she . . . she meant nothing of the kind . . .' It seems as if they can only be accepted again if they are given a new interpretation. For those who think that memories, once taken on board, are stored safely and impregnably, nothing provides a better lesson than unrequited love.

As for cues, Van den Hull had very few, although he made much of them. That Lina blushed when he gazed at her, that her breathing was irregular when she was sitting near him in church, that after the church service she put off her departure for a few days, undoubtedly because the sermon had moved her as strongly as it had moved him, all that dispelled any doubts about her love for him. For Van den Hull there had been two lovers from the very beginning on Nieuwe Gracht. Working on his autobiography thirty-five years later, he was able to reconstruct their love for each other in such a powerful way that later insights were unable to shake it. The reader watches anxiously as a loving heart loses its hold on reality, as Van den Hull reads his own feelings into Lina's, thus managing to project them before Freud was even born. The reader watches a young girl, who could not have had the slightest idea of what was happening, throw the life of a middle-aged man into utter confusion.

Writing about this episode in his seventies, Van den Hull indi-cated that he had come to see his years with Lina in a different light. For why had God really made him suffer so much? If Providence had not wanted him to have Lina, God could have prevented their en-counter. 'Walking up that road just five minutes earlier or later, I would never have seen Lina and would have been spared eleven years of terrible – nigh unbearable – suffering.' Did God perhaps have more than one intention when He inflicted such suffering? The more Van den Hull considered that possibility, the more probable it seemed. His suffering must have been some form of retribution, and soon enough the reader is told for what.

'I was a handsome youth' – Van den Hull felt that at his time of life he could allow himself such an observation. Fair skin, chestnut hair, a rosy complexion, well-formed limbs, his parents' most beautiful child. Moreover, his looks changed so little that he was taken to be no older than forty on his sixtieth birthday. That he was a beautiful boy, 'as they call it in everyday parlance', was something he himself did not realize and had to be told by others. Among the ladies he taught there had been several who had 'given him opportunities to commit impure deeds'. He had always been able to resist their blandishments, but 'at the age of twenty-six he had once succumbed to temptation'. That had been his first sin. When he remained unmarried and attracted the attention of women, in his vanity he began to feel flattered. He was proud in the knowledge that a girl from a distinguished family had fallen in love with him and had blushed when she looked at him. He even took pleasure – a second sin – in stoking the flames of that love, 'not considering how much anguish I was causing, that in a sensitive girl such passion not rarely makes way for incurable suffering and carries many to their grave. And so I might well have been the cause, if not of the early death, then of the sad suffering of this or that young girl.' Through his desperate love for Lina, God had paid him back no more than he deserved; she was the avenger, the retribution for the wrong he had done to women. That he could not capture her heart had been decreed by a higher power. And now the reader might wonder, Van den Hull wrote, if 'Lina ever felt such love for me as I supposed'. But the new interpretation did not go as far as that. 'Oh, let no one doubt it.'

Van den Hull fell in love when he was almost thirty-four. In his autobiography this was the period in which the number of pages he devoted on average to every year of his life had shrunk to fewer than six. If we deduct the thirty or so pages devoted to his love for Lina, we arrive at an average of three pages, which tallies with the pages devoted to the summary account of his years between his middle age and his death at the age of seventy-seven. In other words: his love had helped to spread the years out, making them broader in his memory than they would have been without Lina. There is no doubt that Van den Hull felt these years to be painfully long. His infatuation began one August Saturday in 1821 and ended in April 1831 when he set eyes on the report of her marriage. By the calendar, that was less than ten years; for Van den Hull, they were, as he himself wrote a few times, 'eleven long years'.

But perhaps one ought to say that those years never ended. He did indeed write that he slowly regained some of his composure, but, as he added, he could never forget her: 'My heart had been dealt too great a blow, and whenever I recall her in my loneliness I feel something indescribable, something convulsive, as the relic of that tremendous shock.'

## Once again: the reminiscence effect

Exactly one hundred years after Galton published the results of the study of his own memory in *Brain*, McCormack used Galton's method to study the autobiographical memory of older people. He presented experimental subjects whose average age was eighty with such words as 'horse', 'river' and 'king', dated the memories these words elicited, and showed that most of the memories stemmed from the first and to a somewhat lesser extent from the second quarter of life. The third quarter – for most of the experimental subjects that meant the period between forty and sixty years – showed a sharp drop. The same pattern has been found, with small variations, in dozens of other studies. Combining the results of a long series of experiments, Rubin and Schulkind established that the 'bump' is still absent in forty-year-olds, begins slowly in fifty-year-olds and becomes clearly detectable in sixty-year-olds.

The reminiscence effect is a robust phenomenon, and cannot be expunged completely even under extreme pathological conditions. In an experiment by Fromholt and Larsen, thirty healthy elderly people and thirty Alzheimer patients – all aged between seventy-one and eighty-nine – were given fifteen minutes to relate their reminiscences of events that had meant a great deal to them. The Alzheimer patients recounted fewer reminiscences than the healthy group (eight as against eighteen) but the distribution of these memories over the course of their life did not differ from that of the healthy subjects: Alzheimer patients, too, had most to tell about their adolescence.

The reminiscence effect also cropped up in investigations of quite another kind. In an essay on the generation concept he wrote in 1928, the sociologist Karl Mannheim argued that the experiences gained between the ages of – roughly – seventeen and twenty-five are crucial for the formation of a political generation. On the basis of that theory, the sociologists Schuman and Scott made a quantitative study of differences between generations. In a random survey involving more than 1,400 Americans over the age of eighteen, they asked the participants to mention one or two 'events of national or international importance'. The subjects did not need to have taken part personally in the events, and could even mention something that had taken place before they were born. The answers varied extremely widely. But when Schuman and Scott took the five most frequently mentioned events – in chronological order, the Great Depression, the Second World War, the assassination of President Kennedy, the Vietnam war and the hijackings and hostage-takings in the seventies – and plotted the age of the people who mentioned just these events, they noticed a marked pattern: what people considered an 'event of national or international importance' showed a peak round what they themselves had experienced in their twenties. For people of sixty-five (in 1985) that was the Second World War, for someone aged forty-five it was the death of Kennedy. Put facetiously: world-shaking is what happens when you are twenty.

Though all this counting and dating does reflect a distribution across the age groups, it does not provide an explanation. Three theories about the reminiscence effect can be found in the literature. It is conceivable, first of all, that in neurophysiological respects our memory is at its peak in our twenties. What we experience then is retained without difficulty. In that period we store more memories than in any subsequent period, which explains why, more than half a century later, the likelihood of coming up with memories from that early period is so much greater. This theory may seem tempting but it is probably mistaken. If the quality of a memory were its most important feature, then the reminiscence bump would have to occur some ten years earlier than it does, for the memory then, as experiments show, has the greatest sticking power.

A second theory is that between the ages of fifteen and twenty-five we normally experience more that is worth remembering. This theory is borne out by the finding that when experimental subjects are asked to recount three or four of their most vivid recollections, they come up with a stronger reminiscence effect than during investigations with cue words. Apparently the impression an event has made is an important factor. An explanation along the lines of 'more memorable things happened at that time' invites us not only to date and keep a tally of the elicited reminiscences, but also to identify them. What sort of reminiscences do they happen to be? What do they have in common and why are they less frequent later in life? Research into these questions is rare but not entirely absent. Many recollections during the reminiscence bump, Jansari and Parkin found, are connected with 'first times' of all sorts and types. Not only 'the' first time, but also the first kiss, the first menstrual period, the first public speaking engagement, the first holiday without our parents, the first driving lesson, the first dead person we see, the first day at work – many of these first-time memories have a flashbulb clarity. Of course, first times also occur later in life – the first grey hair, the first hot flush – but they become decidedly rarer as the years progress.

A third explanation of the reminiscence effect has also been proposed. During our youth and early adult years events occur that shape our personality, determine our identity and guide the course of our life. Accidental encounters, a book that made a great impression on us, a penetrating talk that made us suddenly realize what we wanted to do with our life – we are at our most responsive to that sort of event during those years. The effect contrives that someone, once in his life, recalls the events that have turned him into what he now is. The similarities between the present-day self and the experiences that have shaped that self lead the associations of the elderly back to their youth almost automatically. According to this theory, elderly people looking back remember episodes that constitute part of their life history. Conversely, the manner in which they recount that history defines and demonstrates their own identity. According to the psychologist Fitzgerald, most of these life histories have a common feature, namely that the narrator tries to make them look more or less coherent. In old age, people like to look back on their own lives as a story that may hold surprises and sudden changes, but that is nevertheless held together by the characteristic reactions of a stable central character. A second quality, following from the first, is that once fixed patterns have been established, new episodes can be dispensed with gradually. On closer inspection, much of what seems new proves to be routine, repetition, the umpteenth example, something best omitted from a good story. One of Fitzgerald's own studies brought out the repetitive aspect in memories. He asked thirty elderly men to tell five stories about themselves that they would be certain to include if they had to write an autobiography. In this way he was able to obtain a collection of memories distributed unevenly over their lives, with a reminiscence effect that was a mountain rather than a hump: he was told more about events that had happened to them between the ages of ten and twenty than during the years between fifty and eighty taken together.

Willem van den Hull's autobiography ran to eight hundred pages and contained a host of recollections. He distributed the material he dug up from his memory as unevenly over the seventy-four years of his recounted life as Fitzgerald's experimental subjects had done: a mountain at the beginning, with foothills that opened out into a plain. Reading all these memories, you discover that the two main theories found in the literature on reminiscences – roughly expressed as 'more memorable events happened then' and 'the crucial scenes in the story of your life occurred during this period' – overlap like roof tiles. The main chapters about his youth and early adult life comprise scores of 'first time' memories, no matter whether it was the first day in a new school, the first time that he was allowed to go to Maartensdijk, his first day as assistant teacher, his first job as a schoolmaster, or the first time he bought a house. Later, too, there are still 'first times' – for instance the fleeting moment when he saw Lina walking by – but their frequency declines as the autobiography proceeds. At the same time, memories of first times emphasize the 'story' running through Van den Hull's review of his life. For something is only the first time if other times follow, if the first time, so to speak, is the start of a narrative thread. Without the sad story of his unrequited love he would not have seen Lina for the first time. Anyone remembering something is coming from the opposite direction; only later can you see the beginning.

What autobiographical memory has in common with auto-biographies is that the memories in it are fitted into themes, motives, story lines. They emerge gradually as part of a development. What someone reports about his memories, to himself or to others, is aimed at a public, and as such is no longer the bare record of the event itself. For Van den Hull's reminiscences, the memories of what he had experienced, provided no more than the rough material; his interpretation of them needed a retrospective perspective, in his case over a distance of some sixty years. Even his earliest recollections, such as the ritual exchange of greetings with his mother and the fresh milk he was given when his shoes were clean, have their place in a theme; these details were well-nigh too childish to relate, he wrote, but 'far from irrelevant to one's upbringing'. His experience as a young passenger on the night barge to Utrecht, when he climbed up on to the seat and allowed the deep peace of the early morning to move him, have their place in a story that the child does not yet know and that is, in fact, not yet a story. The story only becomes a story thanks to the fact that this sixty-three-year-old diarist remembers repeating the trip half a century later and realized how much had disappeared from his life in the meantime. Thus old age seems to write itself into the memories of youth. Some events Van den Hull, had he been asked about them in his twenties, would no doubt have remembered exactly as he described them in his autobiography, but there were also events he could not have recognized until much later as part of a pattern or of a theme. The narrative character Van den Hull gave to his memoirs is based on what has ceased to be raw material.

The themes Van den Hull brings out through selection, interpretation and colouring do something else as well. They allow time to swell and to shrink. With the humiliations he suffers time almost stands still, the young man freezing under the gaze of the laughing Krijntje, or the gossip of the nursemaids still resounding loudly over the canal so that in his memory we are suddenly thrown back to 3 May 1817. Later in life it is his infatuation with Lina that extends a period of less than ten years into 'eleven long years'. The converse is also true: where the themes begin gradually to drop out of his life, time seems to shrink. 'About what happened next in my story', he writes in the penultimate chapter, 'there is very little to tell from 1841 to 1848: the monotonous life I was leading was barely distinguished by any special circumstance.' A single sentence covering seven years! A few lines further on we find the lament: 'Hours, days and months seemed always to escape me with great speed.'

## 'There I stood, a lost soul in the town of my birth'

The year 1849 brought more to report, albeit news that was bad. In January, his favourite sister, Betsy, died. They had always pulled together, in the boarding school and in raising their adopted son. Her death affected him deeply: 'A thousand times I recalled everything I could remember of those sixty-six years: how I loved to transplant myself back into my youth with my playmates who, alas, had been gone for such a long time; only I had survived!' Now that his sister was no longer with him he felt all alone in the world. In Haarlem, nobody asked him round; good friends 'were all dead or had moved away or married, so there I stood, a lost soul in the town of my birth'. The last twenty pages of the autobiography, covering the four years leading up to his seventy-sixth birthday, tell of a life that is becoming more and more lonely. His only surviving sister breaks her kneecap in a fall and can no longer visit him. One day in October 1849, Van den Hull watches snowflakes pouring down, but when he looks at the ground there is no snow: something must have been amiss with his eyes. In a few months they had become so badly inflamed that he could no longer read or write. Where he had been accustomed to spending the long winter evenings profitably, he was now forced to wait for his bedtime in a dark room without any diversion or useful occupation. Just when his eyes had recovered a little, he was struck by his next misfortune. One morning he climbed up on a chair to take a bottle of ink from the shelf, missed his footing and hit the back of his head against the sharp edge of a marble slab. The blow was so hard that it could be heard in the street. Van den Hull lost consciousness for a moment but got up again without help and looked behind him: 'The pool of blood was as large as from a double blood-letting and, though the brainpan itself was not injured, I nevertheless had a three-inch gaping wound on the back of my head which prevented me for several days on end from putting on my hat and going out.'

Life round Van den Hull grew increasingly quiet. What news he received was almost always obituary notices. Family members, acquaintances, friends, former neighbours and colleagues, old pupils, many of the people who had had a place in his life story are mentioned once more, with the date of their demise and the age at which they died. Van den Hull barely left his house. His right leg was painfully swollen and he could hardly stand. He wondered if he was too old to hope for a cure. He decided, as he had done so often in his life, to place the matter 'under the control of Providence': he knelt painfully down, took up two pieces of paper, and wrote on one: 'Oh, Lord! In your name, Yes', and on the other: 'Oh, Lord, in your name, No', folded the papers, closed his eyes and picked up one of the notes and prayed. He drew 'Yes' and waited patiently for his prayer to be heard. At the time he wrote about this episode – in May 1854 – nothing had as yet happened, to his sorrow, for it was just then that they began to pipe dune-water to Amsterdam and the 'three mighty steam giants, Leegwater, Cruquius and Leynde' drained the Haarlem Lake. He would so have liked to have seen it all with his own eyes.

Van den Hull finished his memoirs in 1854, leaving the last four years of his life, just like the first four, unrecorded. In his final lines he opened up his heart once more: he was still thinking of Lina, who had been widowed in 1844. He still prayed to God for her hand, although he had begun to doubt that his prayer would be answered, 'seeing that I have now reached the age of seventy-five, and those who do not know my story will find it ridiculous that someone should wish for a spouse at such an age'.

## BIBLIOGRAPHY

The widow of the last descendant of Van den Hull's adopted son presented the manuscript of the autobiography to the Haarlem Municipal Archives in 1992. The text was published, with an introduction by Raymonde Padmos and with the bibliography and genealogy of Willem van den Hull, under the title of *Autobiografie (1778–1854)* in the Ego Document series, Hilversum, 1996.

Conway, M. A., and D. C. Rubin, 'The structure of autobiographical memory', in A. F. Collins, S. E. Gathercole, M. A. Conway and P. E. Morris (eds.), *Theories of Memory*, Hove, 1993, 103–37.

Fitzgerald, J. M., 'Autobiographical memory and conceptualizations of the self', in M. A. Conway, D. C. Rubin, H. Spinnler and W. A. Wagenaar (eds.), *Theoretical Perspectives on Autobiographical Memory*, Dordrecht, 1992, 99–114.

Fromholt, P., and S. F. Larsen, 'Autobiographical memory and life-history narratives in aging and dementia (Alzheimer type)', in M. A. Conway, D. C. Rubin, H. Spinnler and W. A. Wagenaar (eds.), *Theoretical Perspectives on Autobiographical Memory*, Dordrecht, 1992, 413–26.

Galton, F., 'Psychometric experiments', *Brain* 2 (1879), 149–62.

Jansari, A., and A. J. Parkin, 'Things that go bump in your life: explaining the reminiscence bump in autobiographical memory', *Psychology and Aging* 11 (1996), 85–91.

McCormack, P. D., 'Autobiographical memory in the aged', *Canadian Journal of Psychology* 33 (1979), 118–24.

Rubin, D. C., T. A. Rahhal and L. W. Poon, 'Things learned in early adulthood are remembered best', *Memory and Cognition* 26 (1998), 3–19.

Rubin, D. C., and M. D. Schulkind, 'The distribution of autobiographical memories across the lifespan', *Memory and Cognition* 25 (1997), 859–66.

Schuman, H., and J. Scott, 'Generations and collective memories', *American Sociological Review* 54 (1989), 359–81.

# 14    Why life speeds up as you get older

Ernst Jünger is sitting in his study. It is late in the evening, almost nighttime. He is working on the manuscript of his study of time, *Das Sanduhrbuch* (The hourglass book). On the desk in front of him is an antique hourglass, a present from his late lamented friend Klaus Valentiner, who disappeared in Russia during the Second World War. The hourglass is set in simple wrought iron. It must have had a great deal of use: at the waist the glass has been scoured to an opaline finish. Jünger watches as a funnel-shaped hole appears in the upper bulb while a cone grows in the lower bulb under the velvet stream of soundlessly falling sand. It is not a comforting thought, he reflects, that though time slips by it does not stop. For what vanishes from above piles up a new supply below. Every time the glass is turned up-side down the reservoir of available time is restored – you have only to stretch out your arm. But no matter how often you can tap the new supply, time passes more and more quickly. In hourglasses the grains of sand increasingly rub one another smooth until finally they flow almost without friction from one bulb into the other, polishing the neck wider all the time. The older an hourglass the more quickly it runs. Unnoticed, the hourglass measures out ever shorter hours. This chronometric imperfection hides a metaphor: 'For man, too, the recurring years fly past more and more quickly, until finally the mea-sure is full. Man, too, is increasingly permeated by impressions.'

*Das Sanduhrbuch* appeared in 1954. Ernst Jünger was approach-ing sixty when he started work on it. The feeling that life seems to speed up as you grow older must have been something with which he was familiar from personal experience. It is a form of acceleration that causes the years to shrink. Once past your fortieth or fiftieth birthday, a year seems to last but a fraction of the years you knew when you were fifteen or twenty. And that mysterious acceleration hides a second puzzle, which William James mentioned in 1890 in his *Principles of Psychology*: how can the years speed up when the hours and days do not and seem to be the same as they always have been?

Fig. 23   Jean-Marie Guyau (1854–88).

For the acceleration of time, metaphors are easier to provide than explanations. 'Time', wrote Gerrit Krol in *Een Fries huilt niet*
(Frisians do not cry), 'is a small chain that you twirl round your fin-
ger.' But why does that chain keep twirling more and more quickly?
Answers expressed in mere numbers are not very satisfactory either.
The French philosopher Paul Janet suggested in 1877 that the apparent length of a period in somebody's life is related to the length of
his life. A child aged ten would experience one year as a tenth of his
life, a man of fifty as a fiftieth. William James considered this 'law' a
description of the subjective acceleration rather than an explanation,

and he was right. He himself attributed the apparent contraction of the years to

> the monotony of the memory's content, and the consequent simplification of the backward-glancing view. In youth we may have an absolutely new experience, subjective or objective, every hour of the day. Apprehension is vivid, the retentiveness strong, and our recollections of that time, like those of a time spent in rapid and interesting travel, are of something intricate, multitudinous and long-drawn out. But as each passing year converts some of this experience into automatic routine which we hardly note at all, the days and the weeks smooth themselves out in recollection to contentless units, and the years grow hollow and collapse.

This explanation places the memory at the centre of our experience of time. Psychological time ticks away on an internal clock, to the accompaniment of our recollections. Duration and tempo are manufactured in the memory. The experience that life speeds up is part of a whole family of time illusions. Some of these occupy a scale of seconds or minutes, others take days, years or even long periods of a human life, but no matter what their length, measured by the clock or the calendar, they all have this in common: they link the experience of time to what takes place in our consciousness. As early as 1885, many of the psychological factors influencing subjective time were described by the French philosopher and psychologist Jean-Marie Guyau (1854–88). In his all too short life, ravaged by tuberculosis, he developed an elegant theory of man's idea of time.

## 'Underneath the streets run subterranean streets'

Guyau was barely twenty when he completed a thousand-page study of the history of ethics; upon his untimely death, thirteen years later, he left an *œuvre* covering ten books and countless articles, on, among other things, aesthetics, sociology, pedagogy and religion. In his life as an intellectual, twice as much as normal seems to have happened to compensate for its brevity. The book that contributed most to his fame, *La genèse de l'idée de temps*, appeared in 1890, two years after his death. It ran, in ordinary print, to just over fifty pages and was based on an article published in the *Revue Philosophique* in 1885. On the occasion of the hundredth anniversary of his death, Michon and a couple of colleagues brought out an annotated edition, preceded by a biographical introduction.

Jean-Marie Guyau was born in 1854 in Laval. One year earlier, his father Jean Guyau had married Augustine Tuillerie, thirteen years his junior. Their union was not a happy one. 'Augustine may have had no clear ideas about Hell when she married', wrote Michon, 'but she was to find out soon.' Augustine was ill-treated and decided eventually to leave her husband. With the three-year-old Jean-Marie she moved in with her cousin, the philosopher Alfred Fouillée.

Jean-Marie received his early education from his mother. Later, Fouillée took over the task. He encouraged Jean-Marie to read Plato and Kant, and even let the fifteen-year-old boy help him write books about Plato and Socrates. On his seventeenth birthday, at the beginning of his university studies, Guyau could already look back on a busy intellectual life. In 1874, he was appointed lecturer in philosophy at the Lycée Condorcet in Paris.

That same year the first symptoms of tuberculosis appeared. It was the beginning of one of those notable nineteenth-century lives that owing to the prospect of a premature end became compressed. Guyau decided to give up his lectureship and to seek enlightenment in a milder climate. With his wife, his mother and Fouillée, he settled in Provence. In 1884, the Guyaus had a son, Augustin. Surrounded by hills and far from the academic hurly-burly, Guyau spent productive and happy years. During this period, he wrote the most important parts of his book on the idea of time.

The basic analogy in Guyau's theory of time is space – not the geometric kind, but that used in perspective – space as it manifests itself to the observer. The experience of time is a case of 'internal optics'. The memory orders our experiences in time much as a painter orders space with the use of perspective. Memories lend depth to our consciousness. As soon as the order in our memory is broken, as happens during the imperceptible transitions between dream images, our sense of time has also gone. Guyau tells us about a student who had suddenly fallen into a lethargic sleep but was quickly reawakened by his anxious friends. In the brief interval he dreamt about a visit to

Italy. The shifting series of images of towns, people, monuments and personal experiences during the visit gave him the impression that he had been dreaming for hours.

Guyau summed up a handful of factors that influence the internal optics of psychological time. Duration and tempo depend on the intensity of our sensations and ideas, their alternation, their number, the tempo with which they succeed one another, the attention we pay them, the effort it takes to store them in the memory and the emotions and associations they call forth in us. However the very same factors that help us to find our bearings in time can also lead to false estimates. Focusing our attention, for instance, works like a telescope: the detail revealed causes the illusion that the object is close by. Guyau borrowed this analogy from the English psychologist Sully, who in his *Illusion* (1881) remarked that a sensational event – say, an abduction or a murder – is estimated to be much more recent than it actually was. By the time the culprit has served his sentence, no one believes that the crime was committed so long ago.

In our personal perceptions, intensity is also a factor of our estimates of duration. Thinking back about an event that has made a great impression on us, we tend to underestimate the time interval separating us from that event. Such illusions have their counterparts in psychiatry. Traumatic events are repeated in flashbacks, memories that penetrate the psychological present and that cannot be removed from it at will. It is as if this type of memory moves with time, Guyau wrote, and refuses to vanish from sight. Standing on the Wengern Alp it looks as if we have only to fling a stone through the clear air to hit the glaciers of the Jungfrau. Deep traumas always seem no more than a stone's throw from the present.

That the clarity of an idea can create the illusion of proximity works in both time directions. Waiting for something we would love to see again, we can imagine it so distinctly that we underestimate the time separating us from it. Tense expectation can last for an infinity. But once it happens the event we have been looking forward to so much seems to fly past; thanks to the contrast with the preceding period, time accelerates.

The part the memory plays in the estimate of duration and tempo means that the past can be found in our current experience:

Under the cities buried beneath the ashes of Vesuvius, traces of even older cities have been discovered, buried in their turn in an even more distant past. Their inhabitants built on the ashes covering the previous city. And so layers of cities are created; underneath the streets run subterranean streets, under crossroads other crossroads; the living city is built on top of sleeping cities. The same thing happens in our brains; our present life covers, without our knowing it fully, our past life that serves it as a support and hidden foundation. If we descend into our inner self, we wander about in the midst of ruins.

The spatial relationships of perspective drawing also apply to estimates of longer periods in our lives. Much as a distance seems greater if objects holding our attention are placed between the start and the finish, so a year with striking and varied events will seem longer than an empty and monotonous year. For Guyau, the apparent length of a period seems to be defined, in retrospect, by the number of clear and intense differences we notice in the events we remember. That is why the years of our youth seem so long and those of our old age so short. Guyau's comment merits being quoted at some length:

Youth is impatient in its desires; it wants to devour time ahead but *time drags*. Moreover, the impressions of youth are vivid, fresh and numerous, so that the years are distinguished in thousands of ways and the young man looks back on the previous year as a long sequence of scenes in space. The back of the stage disappears as it were in the distance, behind all the shifting scenes that follow one another as so many changes behind an open curtain; we know that a whole series of backdrops are hanging ready to be moved into the spectator's view at the right moment. These backdrops are recurring pictures from our past; some have faded, become blurred and misty and create an impression of distance; others serve as wings on the stage. We classify them by their intensity and the sequence of their appearance. Our memory is the stage manager. Thus to a child the last New Year's Day will increasingly recede behind all the events that have followed, and the next New Year's Day will look very far off still to the child so eager to grow up. Old age, by contrast, is more like the unchanging scenery of the classical theatre, a simple place, sometimes a true unity of time, place and action that concentrates everything round one dominant activity and expunges the rest; at other times the absence of time, place and action. The weeks resemble one another, the months resemble one another, the monotony of life drags on. All these images fuse into a single image. In the imagination, time is abridged. Desire does the same: as we approach the end of life we say every year, 'Another year gone! What did I do with it? What did I feel, see, achieve? How is it possible for the three hundred and sixty-five days that have passed to seem no more than a couple of months?'

    If you want to lengthen the perspective of time, then fill it, if you have the chance, with a thousand new things. Go on an exciting journey, rejuvenate yourself by breathing new life into the world around you. When you look back you will notice that the incidents along the way and the distance you have travelled have heaped up in your imagination, all these fragments of the visible world will form up in a long row, and that, as people say so fittingly, presents you with a long *stretch of time*.

Guyau's own early death, at the age of thirty-four, causes a note of regret to sound in his 'if you have the chance'. Exciting journeys were no longer granted him during his last few years, at least not in the geographical sense. You might say that he lived a longer life by renewing his inner world at every turn. His swift, almost obsessive journey through the most divergent branches of philosophy and psychology must have had as mind-stretching an effect as a genuine voyage.

    At the beginning of 1888, an earthquake caused grave damage along the Franco-Italian coast. Guyau's house, too, was damaged. The inhabitants were forced to spend several nights in a damp barn. Guyau's fragile constitution was not equal to this. He caught a cold and his condition deteriorated perceptibly. Three months later, on the eve of Good Friday, he died. Four-year-old Augustin slept in the adjoining room. Next morning he was told that his father had gone on a long journey.

## Inner optics

Guyau took his views of time from personal experience rather than from experiments. Perhaps this is precisely what lends his observations so much cogency. There is something compelling about someone who has a seismic sensitivity to his inner life and knows how to find the right words for what, to others, is no more than a quick tremor. Introspection may mean literally 'looking inside', but beyond a certain point it encompasses the experiences of others and becomes directed to the outside. In that sense introspective observations are reminiscent of internal monologues in novels, and sometimes the one genre seems to resonate in the other. Proust has devoted some splendid passages in *Le Côté de Guermantes* (1920–1), one of the parts of *A la recherche du temps perdu*, to musings about the slowness of time spent in tense expectation. The narrator has just sent a letter to the desirable Mme de Stermaria, inviting her to dine with him. She lets him know that he can expect her reply that same evening before eight o'clock. The afternoon drags on endlessly:

> The time would have passed quickly enough if I had had, during the afternoon that separated me from her letter, the help of a visit from anyone else. When the hours pass wrapped in conversation one ceases to count, or indeed to notice them, they vanish, and suddenly it is a long way beyond the point at which it escaped you that there reappears the nimble truant time. But if we are alone, our preoccupation, by bringing before us the still distant and incessantly awaited moment with the frequency and uniformity of a ticking pendulum, divides, or rather multiplies, the hours by all the minutes which, had we been with friends, we should not have counted.

At long last the letter arrives. Mme de Stermaria agrees to dine with him in three days' time. From that moment on he can think of nothing else but their rendezvous. To be sure, he would simply be dining with her, but what he really wants is to possess her; he feels certain that she will give herself to him that evening and in his imagination he relives from one minute to the next precisely how he will caress her. The effects on the intervening period of time are dire:

The days that preceded my dinner with Mme. de Stermaria were for me by no means delightful, in fact it was all I could do to live through them. For as a general rule, the shorter the interval is that separates us from our planned objective, the longer it seems to us, because we apply to it a more minute scale of measurement, or simply because it occurs to us to measure it at all. The Papacy, we are told, reckons by centuries, and indeed may not think perhaps of reckoning time at all, since its goal is in eternity. Mine was no more than three days off; I counted by seconds, I gave myself up to those imaginings which are the first movements of caresses...

Here Guyau's laws of internal optics are patently at work: desire sharpens the imagination and brings the event – like the view in a telescope – so close that the real distance is felt as disproportionately long and time seems to be lagging. Only once the intervening time has passed at long last do events regain their normal speed – for the narrator, alas, in quite the wrong direction. When the evening of the dinner has arrived, he sends his carriage to fetch her. It returns empty. The driver hands him a card from Mme. de Stermaria, with the news that she has been unexpectedly prevented from coming. She even adds how sorry she is: 'Had been looking so forward to it.' She was not alone in that.

The other monument to time and the memory, Thomas Mann's *The Magic Mountain*, which appeared in its German original in 1924, also alludes to the laws Guyau formulated in 1885. Hans Castorp has been spending a few days in a sanatorium in Davos, visiting a cousin who is taking the cure there. He has been warned that a week 'above' has a quite different length from what it is below, in the midst of the hustle and bustle of healthy people. In an 'Excursus on the Sense of Time', Thomas Mann muses about the effect of boredom on time. It is often said that boredom makes time seem long – hence the German word *Langeweile* for boredom. But that can perhaps apply to an hour or a day – longer periods such as weeks and months are cut short by it; they shrink: 'When one day is like all the others, then they are all like one; complete uniformity would make the longest life seem short, as though it had stolen away from us unawares.' Conversely, a full and interesting content 'will lend to the general passage of time a weightiness, a breadth and solidity which cause the eventful years to flow far more slowly than those poor, bare, empty ones over which the wind passes and they are gone'. Anyone wishing to live long, it seems to follow, must abandon routine as often as possible, change his surroundings, travel, take Guyau's advice to heart. But Thomas Mann, so much more widely travelled than Guyau, also realized that the effect was not lasting:

> Our first days in a new place, time has a youthful, that is to say, a broad and sweeping, flow, persisting for some six or eight days. Then, as one 'gets used to the place', a gradual shrinkage makes itself felt. He who clings or, better expressed, wishes to cling to life, will shudder to see how the days grow light and lighter, how they scurry by like dead leaves, until the last week of some four, perhaps, is uncannily fugitive and fleet.

High up in the mountains, Hans Castorp was to have a great many opportunities to wonder at the opposite of this experience: the power of time to lag disconcertingly. He too was found to have a lung condition and was to spend seven long years in the sanatorium.

Proust and Mann resolve the experience of time into the same factors as had Guyau. The intensity of emotions, their number, the keenness of memories and expectations, the effect of routine or of its opposite – all that lends psychological time its own rhythm and duration. Time speeds up and slows down, shrinks and stretches, in keeping with what happens in our consciousness. According to Guyau, experiences and a memory in which to store them are both needed to develop a grasp of time, since 'from the outset time exists in our consciousness just as it does in the hourglass. Our perceptions and thoughts correspond to the grains of sand escaping through the narrow opening. Just like those grains of sand they displace another in their diversity instead of amalgamating; that trickle of falling sand – that is time.'

## The perception of time

Guyau's image of the 'trickle of falling sand' makes something else clear as well. Our imagination can only come to grips with time by conceiving it in graphic terms. Reduced to its essence, the language of time is the language of space. Before, after, between, short and long are all markings on an imaginary time axis. In the Western view, this axis is a straight line on which we place our units of time as accurately as possible, just like the markings on a ruler, every second, every minute, every hour being of the same length. In some references to time the line runs through our body, so that we 'look forward' to things lying in the future, while past events are 'behind' us. The future is time still to come (*Zukunft, avenir*) while the past is time we have passed (*passé*). Freed of the body, the time axis runs a clear course: later time intervals appear on the right. No matter if it is a time axis on a graph or a time division in a history book, chronology proceeds from left to right. On the 'staircase of life', so often painted in the Middle Ages, youth starts to climb the steps on the left while old age descends on the right. The arrow to the future – 'go to' or 'play' on videos – invariably points to the right. Why our intuitions about time and space work that way is not clear, although there are some indications that the direction in which we write is a factor in the intuitive idea that 'the future lies to the right'. The psychologist Zwaan has conducted a series of experiments in Israel with subjects whose mother tongue was Hebrew, which is written from right to left. Most of them placed a card representing 'before' to the left of 'after'. In the same experiment in the Netherlands almost all the participants placed 'before' to the left of 'after'. The suggestion that the future lies to the right because moving to the right is in keeping with the movement of the hands of the clock, that is, forward in time, simply shifts the problem: there is little rightward movement of the hands in the bottom half of the dial. The fact that we equate 'clockwise' with 'movement to the right' is part of the puzzle, not its solution.

In addition to investing time with a direction, everyday speech also attributes a changing speed and elasticity to it. Time can crawl or fly, speed up, slow down or stand still; time can shrink, expand, contract or stretch. The fact that time in thought and speech fills space and that the experience of time can correspond to the experience of space was a crucial element of Guyau's 'inner optics' and of the ideas of Proust and Mann about the contraction and expansion of time. All three applied the laws of perspective to their inner

Fig. 24 The Taktir Apparatus for time studies, based on a design by Wilhelm Wundt. The apparatus produced ticks whose speed and volume could be precisely adjusted.

perceptions. But the same analogy also has an experimental counter-part. During the last quarter of the nineteenth century, hundreds of psychological experiments with time were conducted. Most of these took place in recently opened German laboratories and were aimed at the pattern of our *Zeitsinn*, or sense of time. The methodology developed for that research can, with a great many variations, still be found in present-day studies of time perception. A common method was to offer experimental subjects a time interval, started and ended with, for instance, a buzzer, and to ask them to recreate that interval by sounding a buzzer themselves. The experimenter would fill the first interval with all sorts of stimuli: loud or soft noises, slow or fast music. Afterwards he compared the intervals marked off by the experimental subjects with the intervals presented to them, and determined whether they had overestimated or underestimated the length of intervals accompanied by, say, slow music. Another method was to present the experimental subjects with two equal intervals filled with various stimuli and to have them say which was longer. To standardize the experiments as much as possible, Wilhelm Wundt, the founder of the Leipzig psychological laboratory, designed the Taktir Apparatus, which produced ticks whose speed and volume could be finely adjusted. With this machine, Wundt's colleague, Meumann, discovered, among other things, the 'law' that if you fill a time interval with ticks produced at precisely the same rate but growing louder and louder, the ticks seem to speed up. Anyone listening to Ravel's *Bolero* has this illusion on a much bigger scale: thanks to the rising volume, the work seems to be quicker at the end than it is at the beginning. It is known that Ravel could fly into a rage if he noticed during a performance that the conductor had speeded up the tempo.

Experiments with the Taktir Apparatus and similar devices always covered a short interval, a few seconds at most; half a minute was very long. Within that interval, stimuli could be provided in relatively strict sequence, and changes in the duration and the tempo of subjective time could be determined with the utmost precision, if necessary in milliseconds. The hope was that the results of a meticulous experiment on a scale of seconds or minutes could be extrapolated to time experiences on the scale of days, months or even years. Over such large intervals the variables can no longer be manipulated; at best life itself can be left to conduct the experiment, as happened on the Magic Mountain, but perhaps the same laws prevailed on the large scale as could be determined accurately on the small scale. The idea was attractive. Much as Guyau and Proust went beyond personal introspection in their descriptions, inasmuch as they resonated in the experience of others, so the endless ticking, buzzing and rattling of the experimental apparatus might be expected to tell us something about the distortions of time outside the walls of the laboratory.

This leap on to a different scale proved to be not without complications. To begin with, there are problems of terminology. Even the simplest experiment in estimating time can cause a veritable confusion of tongues. Someone is asked to mark an interval of precisely one minute without the help of a clock or watch. The true duration of his subjective minute turns out to be fifty seconds. Is that a case of underestimating or of overestimating time? The first, some will say, for the subject has underestimated the real length of a minute. The second, say others, because he has overestimated the speed with which a minute passes. It is a simple matter to exaggerate this confusion of tongues to the point of total incoherence. Someone takes a week's vacation. Before he knows what has happened, it is his last day. On his return home it seems to him that he has been away much longer than a week. Did time pass for him more quickly or more slowly? If holidays pass more quickly than other days, how is it possible that seven of the days rushing by add up to a week that seems to have lasted much longer? In a subjectively long week, time must surely have gone by more slowly? Anyone wishing to use, in addition to short and long or fast and slow, such terms as expanding or contracting, can count on having to cut a Gordian knot. Luckily, time studies rely on several conventions and conceptual distinctions that proffer some help. For what we call underestimating or overestimating, clock time serves as a standard. Someone who reports a subjective 'minute' of fifty seconds possibly overestimates how quickly the time on the clock passes, but even so his answer is considered an *under*estimate. When estimating longer periods we have to distinguish between a primary and a secondary evaluation. The evaluation of the subjective tempo of time *at a given moment* can differ from the evaluation of the length of the interval judged *in retrospect*. During holidays our evaluations often have an inverse relationship, so that 'quick' days (primary) yield a 'long' week (secondary). The same inversion applies to boredom. Time in which 'nothing' happens seems long, as Thomas Mann pointed out, but only in primary judgment; with the secondary judgment time shrinks. Camus, too, was aware of this paradoxical relationship. In *The Outsider* the protagonist is thrown into gaol. With few other diversions than his memories and the alternation of day and night, time passes. 'I hadn't understood how days could be both long and short at the same time. Long to live through I suppose, but so distended that they ended up flowing into one another.' When the warder told him one day that he had been there for five months, he believed it but did not really understand it. 'For me it was for ever the same day that I was spinning out in my cell.'

There is yet another complication that first came to light in experimental studies of time. Writing about the apparent contraction of time as we grow older, William James spoke of 'hollow' years. Thomas Mann wrote about the quick passage of 'poor, bare, empty' years. But what is the experimental equivalent of hollow, empty time? An interval without stimuli? No experimenter can proffer that to his experimental subjects, not even if he should succeed in banishing all sensory stimuli. Nobody can turn himself into a complete blank and experience a completely empty length of time. Empty time is as fictitious as an absolute vacuum; it secretly sucks up snatches of thoughts, observations, memories. The many experiments with 'empty' time – in the weak sense of an interval in which the experimental subject is offered no stimuli – have yielded nothing but incoherent findings.

Meumann found as early as 1896 that an interval filled with ticks is felt to be longer than an equally long 'empty' interval without ticks. But that comparison only held for intervals of less than ten seconds; beyond that the 'empty' time is estimated to be longer. And if you hear no ticks but irritating noises, another investigator discovered, the noisy interval seems longer than a 'quiet' interval.

Anyone reading Leonard Doob's *Patterning of Time*, an elegant and erudite survey of close on a hundred years of time studies, or the more recent *A Watched Pot* by Michael Flaherty, must conclude that the limits of all these studies had been staked out even before the end of the nineteenth century by Wilhelm Wundt and William James. Both were intrigued by the distortions in our estimation of time. Wundt treated them just as if they were visual illusions, which, in fact, they resemble in many respects, such as the interval that seems short after a long interval. With his Taktir Apparatus he meticulously manipulated the variables one by one and waited to see what their effect was on duration or tempo. The questions he asked may have been minor, but the answers were exact and controllable. James asked big questions. He wanted to know why a week's vacation looked longer on one's return home, or why a month of illness shrinks in the memory to perhaps no more than a week. For the answers he consulted his own experiences or that of others recorded in the literature or elicited in conversations. These experiences could be shared or not, but verifying or refuting them experimentally was impossible. Why life passes more quickly as we grow older is not a question Wundt asked. Those who want an answer based on research will have to narrow their search. In recent studies of time and the memory, three mechanisms have been identified and linked to the acceleration of the passing years. The first is a phenomenon known as 'telescopy'; the second is the reminiscence effect discussed in the last chapter, and the third is bound up with the rhythm of the physiological clocks in our body.

## Telescopy

When Ferdi E., the kidnapper and murderer of Gerrit Jan Heijn, was let out of prison on probation pending his permanent release, the general reaction in the Netherlands was: 'You mean he's finished his sentence already? How long is it since that kidnapping, then?' For most people, the answer – Heijn was kidnapped on 9 September 1987 – lay further back in the past than they thought. The psychologist Sully mentioned a similar case as early as 1881, one that also involved a crime attracting a great deal of attention and in which the culprit's three years of hard labour had simply flown by in the public's mind. Sully explained the underestimate of that time interval with the analogy of the binoculars: the details that you can still see clearly give you the impression that an object in the distance is much closer than it actually is.

In 1955 the American statistician Gray discovered a peculiar feature in the answers to questionnaires. With questions of the type, 'How often have you visited your general practitioner during the past two years?', participants tended to overestimate the frequency when their answers were checked. The reason was that they included visits that fell just outside the two years. In other words, Gray found that people in general have the tendency to date events more recently than they actually occurred. This phenomenon has been the subject of a great deal of research and has been called telescopy, with a nod to Sully's binoculars. The suggested explanation, too, does not differ greatly from Sully's analogy: the review of the past magnified by lenses causes the distance in time to shrink, so that the period under consideration appears to be too long.

When personal incidents are involved it is often difficult to judge the extent of telescopy accurately. This is not the case with public events. In 1997, the psychologists Crawley and Pring performed an experiment in which the estimated time interval was compared precisely with the real time interval. They drew up a list of events that anyone in Britain even vaguely familiar with the news was bound to remember. These included such disasters as Chernobyl (1986) and Lockerbie (1988), such major political events as Margaret Thatcher becoming prime minister (1979), the Argentine occupation of the Falklands (1982), the assassinations of John Lennon (1980) and Indira Gandhi (1984), the Harrod's bomb (1983), the bombing of the Grand Hotel in Brighton (1984) and a whole series of other sensational events. The earliest event was the Queen's Silver Jubilee (1977); the most recent the fall of the Berlin Wall (1989). Next, Crawley and Pring asked their experimental subjects to give as nearly as possible the year and the month in which these events had occurred. The answers revealed an interesting difference to do with the subjects' age. Experimental subjects of middle age (between thirty-five and fifty years old) dated the events too recently, thus confirming the telescopy found in earlier experiments. But older subjects (on average aged about seventy) placed the events too far back in time. It was as if they had turned the telescope round, thus extending the interval.

'This can help to explain why time seems to fly by as we grow older', wrote Crawley and Pring. The underlying idea is probably that time in the subjectively longer period must have gone by more quickly. This conclusion shows how difficult it is to interpret the results of research on time perception. For something can also be said for the opposite conclusion. It is precisely those who think something happened three years ago when in fact it was five, who will exclaim, 'Gosh, how time flies.' The speeding up of the years seems to be due to telescopy rather than to reverse telescopy. Crawley and Pring's theory can only be saved by the assumption of a reverse connection between the overestimate of the duration of a period of time and its subjective tempo. That does indeed manifest itself with the quickened pace of a week on holiday, which upon one's return home seems longer than an ordinary week. However, in that case, both telescopy and reverse telescopy will make us feel that time is rushing past, and that robs them of any explanatory value.

## The reminiscence effect

Anyone trying to put a date to a memory, the French physician Théodule Ribot wrote in 1881 in his classic text *The Diseases of Memory*, makes use of markers, events whose place in time is well known. We do not choose these markers, they impose themselves upon us. Generally they are purely individual, but they can also be common to a family or an entire nation. They are made up of series of everyday happenings, important family occasions, professional activities. These series, Ribot asserted, 'are the more numerous the more varied an individual's life. The markers serve as milestones or signposts along our path, all starting from the same point but spreading out in different directions. It is anyway thanks to this peculiarity that the series can be placed side by side, as it were, for purposes of comparison.'

Various present-day authors have included the notion of markers in their theories about time relationships in the autobiographical memory: Conway calls them reference points, Shum 'temporal landmarks'. Such markers determine how long ago something happened, whether it occurred before or after something else, and sometimes even what its precise date was.

Only at moments when we have great difficulty in dating a memory can we see our own time markers at work. Often the memory shifts to and fro on the time axis of one's past, with a 'but' as a pivotal point at every turn: it was after 1993 because X was already working with us – but our neighbour had not yet moved away because I remember talking to him about it, so it must have been before 1995 – but Z was still living at home, so it must have been after September 1994 – but it was a glorious autumn day, so it must have been in about October 1994, oh, that's right, it happened the day before we went on our autumn holiday. Markers allow the memory to bounce between two ever-closer end points. The schema fitting time relationships between memories is as individual as the memories themselves. It has its own colour and mood. It links a series of more specific associations, for instance what friends you had at the time or what your daily activities happened to be. The schema 'when I was working for P' activates other memories than the schema 'when I lived in Q', even if the two schemata were coincident in time. Time markers can indeed, as Ribot contended, be placed side by side and compared.

Shum must also have been inspired by Ribot's casual remark that memory markers are more numerous when life is more varied. He argued that the reminiscence effect, the relative ease with which older people remember events from about their twentieth year, is a consequence of the fact that a greater number of time markers is available for that period. If time markers do indeed order networks of associations, as research seems to indicate, then the same time markers will also be able to call up memories, so that there is a positive correlation between the number of time markers and the density of memories. Typical time markers are 'my first meeting with...', 'the first time I...', 'when I first began to...' – all of them memories that contribute so much to the reminiscence effect. Time markers, in short, do not merely mark periods and dates, they also give rise to reveries in old age.

Shum did not link this theory to the experience that life speeds up as we grow older, but the one follows from the other. A period that brings up many memories will expand when seen in retrospect and seems to have lasted longer than an equally long period comprising few memories. Conversely, time markers will become less numerous at about middle age and later, and in the void thus created time will speed up subjectively. That is an explanation that, at first sight, has much in common with William James's view of the vivid and exciting memories of youth and the uniformity and routine of later years, but what Shum added to that view was that the crucial factor might well be the temporal organization of memories: together with variety the network of time markers disappears, and with it an important access to memories from that period.

## Physiological clocks

Several physiological factors influencing our experience of time have been known since the 1930s. The realization that body temperature can cause subjective time to speed up or slow down is due to a chance discovery by the American psychologist Hoagland. Hoagland's ailing wife reproached him with taking a long time when all he had had to do was to fetch some medicines. In fact, he had been out of the room for a short time only. Hoagland asked her to indicate a time interval of one minute. The actual length of her 'minute' turned out to be thirty-seven seconds. The higher the fever, the longer a minute seemed to her. Baddeley, the memory psychologist, conducted a converse experiment – or rather had it performed – by getting experimental subjects to swim in sea water at 4 degrees Celsius. As expected, they counted the seconds they spent in the water too slowly.

In the absence of manipulation, physiological processes can serve as surprisingly accurate 'clocks', even on a scale of years. In the thirties, Carrel, the French microbiologist, identified various processes at the cell level that had a clock or calendar-like accuracy. The speed, for instance, with which a superficial wound heals varies with age. That variation can be accurately described in equations, from which one may predict that the wound of someone aged twenty is likely to heal twice as quickly as that of a forty-year-old. Anyone performing measurements on a healing wound can conversely deduce the age of a patient from the speed with which the wound heals. For people aged from ten to forty-five, these equations produce reliable estimates.

Dozens of physiological clocks beat in our bodies. Inhalation, blood pressure, pulse, hormone release, cell division, sleep, metabolism, temperature – all these processes have their own cycles, and in turn endow our life with rhythm and cadence. That means no more and no less than that all sorts of physiological processes have a characteristic periodicity. To call these processes 'clocks' is more of a metaphor than an explanation, but is nevertheless a metaphor that raises interesting questions. Can you advance or retard biological clocks? Can you readjust a clock that has gone out of kilter? Is the body governed by standard time, regulated by a master clock? And above all, do biological clocks run faster or slower as we grow older?

A brief tour of the clockwork regulating our internal cycles shows that the fastest rhythms occur in the nervous system. Some neurons fire at a rate of a thousand impulses per second. Less hectic are the cycles of brain activity as recorded on an EEG: from eight to twelve cycles a second. On the opposite end of the scale we find cycles lasting twenty-four hours, such as fluctuations in body temperature and blood pressure. Of the cycles lasting more than a day the menstrual cycle is the most important. The average menstrual cycle takes a lunar month of 29 days. Annual cycles manifest themselves in weight increases and the state of the immune system. Somewhere halfway between the fastest and the slowest cycles the only clock we can hear and feel, namely the heart, ticks away – a pumping muscle whose contractions and relaxations are governed by a carefully adjusted collection of chronometers. An understanding of the rhythm of these natural clocks makes it possible to design pacemakers which, with small bursts of electric impulses, help to control irregular heart beats.

Diurnal rhythms can turn someone into a definite morning or night person. With morning people, the temperature begins to rise in the early morning hours, reaches a peak at about four o'clock in the afternoon, and then begins to fall. Their body clocks are hours ahead of those of night people who are still active and alert after dusk and have a later temperature peak. As we grow older, biological clocks shift towards morning and the differences between morning and night people begin to decrease. This process goes hand in hand with a slowdown in the tempo of life, something that can cause teenagers at railway stations and post offices to long for the introduction of separate counters for old age pensioners.

The problems associated with the cycle of waking and sleeping in older people may well be the consequence of the loss of cells in the suprachiasmatic nucleus (SCN). The SCN – when intact no more than 1 mm³ in size – consists of some 8,000 cells and lies just above the spot where the optic nerves cross. The SCN functions as a mother clock; if it goes wrong a whole set of clocks is thrown out of kilter. Experiments have shown that the SCN is controlled by light. The neurotransmitter dopamine plays an important role in this process, its production decreasing in old age. Cell depletion in the SCN and dopamine deficiency may cause crucial problems in our dealings with time. The American neurologist Mangan considers these problems the explanation of the results of experiments in which older people were asked to estimate how long it took for an interval of three minutes to pass. From earlier experiments it was known that the ability of children to estimate time correctly increases with age, reaching a peak in twenty-year olds, and then falls off. The ability of elderly people drops to the level of young children. Mangan showed that older people invariably *overestimate* lapsed time intervals. He asked three age groups (between nineteen and twenty-four, between forty-five and fifty and between sixty and seventy) to measure an interval of three minutes by counting off the seconds. The youngest group did so extremely accurately – on average they made the three minutes no more than three seconds too long. The middle-aged subjects made the interval sixteen seconds too long. In older people the error ran to forty seconds. That time passes more quickly when you are very busy doing something emerged during the second part of the experiment. All the participants were given a sorting job as a form of distraction and had to estimate three minutes again. Among the youngest group the distraction led to an overestimate of forty-six seconds, in the middle group of sixty-three seconds and in the oldest group of no fewer than 106 seconds. In other words, after the passage of three minutes, the oldest group added almost another two minutes to their estimate.

It seems that with old age we change into slowly ticking carriage clocks. The wheels do not run with more irregularity than before, sometimes too fast and sometimes too slow; they simply turn too slowly and do that with precise regularity. Those who know the extent of their own deviation will be able to judge the time as reliably as before. Just as with Ernst Jünger's antique hourglass, with its eroded waist, we must, as we grow older, take an old-age constant into account in our estimates of time.

Can the three elements – telescopy, or its reverse; the reminiscence effect; and Mangan's experimental findings – be combined into a convincing explanation of the speeding up of the years with old age? The honest answer is no. The results of the experiments simply do not point in the same direction. While the estimated 'minutes' of Mangan's older subjects were much too long, Crawley and Pring's older subjects, who placed events too far back in time, did the same with the period between the event and now, making the 'years' too long. But their relationship to the experienced passage of time was the other way round. If Mangan's experimental subjects had been given a sign after three minutes, they would have thought to themselves, 'Surely three minutes cannot be over yet?' Crawley and Pring's experimental subjects, by contrast, thought to themselves, 'Is it only nine years ago that the aeroplane crashed at Lockerbie [a disaster that on average is judged to have taken place more than two-and-a-half years before it actually did]? I thought it was much longer ago.' It is only when someone thinks that something occurred five years ago when it really happened ten years ago, that the illusion arises that the intervening years have flown by.

What we can rely on most are the reminiscence effect and the slowing down of our physiological clocks. A seventy-year old who wonders if the past five years seem to have passed more quickly to him than earlier years has a tendency not to compare those years with the period between his forty-third and forty-eighth years or between his fifty-sixth and sixty-first, but with the five years he spent at middle school or an equally long period in his youth or adolescence. In a sense this a comparison of extremes. You mentally compare a 'full' part of your memory with a part that has almost inevitably registered, not the events themselves, but their repetition. With many of the organic metronomes slowing down, the outside world may seem to be speeding up.

## A long time young, a short time old

The streets of your youth are smaller than they appear to be in your memory. Back in your old neighbourhood you turn into the endlessly long street of the past and are at the corner in a couple of steps. Lanes, gardens, squares and parks all seem to have shrunk to perhaps half their former size. Even the schools have shrunk; it is a miracle that the teachers, who are the same size as before, still fit into them. A common explanation is that streets seem long to a child because he takes himself as a yardstick. Once he is an adult and twice as tall, the streets seem half their old length. Paced out in the steps of old they are exactly the same length still. Apparently one's memory is duped by an optical illusion ranging over the scale of a human life. Although everyone is conscious of the illusory effect, it is difficult to escape from it. You never hear anybody say: I was back in my old neighbourhood recently and thought everything would be terribly small, but don't you believe it, everything was still the same old size. Just as with genuine optical illusions, comparisons with reality do not lead to the restoration of normal relationships. Streets, once they have shrunk, will never again have their normal length, any more than it helps washing a sweater in cold water once it has been washed in water that was too hot.

Does your memory do the same with the *time* of your youth? An essential difference between time and space is that you can – often – return to the places you used to know but not to that time long past. In the streets of the past, you can no longer walk as a six-year-old. The passage of time you remember can no longer be tested against reality. Perhaps such a test is pointless anyway. Many estimates and judgments of time, such as 'long ago' or 'old', resist correction, just like the streets of yesterday. Perhaps that is because they are based on a particular yardstick: yourself. For a child, a year is a large part of its life; small wonder then that it lasts so long. Children spend long days in their long streets. Throughout our lives we continue to apply a yardstick that keeps changing and is therefore no yardstick at all. Your elders have always been old until you have children yourself and work out how old your parents were when you were your children's age. Teachers, too, are always old – until you meet them twenty years later at a reunion and they seem somehow to have been rejuvenated.

Freshmen grow younger every year (just like their parents). The fact that a period of ten or twenty years is constant as far as the calendar is concerned but has a variable length in personal experience, may mean that a period from the past which, to go by the calendar, you leave further and further behind, seems subjectively to have become nearer instead. Those born ten years after the war see the time lapse since then differently on their fifteenth birthday from the way they do on their fiftieth. Even in judging future events, the personal yardstick plays a significant part. Once having reached the age in which one has become familiar with the speeding up of time, ten years can seem short, while the same period still strikes a twenty-year-old as a small eternity. Everyone, in short, is his own sliding yardstick, and just as with an old-fashioned slide rule the result of the calculation depends on the position of the slide.

However, there is no doubt about the direction of the shift as we grow older. Objective slowing down creates subjective speeding up and in this process the rate of our biological clocks has a part to play. Many of these clocks happen to run more quickly in a young body than they do in an old. If we were to express our age in terms of the revolutions of physiological clocks, as Carrel, whom we quoted earlier, put it, we should have to say that we are a long time young and a short time old. Perhaps that explains why our days as a child were so long while in old age time passes so alarmingly fast: unconsciously we read clock time against the background of physiological time. Objective time, clock time, Carrel explained, passes at an even rate, like a river through a valley. At the beginning of his life man still runs briskly along the bank, more quickly than the river. At around midday his speed is somewhat slower and he keeps pace with the river. Towards evening, as he tires, the river flows faster and he falls behind. In the end, he stands still and goes to lie down beside a river that continues along its course at the same imperturbable rate at which it has been flowing all along.

BIBLIOGRAPHY

Baddeley, A. D., 'Reduced body temperature and time estimation', *American Journal of Psychology* 79 (1966), 475–9.

Why life speeds up as you get older

Camus, A., *L'étranger*, 1942. Quoted from A. Camus, *The Outsider*, translated by J. Laredo, London, 1982.

Carrel, A., *Man, the Unknown*, London, 1953.

Conway, M. A., *Autobiographical Memory*, Milton Keynes, 1990.

Crawley, S. E., and L. Pring, 'When did Mrs. Thatcher resign? The effects of ageing on the dating of public events', *Memory* 8 (2000), 111–21.

Doob, L. W., *Patterning of Time*, New Haven and London, 1971.

Flaherty, M. G., *A Watched Pot: How We Experience Time*, New York and London, 1999.

Gray, P. G., 'The memory factor in social surveys', *Journal of the American Statistical Association* 50 (1955), 344–63.

Guyau, J.-M., *La genèse de l'idée de temps*, Paris, 1890.

Hoagland, H., 'The physiological control of judgments of duration: evidence for a chemical clock', *Journal of General Psychology* 9 (1933), 267–87.

James, W., *The Principles of Psychology*, New York, 1890.

Janet, P., 'Une illusion d'optique interne', *Revue Philosophique* 3 (1877), 497–502.

Jünger, E., *Das Sanduhrbuch*, Frankfurt am Main, 1954.

Krol, G., *Een Fries huilt niet*, Amsterdam, 1980.

Mangan, P. A., *Report for the Annual Meeting of the Society for Neuroscience*, Washington, DC, 1996.

Mann, T., *Der Zauberberg*, 1924. Quoted from *The Magic Mountain*, translated by H. T. Lowe-Porter, New York, 1968.

Meumann, E., 'Beitrage zur Psychologie des Zeitbewusstseins', *Philosophische Studien* 12 (1896), 127–254.

Michon, J., V. Pouthas and J. Jackson (eds.), *Guyau and the Idea of Time*, Amsterdam, Oxford and New York, 1988.

Orlock, C., *Inner Time*, New York, 1993.

Proust, M., *The Guermantes Way, Part II*, translated by C. K. Scott Moncrieff, London, 1941.

Ribot, T., *Les maladies de la mémoire*, 1881. Quoted from *The Diseases of Memory*, London, 1882.

Shum, M. S., 'The role of temporal landmarks in autobiographical memory processes', *Psychological Bulletin* 124 (1998), 423–42.

Sully, J., *Illusion: A Psychological Study*, London, 1881.

Zwaan, E. J., *Links en rechts in waarneming en beleving*, Utrecht, 1966.

# 15   Forgetting

Our memory is both fragile and resilient at the same time. It does not take much to throw it out of gear. A small blood clot, a shortage of oxygen, an infection of the cerebral membrane – the slightest organic defect can cause irreparable damage. Yet even in the most drastic forms of memory loss, much is left intact. People with amnesia can still recall the meaning of words and symbols, and still know what movements to perform in order to dress themselves or to eat. However great the ravages associated with brain injuries look at first sight, some parts of the memory seem afterwards to have escaped strangely unharmed.

Of all forms of memory, the autobiographical memory is the most susceptible to disruption. Memories can go wrong in the wake of two types of memory loss that can be fitted on to a timescale. In the case of retrograde amnesia, recollections of events before the injury are impaired. In the most drastic case, everything has gone: where you have just come from, what you were doing, who you are. You know as little about the past as you do about the future, are as unfamiliar with yourself as you are with a stranger. The other form, anterograde amnesia, prevents the storage of memories after the injury. You keep your past, but your future will never become your past. If autobiographical memory were really a diary, all the blank pages would have been torn out with anterograde amnesia, while retrograde amnesia would leave you with nothing but empty pages.

It makes no difference whether a patient suffers from the one form of amnesia or the other, in both cases time is cut off from him in one direction. Whereas before, to use an image of William James, he was astride the saddle of time and could look ahead and backwards with equal ease, he is now sitting with his back permanently to the past or to the future. The unfortunate person afflicted with a combination of both amnesias, as happens in dementia, ends his life in a segment of time that begins to close in both directions and finally narrows down into a present without breadth, a now with neither retrospect nor prospect.

## Remembering and forgetting

We are used to thinking of remembering and forgetting as mutually exclusive. What you remember you did not forget and what you have forgotten you cannot recall. Where the one stops, the other starts. But where in this dichotomy do you fit the memory of what you have forgotten? Not the memories of the events themselves – those you have forgotten – but the knowledge that you used to know something that has now gone? If you can remember that you have forgotten, something has plainly stayed behind in the memory, something like the discoloured patch on the wall whose outlines tell you what used to hang there for years.

The relationship between remembering and forgetting is far more complex than mere mutual incompatibility. Sometimes we cannot remember something while we know for certain that it is stored in our memory. Everyone knows what it is like to to have a word on the tip of your tongue, but the sounds and syllables fail to fall into the right place. The most remarkable thing of all is that the word refuses to come to you at that very moment, but that it hints at its presence. As William James put it:

> Suppose we try to recall a forgotten name. The state of our consciousness is peculiar. There is a gap therein, but no mere gap. It is a gap that is intensely active. A sort of wraith of the name is in it, beckoning us in a given direction, making us at moments tingle with the sense of our closeness, and then letting us sink back without the longed-for term. If wrong names are proposed to us, this singularly definite gap acts immediately so as to negate them. They do not fit into its mould and the gap of one word does not feel like the gap of another, all empty of content as both might seem necessarily to be when described as gaps. When I vainly try to recall the name of Spalding, my consciousness is far removed from what it is when I vainly try to recall the name of Bowles.

That 'gap' can prove very enduring and continue to claim our attention with a provoking pertinacity. The psychologists Brown and McNeill presented their experimental subjects with definitions of relatively uncommon words such as 'small Chinese skiff' (*sampan*) or 'blood feud' (*vendetta*). When the experimental subject had the feeling that the wanted word was on the tip of his tongue, they asked him a number of questions. With what letter does it start? How many syllables does it have? What vowels are in it? Can you name words that resemble it? The contours of the 'gap' do indeed hold information. In half the cases the subjects seemed to have a good idea of the first letter and the number of syllables. However, the same 'gap' also introduced a new phenomenon. Often the sound, the syllables and the separate letters combined into a word that also fitted the description and that repeatedly jumped the queue: the 'ugly sister'. For someone looking for 'sampan', a word such as 'saipam' underpins the irony of your being unable to find a word while you know exactly where you should be looking: right behind the ugly sister.

Equally common is the mistaken memory that you positively believe you have forgotten something you could not possibly have remembered. This mistake is something with which I am familiar from personal experience. In 1979, Anne Vondeling, the Dutch Labour Party politician and former president of the Second Chamber, had a fatal accident. The obituary, signed, as far as I can remember, by the party leadership, contained four lines of a poem. The first was 'Over the heath, through the tenuous mist'; there followed a line I did not like all that much and quickly forgot, and then the final lines:

> with a rattling of chains comes the night's descent
> and the lid of the world slams down.

It was signed: Gerrit Achterberg. That image, a lid that has to be hoisted up by chains and that you cannot raise by yourself once it falls shut over you, was fixed firmly in my memory, or rather could not be cast out from it. When later, in the year of our daughter's birth, I was given Achterberg's *Verzamelde gedichten* (Collected poems) I searched for these lines for hours. Nothing. Not even anything like them. Four or five Achterberg connoisseurs whom I asked could not help, and some insisted categorically that the lines had not been written by Achterberg. Strange, the party leaders would surely not have written the lines themselves and then put Achterberg's name to them.

Twenty years later – by which time our daughter had left home – I again came across an obituary with these lines. There were two differences: the line I had forgotten had been omitted and the lid did not slam down but went down. Once again it was signed Achterberg. To make absolutely certain I once again went through the collected poems page by page. In addition I consulted the index of Hazeu's Achterberg biography – again with no result. I cut the obituary out, left it lying around for a short while and then rang the first signatory of the obituary. He was very obliging. In answer to my question of how they had come by those lines, he told me that the deceased, his partner, had read them in Anne Vondeling's obituary.

I was looking for an answer and was left with the old riddle. What sort of ghostly lines were looming out of the tenuous mist? *Were* they indeed by Achterberg? I wrote a piece about it all for a Dutch newspaper and awaited further developments. One week later I was in receipt of a handful of letters from Achterberg devotees. What they wrote made me feel humble, a mood that lasted for several days. I had truly got the whole thing wrong. To begin with, the text is indeed by Achterberg; it is the penultimate strophe of 'Fait accompli'. The poem ends with:

> The decision today cannot be missed.
> Tomorrow my papers The Hague will have sent.
> There, where the last post has just gone.

Moreover, the poem *is* included in his collected poems (on page 955). Furthermore it was an obituary notice not by the party leaders, as I thought, but by the Vondeling family. And finally, with Achterberg the lid does not 'slam' down but 'goes' down. Peter de Bruijn, the editor of the historico-critical edition of Achterberg's *Gedichten* (Poems) let me know that in his last rough manuscript, Achterberg originally wrote 'let' instead of 'goes'. With 'slams', my memory had vulgarized that line, something that Achterberg did not do. No wonder then, in retrospect, that the Achterberg experts I consulted could not place the strophe.

But things were worse still. Of the one line I had forgotten, I could only remember that it was not very beautiful. In reality there was no fourth line at all. I must therefore have made it up and then have forgotten it. Various correspondents also pointed out that 'Fait accompli' originally appeared in another collection, the title of which translates as *Forgotten*.

## Forgotten forgetting

Anyone worried about their memory might like to complete the 'Everyday Memory Questionnaire' compiled by Alan Baddeley, a British memory researcher, and several of his colleagues. The questionnaire describes twenty-seven common situations in which memory fails. For each item the subject has to indicate on a nine-point scale whether this has happened to him 'not at all in the last six months' (1) or 'more than once a day' (9). Standardized on a sample of the general public without any specific disorders of memory, the test indicates that situations like having to go back to check whether you have done something that you meant to do, forgetting where you have put something, failing to find a word that is 'on the tip of your tongue', forgetting what you have just said ('What was I talking about?'), or forgetting whether something happened yesterday or last week, happen to practically all of us once or twice a month. Situations like forgetting to do things you said you would do, forgetting to pass on an important message, forgetting where things are normally kept, getting lost in a building where you have often been before or repeating what you have just done ('Why is this toothbrush wet?') are less frequent: about once in a half year. If you fail to recognize places that you have often been to before, start reading an article in a newspaper without realizing that you have already read it before, forget important details of what you did the day before, fail to remember your birthdate, lose track of what a newspaper article is about or even do something as innocent as asking someone the same question twice, you will fail to find any consolation in the statistics of the general public: this hasn't happened to them, they indicate, in the last six months. As happens with all norms typical of the average person, for a long time they provide relief ('I weigh, drink, forget just a little bit more than the average'), but later the lapse is all the more worrying.

With such questionnaires, a curious methodological artefact appears. In diagnostic practice various methods are used to determine the seriousness of a memory disorder. One therapist will ask his patients to keep a diary, another will interview them in some detail, a third will give them a standard memory test or even ask them to fill in questionnaires. Baddeley and his team were trying to determine if these different methods yielded the same answers. Their experimental subjects were people who had suffered a brain injury, generally through a traffic accident, and as a consequence had problems with their memory. To his regret, Baddeley found that his own questionnaire did not correlate all that well with other tests. In retrospect, the cause seems obvious: those who have a bad memory forget what they have forgotten. Baddeley quotes from a diary, kept by a law student who had become amnesic following a brain haemorrhage: 'Late last night I remembered that I'd forgotten to list those things that I had forgotten. But then how do I know what I'd forgotten?' In research with older people – but without a brain injury – the same defect came to light: the point at which the scores went on getting better marked the moment when the memory mercifully forgot its own failure. Some people have so bad a memory that they can remember no reason at all for complaint.

## Writing in the dark

By far the strangest relationship between remembering and forgetting occurs in a phenomenon known as 'implicit memory'. This form of memory comprises the layer of experiences of which we have no conscious memory but which nevertheless influence our actions. This is one compartment of the memory that introspection cannot penetrate, its existence being inferred from its effects on our behaviour. It works underground and is practically indestructible. Even in the most drastic forms of amnesia the implicit memory remains intact.

The first indications that something like an implicit memory must exist cropped up with patients suffering from anterograde amnesia. When these patients were given exercises involving the reading of texts in mirror writing they learned to do so as quickly as people without memory disorders. The odd thing was that they forgot the texts and the exercises – presenting themselves politely to the experimenters every morning – while progressing in the reading of mirror writing as quickly as healthy subjects. They remembered what they had learned, not how they had learnt it. Originally it was thought that the implicit memory remained confined to simple motor and perceptual skills, but Daniel Schacter and his colleagues also investigated 'higher' mental functions such as the understanding of sentences. The results were equally counter-intuitive. In one of the tests, people with serious memory loss were given sentences that made no sense without further explanation. An example would be: 'The haystack was important because the canopy ripped.' Only after adding 'of the parachute' can you fathom the meaning: the parachute tore, but luckily the parachutist landed on a haystack. In the same way, you can only understand the sentence, 'The notes were wrong because the seams burst' after adding 'of the bagpipe'. Patients with memory disorders were presented with a series of such sentences, together with the solution. When they were shown the same sentences a few days later, without the amplification, the sentences appeared completely unfamiliar to them: 'Never seen it before.' In view of their disorder, that is as you would expect. Yet they did not have any problem with the meaning. Asked how they could possibly understand such cryptic sentences they seemed astonished; surely the meaning was clear and entirely logical? Underneath a layer from which everything was wiped out within a few minutes, something seemed to have been registered that could no longer be elicited through the conscious mind, but did have an influence on the processing of language.

In 1880, Théodule Ribot published an article on the biological basis of the memory. In everyday speech, he explained, the memory comprises three elements: the storing of experience, its recall, and the location of the experience in the past. The first two are indispensable – if they are lost, for whatever reason, the memory is destroyed. But if the third disappears, 'the memory ceases to exist for itself, without ceasing itself to exist'. That sentence describes very precisely what remains and what goes. Even if, to the conscious mind, the memory seems to have been put out of action, it nevertheless continues to register something, so many inscriptions in the dark.

It is tempting to include this notion of inscriptions in the dark in the wider theory of the perfect memory. Might our memory not be able to capture *everything* we see, experience, think, dream or imagine? In 1980, Elizabeth and Geoffrey Loftus published the results of an enquiry among psychologists. The answers showed that a great majority (84 per cent) believed that our brain contains a complete record of all our experiences. Now it cannot be denied that the memory is able to preserve some types of information for an indefinite period of time. Bahrick's experiments with foreign languages unused since youth showed that a large part of the vocabulary was found intact in the memory fifty years later, a form of storage to which Bahrick referred as the 'permastore'. Wagenaar, too, failed to find any evidence in his diary experiment that autobiographical recollections disappear from the memory: he was able to remember all the events. Now it must be stressed that these were events Wagenaar had put in writing for the sake of the experiment and which, for that reason alone, may well have been stored more securely than others. Wagenaar ascribed the cause of forgetfulness to the inability to get access to stored experiences; perhaps they are still there – there is no proof to the contrary – but our powers of recollection can no longer reach them. We may well have a perfect memory without realizing it. It would have to be a memory made up exclusively of the first of Ribot's three elements. In biological terms, the hypothesis that the memory stores all experience seems improbable. Memories are stored in brain tissue that undergoes all sorts of changes: growth, metabolic processes, damage, decay, death. That some traces of experiences remain intact throughout a person's life is beyond any doubt; that *all* traces survive is doubtful.

## Horror vacui

Anyone who suffers a serious memory disorder loses a large part of their mental capital, either at once or in the longer term. A neurological injury, lack of oxygen, an infection or one of the pathological conditions to which Alois Alzheimer or Sergei Korsakoff have given their names – no matter what the cause, the consequences are disastrous: much of what has been acquired or learned, what has been appropriated with care and discipline, has gone. A patient with anterograde amnesia loses the ability to store new experiences in such a way that they can be recalled later. His future has been wiped out while he is still alive. In a patient with retrograde amnesia, the past has been erased or rendered inaccessible. The person he once was, with abilities, talents and character traits, with an inner life fed by what he has experienced, has vanished. In both cases the patient has lost a good deal of his mental assets and lacks the means to make good the loss.

With the amnesia that has most in common with an armed hold-up of the memory some restoration may be possible. Electroshocks or a very hard blow to the skull can cause retrograde amnesia. Awakened from unconsciousness, the patient finds that a part of the past is gone. The one cut-off point is relatively clear: the moment of coming to. The other cut-off point is vague, the time it takes to recover varying with the seriousness of the injury. Recovery follows a fixed course first formulated by Ribot and since investigated more closely on the basis of case studies. The oldest memories, he wrote in *Les maladies de la mémoire*, are the first to return, memory loss shrinking from earlier to later. In memory loss caused by what he called 'senile dementia', the most recent memories go first and the oldest are the last to disappear. We must not form an oversimplified idea of that process, Ribot warned. 'It would be childish to assume that memories are laid down in the brain in layers, in accordance with their age, like archaeological strata, and that the illness, descending from the surface to the deeper layers, acts like an experimenter who removes the brain of an animal slice by slice.' He himself sought the explanation of what is nowadays called 'Ribot's law' in the stronger associative links between older memories that are often repeated and hence more closely linked with other memories. In current theories about the course of amnesia, the strength of associations is still an important hypothesis about the relative invulnerability of older memories. It has also been suggested that older memories are stored in a part of the brain that is less easily disturbed. The absence of memories of what happened just before the injury is said to indicate that the trauma has interfered with the chemical processes involved in the consolidation of memory traces.

In memory disorders that are not the result of such sudden attacks but seem to be a creeping invasion, something occasionally remains that is adequate for an apparently normal life. In a chapter on the effects of brain disorders on the memory, Daniel Schacter has described his experiences during a game of golf with Frederick, a man in his fifties with incipient Alzheimer's disease. Frederick had been a golfer for thirty years. During the two rounds they were playing, Schacter was impressed with what Frederick could still achieve: the quality of his strokes was in keeping with his handicap, he chose the correct clubs, managed his golf terms without difficulty, and spoke

enthusiastically about birdies. His golf etiquette too was beyond re-
proach: when his own ball was lying between the hole and Schacter's
ball, he picked it up, marked the spot with a coin and waited politely
until Schacter had finished. Finding the ball posed no problem for
Frederick: he hit the ball and followed behind. Halfway through the
first round, Schacter decided to make an experiment; he was a psychologist after all. He proposed to change the order of teeing off –
Frederick first, then himself. Immediately there were problems. The
time Frederick had to wait while Schacter was having his turn proved
just too long for him to remember where his own ball had ended
up. When they moved on after playing their strokes, Schacter had
to help him to find his ball. After the game, back in the clubhouse,
all memories of the game had been expunged and Frederick kept up
appearances by talking about such generalities as 'my putting today
wasn't great'. A week later, when Schacter fetched him for another
game, Frederick warned him not to expect too much: he hadn't been
on a golf course for months.

Memory failure causes holes, gaps, voids. No one can live with
a vacuum. Often it is refilled, not with memories but with made-up
stories. Korsakoff patients can tell you convincingly what allegedly
happened to them during the previous week: confabulation is one of
the characteristic symptoms of their syndrome. Some memory disorders can be 'felt' within, even if they do not lead to a void. You do not
miss much of what you have forgotten. Just as someone only discovers
during a visit to an ophthalmologist to what extent his visual field has
shrunk – you don't see any edges, after all – so a deterioration of the
memory sometimes does not come to light before a diagnostic test is
made. Routine, repetition, an environment in which you react in fixed
patterns, often continue to serve for a long time as the supporting
tissue of a memory that could barely be kept up with its own strength.

The first sign that all is not well is often a deterioration of a
form of memory directed at the future: the prospective memory, that
is the ability to remember what you were *about* to do. Even in healthy
people, this is a problematic form of recall: telling yourself, 'I musn't
forget...' sometimes looks like the secret code that ensures that you
*do* forget. In a more serious form, problems with one's plans, with
remembering one's intentions as well as with remembering in time
to carry them out, not only have a disorganizing effect on daily life

but are also sensitive indicators of decay and decline. For the sufferers themselves, memory loss is hard to bear, particularly during the initial phase. Patients with incipient Alzheimer's disease go through every stage between slight anxiety and downright panic once they realize that they no longer know what a healthy and normal person knows perfectly well. The prospect that ultimately you will forget all you have forgotten and that you won't miss it either, is no consolation, for it means that you will have ceased to exist as a person. Your nearest and dearest, too, cannot live with the emptiness of memory loss. What makes contact with close relatives who begin to lose their memory so painful is that the instruments needed for a conversation – words and the ability to understand them – remain intact for a long time, while feeling and depth vanish from what they have to say. References to shared experiences reveal that these experiences are not really shared. The words still mean what they used to mean but no longer elicit the same associations; no past resonates in them and it is a little like plucking strings that are no longer stretched over a sound box.

Even in the more serious stages of memory loss, when there is hardly any contact with the patient's own past or the surroundings, the conscious mind continues to make desperate attempts to find answers to what, in the circumstances, are the most pressing questions: where am I, who are those people, what is happening to me? A woman of eighty-three has been living in a nursing home ever since her husband's death. She is suffering from Alzheimer's disease and no longer remembers that her husband died eight years ago. When she is agitated, she writes letters to her husband.

Den Helder

My dear husband,

As you can see, here we are on holiday in Den Helder with the old folk from Alphen, and we're looking forward to spending a nice week here together. I just found the parting from you a very sad business, and I hope everything will turn out all right for us again in the end. We're here in Den Helder with the old folk from Alphen. I hope everything turns out all right for us in the end because parting like that was so sad. We didn't take that into account. It's a very nice crowd here. It's just that I thought it was sad to part so coldly. I hope that when I come home everything will be all right again. It was sad we had to part like that. It's very nice here, all of us together. There isn't much more to write, I just hope that we'll be in a better mood when I come home. It's very nice here, all of us together. Well, dear husband, there isn't much more to write and I hope to be back home in a week's time and hope that we'll be in a good mood then too. Well, dear husband, my thoughts are with you, believe me, and a big kiss from

Your still loving wife.

What is so touching about this letter, first of all, is the repetition. Quite obviously, her memory has left just a very small window of time open; everything that slips out reappears in less than a minute. Perhaps you cannot even call it a window; it is a narrow slit of at most two or three sentences. Also touching is *what* she keeps repeating. Why did the needle have to be stuck in so unhappy a groove? A few grooves earlier she possibly lived in perfect harmony with her husband; a few grooves further on and the quarrels will be forgotten. Or is this view of her memory naïve and a fitting memory has simply joined her disorientated feelings? Perhaps it is not even that; perhaps the cold parting from her husband is no memory at all, any more than her stay in the nursing home is a holiday. She is there without her husband in the exclusive company of old people and is disturbed for a reason she cannot understand herself: surely this must be an old people's outing and her husband will be waiting for her at home. What appears on paper are shreds of the past, repeated for just as long as it takes to fill the paper, and she can take her leave with a big kiss.

## BIBLIOGRAPHY

Achterberg, G., *Verzamelde gedichten*, Amsterdam, 1963.

Baddeley, A. D., *Human Memory: Theory and Practice*, Hove, 1990.

Bahrick, H. P., 'Semantic memory content in permastore: 50 years of memory for Spanish learned in school', *Journal of Experimental Psychology: General* 113 (1984), 1–29.

Brown, R., and D. McNeill, 'The "tip of the tongue" phenomenon', *Journal of Verbal Learning and Verbal Behavior* 5 (1966), 325–37.

James, W., *The Principles of Psychology*, New York, 1890.

Loftus, E. F., and G. R. Loftus, 'On the permanence of stored information in the human brain', *American Psychologist* 35 (1980), 409–20.

Ribot, T., 'La mémoire comme fait biologique', *Revue Philosophique* 9 (1880), 516–47.

*Les maladies de la mémoire* (1881). Quoted from *The Diseases of Memory*, London, 1882.

Schacter, D., *Searching for Memory: The Brain, the Mind, and the Past*, New York, 1996.

Sunderland, A., J. E. Harris and A. D. Baddeley, 'Do laboratory tests predict everyday memory?', *Journal of Verbal Learning and Verbal Behavior* 22 (1983), 341–57.

Wagenaar, W. A., 'My memory: a study of autobiographical memory over six years', *Cognitive Psychology* 18 (1986), 225–52.

# 16 'I saw my life flash before me'

In 1836 the German physicist and philosopher Gustav Fechner (1801–87) published a comforting theory on what awaits us after death. He confided his ideas in the *Büchlein vom Leben nach dem Tode* – 'The little book about life after death'. About halfway through the text Fechner discusses the limitations of man's intellect during his life on earth. In normal life consciousness can accommodate just one thought and one memory at the same time. We can never access the entire contents of our mind all at once. Our powers of recall can only be in one place at a time; if we want to bring something to mind we have, so to speak, to search our memory with a feeble lantern that throws light in a narrow beam and leaves the rest in the dark. Man thus wanders about like a stranger in his own mind, 'feeling his way as if along a wire, and ignoring the large shadows that lie buried in the darkness beside the illumined path of his thoughts'.

This is a poignant picture. There is also something depressing about it: a slowly moving pool of light, lost in an enormous repository. That which enters the circle of light of our consciousness always stands on its own and as soon as our thoughts move on it returns to darkness. The edges of the circle of light are sharply defined; anything that falls just outside them is as dark as the furthest object. We have no idea of the things we brush past with our lantern. According to Fechner this all changes when we die. The moment our eyes are shut to the outside world and we suppose that eternal night is about to descend upon us, the light will in fact be beginning to shine in our inner world. We shall be able at a glance to take stock of everything that has ever interested us, everything we have stored in our memory. During the moments just before death we already have an inkling of that, Fechner states. As we look back on life, memories return that had seemed completely lost. People who are about to drown experience 'a brightness suddenly lighting up the contents of our mind'.

What Fechner was writing about is often described nowadays by the phrase 'I saw my life flash before me like a film.' Quite a few accounts have been written over the years about people who have had near-death experiences and saw a series of images pass quickly before their mind's eye in what they thought were their final moments. These incidents include near-drowning, but also falling from great heights or other last-minute escapes by people who lived to tell the tale. In 1825, at the request of the English naturalist Dr W. Hyde Wollaston, Rear Admiral Sir Francis Beaufort (1774–1857) described in a letter what he experienced in 1795 as a young sailor when he fell into the water in Portsmouth harbour and was in danger of drowning. During the agitation of drowning, Beaufort granted, he may have been too occupied

to mark the succession of events very accurately. Not so however with the facts which immediately ensued; my mind had then undergone the sudden revolution which appeared to you so remarkable – and all the circumstances of which are now as vividly fresh in my memory as if they had occurred but yesterday.

From the moment that all exertion had ceased ... a calm feeling of the most perfect tranquillity superseded the previous tumultuous sensations – it might be called apathy, certainly not resignation, for drowning no longer appeared to be an evil. I no longer thought of being rescued, nor was I in any bodily pain. On the contrary, my sensations were now of a rather pleasurable cast, partaking of that dull, but contented sort of feeling which precedes the sleep produced by fatigue. Though the senses were ... deadened, not so the mind; its activity seemed to be invigorated, in a ratio which defies all description, for thought rose after thought with a rapidity of succession that is not only indescribable, but probably inconceivable by any one who had not himself been in a similar situation. The course of those thoughts I can even now in a great measure retrace – the event which had just taken place, the awkwardness that had produced it [Beaufort had been sculling about in a small boat and, on returning to his ship, attempted to fasten his cockleshell to one of the scuttle-rings. 'In foolish eagerness I stepped upon the gunwale, the boat of course upset, and I fell into the water ... '], the bustle it must

240

have occasioned (for I had observed two persons jump from the chains), the effect it would have on a most affectionate father, the manner in which he would disclose it to the rest of the family, and a thousand other circumstances minutely associated with home, were the first series of reflections that occurred. They then took a wider range – our last cruise, a former voyage, and shipwreck, my school, the progress I had made there and the time I had mis-spent, and even all my boyish pursuits and adventures. Thus travelling backwards, every past incident of my life seemed to glance across my recollection in retrograde succession; not, however, in mere outline, as here stated, but the picture filled up with every minute and collateral feature. In short, the whole period of my existence seemed to be placed before me in a kind of panoramic review, and each act of it seemed to be accompanied by a consciousness of right and wrong, or by some reflection on its cause or its consequences; indeed, many trifling events which had been long forgotten, then crowded into my imagination, and with the character of recent familiarity...One circumstance was highly remarkable; that the innumerable ideas which flashed into my mind were all retrospective...I had been religiously brought up...yet at that inexplicable moment, when I had a full conviction that I had already crossed the threshold, not a single thought wandered into the future – I was wrapt up entirely in the past. The length of time that was occupied by this deluge of ideas, or rather the shortness of time into which they were condensed, I cannot now state with precision, yet certainly two minutes could not have elapsed from the moment of my suffocation to that of being hauled up.

Beaufort ended his report to Dr Wollaston with a courteous line: 'If these *involuntary experiments* on the operation of death afford any satisfaction or interest to you, they will not have been suffered quite in vain by Yours very truly, F. Beaufort.'

Beaufort was rescued at the last moment and went on to gain immortality with his windforce scale.

Can a report like this be trusted? Or was Beaufort simply repeating what his biographer, A. Friendly, termed 'the folklore of a

Fig. 25   Daguerrotype of Sir Francis Beaufort (1774–1857).

drowning man's total recall'? That seems unlikely. In his capacity of 'the King's Hydrographer', Beaufort had a passion for accuracy; in his profession, precision and reliability were defining values. His report to the celebrated Dr Wollaston was intended as a contribution to science, and as such was not taken lightly by him. Although Beaufort was a believer, he did not seize the chance of presenting what had befallen him as a religious experience; rather he seemed astonished that his mind should have turned resolutely to the past instead of to the imminent future of life after death. And last but not least, much of what befell Beaufort agrees with reports written later that were independent of his own account.

Nearly every line in his report raises questions. Why the rapid succession of thoughts? How was Beaufort able to recall the long series of images years later? Why did his thoughts first run 'forward' to the effect of the news of his death on his father and then resolutely 'backwards' to his past life? Why did his memory project his life in reverse order? Was it really a review of 'the whole period' of his existence? Can that also be reconciled with remembering 'trifling events' and 'every minute and collateral feature'? And why was it that

242

all his actions were accompanied by a sense of right and wrong, of their motives and consequences? His account also raises the question of whether certain constants can be found in all such reports. Does the sequence of events always 'travel back in time' as it did with Beaufort, or is it sometimes in chronological order? *Is* there always a sequence of events? Is it always images that people on the point of death recall or do they also have non-visual memories at times? Are words used in the review of one's life? Does the cause of the mortal danger make a difference? Is there a difference between the experiences of people who fall and those who deliberately jump from great heights? Does the experience of a rapid review of their life also happen to people who are not in mortal danger?

Underlying all these questions is the further problem of the *representation* of the experience. Beaufort's report makes it clear that he has suffered something completely outside his normal experience. It follows that, while writing his report, he had to find words for something quite beyond his own powers of imagination. That too is a constant in all the accounts: the author's frustration that he has to conjure up a language to describe a series of happenings that occurred outside the usual course of time. This is the point at which the reports resort to metaphors. Fechner suddenly casts an all-pervading light into the storehouse of the memory; Beaufort sees his life in a 'panoramic review'. The expression 'I saw my life flash before me like a film' is a metaphor. English technical literature speaks of 'panoramic memory', a name introduced in 1928 by the English neurologist S. A. Kinnier Wilson.

The experience of panoramic memory is fleeting and unforgettable at the same time. The conditions of the experience preclude experimental studies. Yet a surprising amount of work has been devoted to it. Psychiatrists have questioned people who have jumped off high bridges. Physicians have examined people who have had a near-fatal accident, had been on the point of drowning or had been shot. Research has been done into psychiatric and neurological disorders capable of producing a similar series of images. The study of neuropharmacological substances has also revealed interesting parallels with the time experience involved in panoramic memory. But as a sign of respect it is only fitting that we begin with the first systematic study of experiences during moments of mortal danger. It was done by a scientist with personal experience of the subject, the Swiss geologist Albert Heim (1849–1937).

## The fall of Albert Heim

In the spring of 1871, Albert Heim, accompanied by his brother and three friends, went climbing in the Säntis mountains, east of Zurich. Heim, though only twenty-one years old, was already an experienced mountaineer. He had been keen on geology since early youth. When he was sixteen, he built a prize-winning relief model of the Tödi mountains. He studied geology at Zurich University, and five days after this climb was due to deliver an inaugural lecture to mark his appointment as *Privatdozent*, an unsalaried university lecturer, in geology. Heim was the leader of the mountaineering party. The five men were above the Fehlalp at a height of 5,900 feet in a heavy snowstorm when they reached the shoulder of a steeply descending layer of snow. The others hesitated, but Heim decided to start the descent. The accident happened almost immediately. Heim wrote:

> Then a draught blew off my hat and instead of letting it go, I impulsively made the mistake of grabbing for it. This movement caused me to fall and to be unable to govern my direction. Propelled by the wind, I dove toward the leftward crag-point, rebounded from the crag-face, sailed back-first and with my head downwards over the crag. At the last I flew freely through the air about 66 feet until I landed on the border of snow under the wall of the crag.
>
> As soon as I began to fall I realized that now I was going to be hurled from the crag and I anticipated the impact that would come. With clawing fingers I dug into the snow in an effort to brake myself. My fingertips were bloody but I felt no pain. I heard clearly the blows on my head and back as they hit each corner of the crag and I heard a dull thud as I struck below. But I first felt pain some hours afterward. The earlier mentioned flood of thoughts began during the fall. What I felt in five to ten seconds could not be described in ten times that length of time. All my thoughts were coherent and very clear, and in no way susceptible, as are dreams, to

obliteration. First of all I took in the possibilities of my fate and said to myself, 'the crag point over which I will soon be thrown evidently falls off below me as a steep wall since I have not been able to see the ground at the base of it. It matters a great deal whether or not snow is still lying at the base of the cliff wall. If this is the case, the snow will have melted from the wall and formed a border around the base. If I fall on the border of snow I may come out of this with my life, but if there is no more snow there, I am certain to fall on rubble and at this velocity death will be quite inevitable. If, when I strike, I am not dead or unconscious I must instantly seize my small flask of spirits of vinegar and put some drops from it on my tongue. I do not want to let go of my alpenstock; perhaps it can still be of use to me.' Hence I kept it tightly in my hand. I thought of taking off my glasses and throwing them away so that the splinters from them might not injure my eyes, but I was so thrown and swung about that I could not muster the power to move my hands for this purpose. A set of thought and ideas then ensued concerning those left behind. I said to myself that upon landing below I ought, indifferent to whether or not I were seriously injured, to immediately call to my companions out of affection for them to say, 'I'm all right!'. Then my brother and three friends could sufficiently recover from their shock so as to accomplish the fairly difficult descent to me. My next thought was that I would not be able to give my opening university lecture that had been announced for five days later. I considered how the news of my death would arrive for my loved ones and I consoled them in my thoughts. Then I saw my whole past life take place in many images, as though on a stage at some distance from me. I saw myself as the chief character in the performance. Everything was transfigured as though by a heavenly light and everything was beautiful without grief, without anxiety, and without pain. The memory of very tragic experiences I had had was clear but not saddening. I felt no conflict or strife; conflict had been transmuted into love. Elevated and harmonious thoughts dominated and united the individual images, and like magnificent music a

divine calm swept through my soul. I became ever more surrounded by a splendid blue heaven with delicate roseate and
violet cloudlets. I swept into it painlessly and softly and I saw
that now I was falling freely through the air and that under
me a snow field lay waiting. Objective observations, thoughts
and subjective feelings were simultaneous. Then I heard a dull
thud and my fall was over.

In moments a black object whisked away from my
eyes and I shouted to my companions three or four times 'I'm
all right!' I took some of the spirits of vinegar, I grasped my
glasses that lay unbroken next to me in the snow, and I felt
my back and limbs to confirm that no bones had been broken.
Then I saw my companions, who already appeared quite near
me, hewing their way slowly step by step to reach me in the
corridor of snow beneath the crag-point off which I had flown.
I could not understand why they were still so far away. But
they told me that for fully a half hour I had made no reply to
their calls. It was at this point that I first realized that I had
lost consciousness upon impact. The black object had been
unconsciousness that evidently had registered in perception
a fraction of a second after it had been effected in my brain;
and without my observing the interruption, my thoughts and
activities had gone on just as they had before. In between
there had been subjective absolute nothingness. I experienced
the lovely, heavenly representations only as long as I still flew
through the air and could see and think. With the loss of
consciousness upon impact they, too, were suddenly erased
and afterwards no longer continued. After my friend, Andreas
Anton Dorig, had set me on my feet I was able to move. Many
screams, however, were torn from me by pain in my head and
from bruises on my back until, wrapped in ice coverings, I was
carried to the Meglisalp. Even so, I gave my opening lecture
at the previously agreed-on time.

Quite certainly it is incomparably more painful, both
in the feeling of the moment and subsequent recollection to
see another person fall than to fall oneself. This is attested to
by innumerable narratives. Often the spectator, incapacitated
by paralysing horror and quaking in body and soul, carries

Fig. 26   Albert Heim (1849–1937) shortly before his seventieth birthday.

away from the experience a lasting trauma, while the person whose fall was watched, if he is not badly injured, comes away from his experience free of fright and pain. To be sure there soon follow subsequent reactions of severe headache and immense fatigue. I have seen others fall several times though I have not seen them fall to their deaths. But these memories remain ever dreadful. I must even testify that the memory of a cow's fall is still painful for me, while my own misfortune is registered in memory as a pleasant transfiguration without pain and without anguish – just as it actually had been experienced.

## 'Falling into heaven'

Albert Heim was taken aback by what he experienced during his fall. He had expected mortal fear, panic or distress, but certainly not his sudden lucidity of mind as he weighed up his chances of survival and serenely watched his life pass before him. In the years that followed, he tried to track down other case of people who had been in life-threatening danger but had survived. For more than twenty years he asked people, face to face and in letters, about their last moments before they lost consciousness. After his appointment to the chair of geology at Zurich University in 1875, he conducted large-scale geodetic projects in the Alps, which brought him into regular contact with fellow climbers. Some had survived a fall just as he had. He also questioned roofers, bricklayers who had fallen off high scaffolding, and workers who had been involved in accidents while laying railway track high up in the mountains. Heim did not confine himself to acute life-threatening danger caused by a fall. He spoke to survivors of the mountain railway disaster on the Mönchenstein, went to a military hospital in Hamburg to seek out soldiers who had been badly wounded in the Franco-Prussian war of 1870, and interviewed a fisherman who had nearly drowned. In 1892, Heim presented his findings in a lecture to fellow climbers.

Heim started with a tricky question: how can we tell what someone experienced during the last moments of his life when they were not really his last moments? In the end, we can only question survivors and for them those moments were not the last. Heim felt that this was not a valid objection. Unconsciousness followed by death does not differ from unconsciousness followed by miraculous rescue, except that in the second case it is possible to tell what preceded unconsciousness. Someone in that situation 'will have died twice in his life'. And so, he returned to the question: what does someone feel just before he dies? According to the testimony gathered by Heim, almost everybody, regardless of education, was thrown into the same state of mind by a sudden fall. That state resembled what Heim himself had experienced: no dread, no regret, no confusion, no pain; no one felt the paralysing fear that can accompany less acute life-threatening danger, as, for instance, during a fire. Thinking became a hundred times as rapid and intense. Events and their consequences were surveyed with objective clarity. Time stood still. Often there followed a sudden review of the survivor's entire past and finally the falling person heard glorious music. 'Then consciousness was painlessly extinguished, usually at the moment of impact, and the impact was, at the most, heard but never painfully felt. Apparently hearing is the last of the senses to be extinguished.'

The clarity of mind during the fall conflicts with the belief that people lose consciousness before they land. Heim's fellow mountaineer Sigrist, who had fallen over backwards from the top of the Kärpfstock, insisted that he could think and see things clearly until the last moment: 'Without pain or anxiety I surveyed my situation, the future of my family, and the arrangements I had already made for their security with a rapidity of which I had never before been capable. There was no trace of the loss of breath that people often speak of, and I painlessly lost consciousness only upon the most powerful impact on the cushion of snow covering the crag below.' A man who had fallen off a 72 foot high rocky peak at the age of eight reported that he had turned three or four somersaults in the air and had been worried that the pocket knife his father had given him would fall out of his trouser pocket. A theology student who made a train journey and, after the collapse of the bridge across the Birs, was in danger of being crushed by the carriages that fell on top of his own, wrote to Heim that in the midst of all the pandemonium of splintering wood, 'I had a whole flood of thoughts that went through my brain in the clearest way' and that 'a series of pictures showed me in rapid succession everything beautiful and lovable that I had ever experienced'.

What was common to all of Heim's reports, his own included, was the clarity and peacefulness of the experience. Not a single person cried out in terror during his fall, no one was in despair because his life would be over in a few moments. 'Those of our friends who have died in the mountains have, in their last moments, reviewed their individual pasts in states of transfiguration.' Their loved ones could take solace from that fact. At the end of his lecture, Heim told his listeners that his discoveries had helped to reconcile a mother who had lost two sons in a fatal fall in the mountains. 'Reconcilement and redeeming peace were the last feelings with which they had taken leave of the world and they had, so to speak, fallen into Heaven. In spirit, dear comrades, we lay a wreath on the graves of those who have died in falls!'

## When the unconscious takes over

In 1929 Heim was asked by his fellow townsman Oskar Pfister to answer a few more questions about his fall. Heim was by now eighty years old but was still busy with geological publications. Although the fall had happened sixty years before, Heim wrote a lengthy reply, giving as many further details as possible. Pfister (1873–1956) was a theologian. He was an old friend of Freud's and had applied psycho-analysis to pastoral care as a clergyman. He himself had had two near-fatal accidents while mountaineering. On both occasions he had been able to save his own life, the first time by grasping a branch at the last moment and the second time by driving his pick quickly into the ice. He, too, had had the experience of thoughts rushing by at lightning speed: first, an incredulous, 'This can't be true; you're imagining that you're falling'; then a correct assessment of the situation ('It's true, I am falling'), followed by the life-saving action. Pfister wrote up the experiences of Heim and an officer whom he had had in analysis for some time after he was nearly killed in action in an article on what he called 'shock-thinking'.

Asked about the sequence of his feelings, Heim replied that he could not give it precisely: 'I believe that it was almost instan-taneous. I can perhaps compare it best to rapidly projected images or with the rapid sequence of dream images.' Later in the letter he added, 'I saw the images as though projected on a wall. One gave way to another, but all without haste, in a pleasing sequence and with copious changings, without any emotional interruptions. I felt as though the seconds were practically five minutes.' Heim wondered if the series of images might have become regressive upon his fall, 'and because of that the images of my school days would have been a portion of this thread of thoughts. But I don't think so. When I think back to that minute, it seems to me that the theatrical performance of my life began with school and ended with the fall backwards into emptiness or sky.' At Pfister's request he also wrote in greater detail about *what kind* of images he had seen:

As though I looked out of the window of a high house, I saw myself as a seven-year old boy going to school (the old school house, city of Zurich, 'in Kratz'), then I saw myself in the classroom of my beloved teacher, Weisz, in 4th grade. I acted out my life, as though I were an actor on a stage, upon which I looked down as though from practically the highest gallery in the theatre. Both hero and onlooker, I was as though doubled. I saw myself industriously working in the sketching studio of the Canton school, in matriculating examinations, making a mountain journey, modeling on my Tödi-relief, sketching my first panorama from Zurichberg. My sisters and especially my wonderful mother, who was so important in my life, were around me. Suddenly, through the images of the moment, there came the thought: 'In the next moment I will be dead.' Then I saw a telegram or letter messenger who gave my mother, at the door to her house, the notice of my death. She and the older members of my family took the news with the deepest sorrow, but with an elevatedly pious greatness of soul; no complaining, no wailing, no weeping, just as I myself felt no trace of anxiety or pain, but went to death matter-of-factly and without anxiety.

Pfister did not analyse Heim's experiences. Instead he discussed those of a man aged forty-five who had, thirteen years before, during the First World War, been put in mortal danger by an exploding shell (mention was made of this man in the chapter on déjà vu). Pfister based his theory on what the officer who had nearly been killed in action told him about his 'last' moments, and used Heim's experiences as confirmation. Following the explosion, the officer had seen a series of images, among them one of himself at about two years old riding in a small cart of some sort, and ending with an image of his travelling in a car or a train through magnificent scenery, feeling that he was living a wonderful life. The first memory was one the man himself could not place; later his mother told him that as a toddler he regularly took rides in a cart drawn by their dog. The ride would sometimes take him a kilometre from home, without anyone accompanying him. The man added that he himself would never allow a child to go so far from home without supervision. After this explanation, Pfister ventured an interpretation along psychoanalytic lines.

The image of a toddler being driven about in a cart seems totally irrelevant at first sight. However, the mother's confirmation of the story suggests an explanation. He was in some danger in the cart at the time. The dog might have been attacked by another dog, or could have been frightened by a passing carriage. But something or somebody had protected him against danger. After the explosion in the trench, the man's unconscious sought a parallel that, by means of a transparent analogy – you were in danger then, yet nothing happened to you; you are in danger now and you will be protected again – brought solace in a moment of life-threatening danger. All the man remembered consciously was the toddler in his little cart; he could not even remember the dog – it was the unconscious that lent the event its emotional significance.

According to Pfister, incidentally, the last image of riding through magnificent scenery agrees with Heim's last images: while the mountaineer had the feeling that he was floating in a blue sky with roseate clouds, the officer passed through a paradisiacal landscape. Both were free of anxiety and grief; everything felt delightful and pleasant. Their last images, in short, belied the hideous danger in which they found themselves and were selected by their unconscious expressly to distract them from an unbearable reality.

The question – which Pfister put to himself – is why the human mind behaves in this particular way. Where do the speeding up of thoughts, the review of the past and the sense of intense peace come from? Pfister thought that the answer lay in Freud's idea of the 'stimulus barrier'. Much as our senses are protected against too powerful stimuli, so the mind has a way of defending itself from too powerful mental stimuli. One of these ways is 'de-realization', the feeling that the situation in which one happens to be is not real. Pfister mentioned the case of a mountaineer who saw his friend fall to his death.

As he saw his friend lying prone, bleeding from mouth and nose, and rattling in his throat, he laughed to himself, 'It doesn't matter, it just seems this way; it is only a dream.' Afterwards, he waited for a full hour and wandered far from

252

the corpse, his mind dimmed, and he repeatedly asked his companion, 'Where is Fischer? There were three of us!' Only after the leader told him that Fischer was dead did he begin to feel the pain from fractures of his sternum and ribs.'

Pfister himself felt the same kind of de-realization – 'this can't be true' – for a short time during his two near-falls. That Heim saw his life being played out on a stage as if from a distance was a similar means of warding off too powerful stimuli.

According to Pfister, the stimulus barrier has a biological function. The enormous speeding up of thoughts wards off the normal reactions of fear and dread – and their paralysing effects on our actions. The flood of ideas and the review of one's past life spare the man who is falling, drowning, crashing or being shot from the traumatic reality of a rapidly approaching death. At the same time they prevent the victim from losing consciousness; were he actually to faint, any form of life-saving action would be in vain. What people experience during their last moments is therefore the result of a protective barrier which acts in two ways: to prevent paralysing panic, reality is stripped of its frightening character, and in order to prevent loss of consciousness the unconscious stages a comforting make-believe act. If conscious thought cannot provide a solution despite its immensely accelerated tempo, then the unconscious takes over.

Towards the end of his article Pfister slipped more and more into the personifications and political metaphors in which Freud also excelled. In sudden mortal danger, consciousness must put up with one humiliation after another; it is impotent, 'like a banished king subsisting only on scanty, unintelligible news from his former land; who having given up his kingship, must play a passive role while awaiting help from fortune'. This reminds consciousness that 'even in the political life of the individual soul there is no such thing as absolute despotism'. To Pfister, therefore, 'Freud's psychology is democratic.'

The idea of panoramic memory as a takeover by the unconscious conjures up a ticklish problem, to which Pfister himself drew attention. If certain perceptions and ideas have to make way for consolation and reassurance because of their traumatic character, then somewhere in our mind the danger of these perceptions must nevertheless have been grasped. Pfister explained that this 'somewhere' was the preconscious. It is aware of the threat, but tries to keep it out of consciousness. Like a devoted secretary, it intercepts unwelcome visitors in the waiting room and sends them packing. Or, to use another metaphor, the preconscious is the doorman who protects the hotel guests from intruders, but cannot, alas, save them completely from their noisy presence. The conscious hears nothing but a distant noise. It deludes itself into thinking that it is safe, has no knowledge of approaching death. It spends its last moments in a pleasant delusion.

## Metaphors

The older accounts of panoramic memory strike the reader as having a somewhat rustic quality. They concern the sort of accidents that reflect the daily life of nineteenth-century man: a horse shies without warning and all the passengers in the carriage land in the water; a boy drawing water falls down the well. Our age has new types of mortal danger: aeroplanes crashing, parachutes failing to open, the threat of head-on collisions. Last-minute rescues have also taken on new forms. People survive acute cardiac arrest thanks to modern equipment. Others are given an injection that neutralizes the effect of an overdose just in time. Whether the experience of panoramic memory has been changed as well is impossible to say. The conscious is a theatre with a single seat, and what is being performed in another's theatre is something we only know at second hand. What has certainly been changed is the language in which panoramic memory is described. The experience itself may be timeless but the metaphors people use to convey their experience to others are the products of their own age. Even without knowing that Dr Forbes Winslow wrote his book 'on the obscure diseases of the brain' in the 1860s, it is not hard to date descriptions such as the following as having been written after the invention of photography but before the invention of cinematography:

> It has occurred, that persons in the act of drowning ... have had presented to their minds, whilst in the agonies of death, a series of striking *tableaux* of the most minute and remarkable occurrences of their past lives! ... Events associated with the period of childhood have been, under these circumstances,

recalled to the mind, and presented to it like so many exquis- itely executed artistic photographic representations.

In older accounts, too, written before the advent of photography, we find metaphors emphasizing the visual character of the experience. In 1821, De Quincey wrote in his *Confessions of an English Opium-Eater* about a young relative who had fallen into a river. On the verge of drowning, 'she saw in a moment her whole life, in its minutest inci- dents, arrayed before her simultaneously as in a mirror; and she had a faculty developed as suddenly for comprehending the whole and every part'. De Quincey fully trusted in her testimony, for she 'reverenced truth no less than did the Evangelists' and had 'a masculine under- standing'. Francis Beaufort compared his experience to a 'panoramic review', a metaphor that, at the time, was relatively new. The first circular painting that could be viewed from the centre was patented in 1787. In the patent, that type of painting still had no proper name; the term 'panorama' (from 'pan' meaning all and 'horama' meaning view) did not come into use until about 1800. Panorama in the sense of an extensive and unbroken view of a landscape *followed* the advent of the painted panoramas. When Beaufort wrote his report, in 1825, the panorama was still a relatively recent metaphor for a wide view that could be taken in at a glance.

More recent accounts compare the panoramic memory with a host of visual media. A motorcyclist who was on the point of head-on collision on a dimly lit road compared his experience to a hectic slide show, a series of loose images projected at a very fast pace. A man who survived a jump with a parachute that failed to open said that it seemed as if his head was a computer and that someone was feeding it the images of a lifetime in just a few seconds. A severely wounded Vietnam soldier remembered that his life unfolded like a very fast computer. But these metaphors are all – in a sense – exceptions; by far the most common metaphor in recent descriptions of panoramic memory is *film* and its associated terms like flashback, replay and slow motion. The following examples are taken from surveys of near-death experiences:

- 'During the instant *replay* of my life I lost track of time...'
- Memories passed by as though 'on a *film sprung loose* from the camera'.

- Only memories of warm relationships 'were selected for *slow motion*'.
- 'Like in *a swift film* each picture appeared in quick succession, framed and distinct.'
- '*Very fast movie*. Just highlights, just certain things.'
- 'It was *like a picture*, it was *like a movie camera* running across your eyes.'

These are just a few examples. Clearly, film metaphors have a mesmerizing appeal. In fact, this was already demonstrated by Albert Heim, whose fall in the Alps led to such a detailed report. Thanks to Pfister, who asked Heim to answer some further questions on his experience during the fall, we have two reports by Heim, one pre-film and one post-film. In 1892, Heim wrote that he saw his life 'in many images, as though on a stage at some distance from me'. In his 1929 report he still stuck to his theatrical metaphor, but he now added that he could perhaps 'best compare it to rapidly projected images' and that he saw 'the images as though projected on a wall'.

We should not be surprised. Film is a metaphor that excellently evokes both the visual nature of panoramic memory and the sensation that the images are seen from the outside. When someone says that his life 'flashed by like a film', he is activating a dense network of associations. Films have a relationship with the passage of time at many levels. The projection of films may be speeded up or slowed down – both affect the emotional colour of scenes. Even when projected at a natural speed, films may still be 'slow' or 'fast' due to the editing. Films may respect the chronology of events or breach it by means of flashbacks and flash-forwards. Aspects of panoramic memory that have to do with the subjective speed and direction of time will find a most natural expression in film metaphors.

In the final scene of the film *American Beauty* (1999), these various layers of time are subtly manipulated. *American Beauty* chronicles, roughly speaking, the midlife crisis of forty-two-year-old Lester Burnham, played by Kevin Spacey. Towards the end of the film he is shot in the head by one of the other characters. After the sound of the shot has echoed away, all is quiet. Then a piano begins to play, slowly and softly, a violin joins in, and we hear a voice-over, Lester's voice, saying: 'I had always heard your entire life flashes in front of your eyes the second before you die. First of all, that one second isn't a second at all, it stretches on forever, like an ocean of time. For me it was: lying on my back in boy-scout camp watching falling stars. And yellow leaves from the maple trees that blind our street. Or my grandmother's hands and the way her skin seemed like paper.' Meanwhile the camera pans over scenes in black and white: a boy lying on his back, maple trees, a pair of wrinkled hands: a series of disconnected images passing very slowly, suggesting this one second had indeed become an ocean of time.

There is something strangely cyclical about scenes like these. Peaceful episodes from someone's past, slow motion, flashbacks, black-and-white scenes, eerie light – this is all film-language to express the fact that someone is dying. The metaphor of film for the experience of panoramic memory has *itself* become a cinematographic convention. This involves a twofold risk. Metaphors that become commonplace tend to have a unifying effect on the way people describe their experience and perhaps also on the way they see their experience in retrospect. The metaphor of the film selects – as does any metaphor – its own specific set of associations, thereby organizing its own perspective. Perhaps we should be sensitive to the possibility that this particular cinematographic convention may in turn shape the way people look back on an experience for which it is so hard to find words. The second risk is that the new metaphor may eclipse specific aspects. If there are features of panoramic memory that *cannot* be expressed in terms of film, they may silently slip from the description. An example would be the sensation that all memories seem to be present simultaneously, all at once. This experience would fit in De Quincey's metaphor of memories 'arrayed as in a mirror' and also in Beaufort's 'panoramic review', but not in a sequential metaphor like the film.

## Statistics of panoramic memory

On a much larger scale, similar effects seem to occur in accounts of more recent near-death experiences. After the publication of *Life after Life* (1975) by the American physician Raymond Moody, a canon of near-death experiences emerged very quickly. Moody collected a large number of accounts by people who had been resuscitated after cardiac arrest or who had been clinically dead for some time during an operation. According to Moody, the similarities in the experience – feelings of being at peace, entering a tunnel, release from the body, meeting a luminous being, the decision to return to life – reflect a universal pattern during the process of dying. One stage in this process, according to Moody, is the 'life review', which he situated between the meeting with the luminous being and the return to life. With the help of the luminous figure, the nearly dead person is shown images of his life, a display that is accompanied by the feeling that the balance of his life is being drawn. According to Moody, many reports about panoramic memory resemble a calm review of one's life, with the luminous being as an element that did not appear in any of the older accounts. In his influence on the language in which people express panoramic memory, Moody was nearly as influential as the Lumière brothers.

The stereotypical near-death experience was borne into the collective consciousness on the wave of eastern mysticism towards the end of the 1970s. The literature that followed *Life after Life* is oceanic in compass and consists predominantly of endless reports of meetings with beings said to reside in the beyond. During the same period, various, more systematic studies of near-death experiences were carried out. Most of these studies were made by cardiologists, psychiatrists and clinical psychologists, whose professional work gave them access to people who had been close to death. Questionnaires and interviews yielded so many reports about panoramic memory that a few tentative conclusions can be drawn about the frequency of, and the links with, such variables as age, sex, type of life-threatening danger, and so on. The psychologist Kenneth Ring collected 102 cases of people who had been in mortal danger. The circumstances varied: serious illnesses (52), serious accident, near-drowning or falls (26), attempted suicides (24). Twelve persons reported panoramic memory. Ten of them had been in unexpected and unintentional life-threatening danger. Life-threatening danger following a suicide attempt led to panoramic memory in just one case. These findings agree with those of an investigation by the psychiatrist David Rosen. He interrogated seven people who had jumped off the Golden Gate bridge and survived. (Those who jump off the bridge, Susan Blackmore has calculated, hit the surface of the water with a speed of 120 km per hour after a drop of

75 metres. Only 1 per cent of them survive.) None had had a panoramic memory experience. It would seem that such an experience is only brought about by acute but unsought mortal danger.

The American psychiatrist Russell Noyes, Jr. and the clinical psychologist Roy Kletti interviewed or took questionnaires from over 200 persons who had encountered life-threatening danger. They distinguished the causes of life-threatening danger more widely than Ring had done: falls (57), automobile accidents (54), drownings (48), serious illnesses (27) and various other accidents (29). Sixty persons said that they had experienced panoramic memory. Age seemed to make a difference: those under twenty had a significantly greater chance of experiencing panoramic memory than older people. The same applied to the speeding up of thought. In that respect Beaufort and Heim – aged seventeen and twenty-one – were representative of that age group. Noyes and Kletti also asked their respondents whether they had believed that they were about to die at the time of mortal danger. This is far from obvious: some people do not think about life and death at such times or are certain that they will come out alive. The belief that death was inevitable within a few moments turned out to be an important consideration. People with that belief reported four times as many cases of panoramic memory as the rest. Feelings of understanding, happiness and detachment were more common among them as well. Finally, the cause of the life-threatening danger made a difference. Near-drowning produced the largest number of cases reporting panoramic memory (43 per cent), followed by car accidents (33 per cent) and by an unexpected fall (9 per cent). This last finding is hard to reconcile with Heim's claim that almost all falling mountaineers had experienced panoramic memory. That near-drowning creates favourable conditions for experiencing panoramic memory was also the impression that Ring gained from his material.

These reports revealed constants as well as differences. For every subject, panoramic memory was a predominantly visual experience. The images were clear and detailed. Everyone saw them 'outside' and felt like a spectator. No one thought he had any influence on the choice of the tempo with which the images appeared; people watched them obsessively but passively. The images generally evoked pleasant emotions. Many youthful memories occurred, and people often saw themselves as part of the action. The differences were mainly due to the sequence of events in time. Some remembered a backward course, others a chronological sequence. With some, the images merged seamlessly; to others it seemed as if isolated images jerkily succeeded one another. Not everyone saw pictures from the past alone; some saw flash-forwards as clear as their memories and nearly always including the sadness of their dearest and nearest.

## Explanations

As early as the 1860s, Winslow drew attention to the consoling force of childhood memories during the last moments of life. On their deathbeds, old people sometimes think they are back amidst the friends of their youth:

> How often the mind, during the last struggle with life, is busily occupied in the contemplation of pastoral imagery and pleasant early remembrances, associated with the innocent recreations and unmatched beauties of country life! All the unsophisticated aspirations, and fond reminiscences of the youthful fancy appear, occasionally, at this awful crisis, to gush back to the heart in all their original beauty, freshness, and purity!

Panoramic memory, he believed, might well be an accelerated version of the natural process, imposed by suddenly approaching death. Noyes and Kletti's hypothesis is of a similar kind. They, too, were struck by the peaceful character of the images and the many memories of a safe and happy youth. It was precisely the contrast between the images and the life-threatening reality that served them as an indication that panoramic memory has a vital biological function. In that sense it is said to resemble 'depersonalization', an adaptive reaction serving to protect consciousness against panic and disintegration in traumatic circumstances. Depersonalization is accompanied by distorted time perception, the speeding up of thought, a sense of detachment, the impression of suddenly standing outside reality and being a spectator of one's own actions (cf. pp. 156–8). For Noyes and Kletti, the similarities were so suggestive that they treated panoramic memory as a special case of depersonalization. Panoramic memory proffers the safety of a timeless sphere in which death does not seem to exist. The threatened person seems to split into separate parts instantaneously. One part appears in the scenes he remembers; the other part looks on like a disinterested third party. In that way there arises the sense of detachment that helps to keep mortal fear effectively at bay.

The detachment hypothesis has much in common with Pfister's idea of a subconscious takeover. The underlying idea, too, that it is an instinctive biological reaction agrees with this view. However, that the depersonalization hypothesis adds a new factor has not been widely accepted. With depersonalization, the images are in fact lifeless and pale, and if they elicit any feeling it is mainly one of indifference, while the detachment that goes with the experience of panoramic memory stems from the comforting feeling that all is well.

Towards the end of the nineteenth century, the neurologist Hughlings Jackson devised a new theory about the origins of hallucinations, a theory that is nowadays also proffered as an explanation of panoramic memory. The human brain is barely able to cope with the absence of sensory stimuli. If the senses are disabled or stunned by monotonous stimuli, and the external supply of stimuli is eliminated, then the brain comes up with an emergency supply. It turns to the stimuli that were stored in the past and reprocesses them. This happens with so much intensity that the dying person thinks he is looking on it all from the outside, as if the whole scene were being played before his eyes. Where normal memories are experienced 'from inside', as if you could see them 'in your head', the images of the panoramic memory have a sharpness and vividness that only images 'from outside' have under normal circumstances. The psychiatrist L. J. West has compared the brain with a man standing at a window. Behind him the fire in the hearth is burning. During the day he looks out on the world outside. But when night begins to fall the interior of his room is gradually reflected in the windowpane. Finally and without realizing it he is looking at himself standing in his brightly lit room. Against the dark of the night, inside the window frame, the images are projected from his inner self.

The experience of panoramic memory as a hallucination triggered off by the loss of sensory stimuli seems to fit in well with the experience of near-death by drowning. Beaufort wrote that after the 'tumultuous sensations' and the panic of suffocation there followed 'a calm feeling of the most perfect tranquillity' – he added that his senses had been deadened. Then extremely vivid pictures seemed to pass through his mind, 'filled up with every minute and collateral feature'. Others, too, have reported that they began to look back on their past after the tumult stopped. In 1896, the *Revue Philosophique* published the report of a man who had fallen into a well when he was eight and had been saved at the very last moment. He remembered that at first he had done his very utmost to reach the edge as the water swirled into his mouth and ears, and finally, certain that he was about to die, he had stopped thrashing about and allowed himself to float motionless in the water. At that moment there began an 'extremely rapid, kaleidoscopic procession of countless events from my past life'. The images were 'exceedingly powerful and sharp, external; I saw myself from outside as somebody else'. Once again: images in the memory that seem to originate outside and only become visible when no more stimuli enter from the world outside.

For cases other than near-drowning, the hallucination hypothesis seems at first sight less plausible. The brains of those who fall from great heights or who have had a head-on collision lasting two or three seconds had no shortage of sensory stimuli. On the other hand, Albert Heim wrote that he felt no pain when he clawed at the snow with his fingers or hit his head against the rocky crag. The only sense that was still working was his hearing: Heim heard the thud as he landed. Perhaps in the extreme circumstances of mortal danger so many senses are dulled or switched off that even within a few moments a reflecting screen of hallucinations can be set up.

What the interpretation of panoramic memory as a hallucination leaves unexplained is why the images are attended by the serene feeling that all is well. If the hallucination is made up of what is stored in the memory, then why are predominantly peaceful and carefree youthful memories projected during the last moments? What has happened to pain, sorrow and weariness? Why does the brain see nothing but good and beautiful reflections in the window? Nor can the hallucination hypothesis explain why the images change so fast. No matter what the sequence of images experienced – backwards or in chronological order – all the reports mention that the 'film' is reeled off so quickly that it seems that the pictures do not take place in normal time. Why should time, too, change with the change from 'inside' to 'outside'? Hallucination can at best be a part of the story.

The theory that casts the widest net over panoramic memory is based on three lines of research: the biochemistry of the brain, epilepsy and hippocampal activity. In the 1970s proteins with opium-like properties were discovered in brain extracts. These endorphins are neurotransmitters produced by the body in response to pain and stress; they are *endogenous morphins*. They attenuate pain stimuli and produce a sense of well-being and euphoria. They are responsible for the 'runner's high' and for the euphoric high following parachute jumps. However, with epileptic patients, endorphins have an unfortunate side effect: they lower the seizure threshold. The underlying mechanism is not clear; it is possible that endorphins subdue the activity of neurons involved in inhibiting epileptic seizures. In a specific form of epilepsy, namely temporal lobe epilepsy, which was mentioned in the chapter on déjà vu, the attack is sometimes heralded by phenomena that have much in common with panoramic memory: time distortion, hallucinations, the feeling of looking at oneself from the outside, a sense of familiarity, flashbacks. The French neurologist Féré mentioned the similarities with panoramic memory as early as 1892. This suggests a link with activity in the temporal lobe.

Besides the role of endorphins and the part played by the temporal lobe, there is yet a third element in the neurological explanation of panoramic memory. Electrical stimulation of the amygdala can provoke feelings of anxiety or, on the contrary, of peaceful relaxation. The adjoining hippocampus is indispensable for the storage of autobiographical memories. Stimulation of the hippocampus produces extremely clear and detailed flashbacks. The neurons in the hippocampus are more sensitive to spontaneous discharges than neurons elsewhere in the brain. Many forms of epilepsy, temporary memory loss and twilight states have their origin in a disturbance of the delicate balance prevailing in the hippocampus.

All these neurological findings, assumptions and analogies can be combined to suggest the following course of events: during the first few moments of shock and horror a large quantity of adrenaline is released; the brain is thrown into a state of extreme activation;

thoughts and reactions follow one another in such quick succession that time seems to expand. Next, the stress, the pain, the oxygen deficiency or whatever else the specific circumstances of mortal danger may bring, lead to the production of endorphins. These dull the pain, subdue the senses and ensure that the tumult of instinctive fear reactions is followed by a sense of calm. However, the same numbing effect releases the activity of brain areas associated with memories and the sense of time. The spontaneous activity of neurons in the hippocampus, the amygdala and other parts of the temporal lobe projects into consciousness a series of pictures, presented at top speed and carelessly assembled. Alarming scenes are not shown, or rather, in his state of relaxed stupefaction or downright euphoria, the spectator sees everything in a benign and serene light. With these images before him, he finally loses consciousness or else the pain returns. In both cases the images vanish.

What Albert Heim experienced during his fall fits this description almost from moment to moment. When Heim lost his balance and to his horror slipped to the edge of the abyss, he clawed at the snow in a reflex response. He was insensitive to pain stimuli and his hearing alone told him that he was hitting the crag with his head. In his state of heightened activation, thoughts about his chances of survival rushed through his consciousness with lightning speed. He thought of his bottle of spirits of vinegar, his alpenstock, his glasses, of what he should do when he landed, of his brother and friends, of the lecture he would be unable to give, of his family's reaction to the report of his death. Once he was falling, no external stimuli reached him. His thoughts shifted to the images he saw before him and which he recognized as scenes from his past. His mood was now peaceful and calm. The images were guided by associations outside his control; he was passively in their grip, not their director but simply a spectator. He also remembered a tragic event but could not feel sad about it. Even the thought of his mother receiving news of his death by express messenger was in no way alarming. He saw memories as clearly spread out before him as he did the fantasy about the messenger. In the serene enchantment of the moment, his normal sense of time had vanished. Later he was not even sure whether the images were projected chronologically or back in time. According to the neuropharmacological explanation of panoramic memory, Heim was indeed a spectator. He saw a performance in his consciousness, the props and scenery of which came from his own memory while the direction of the play was in the hands of adrenaline, endorphins and spontaneously firing neurons in his temporal lobe.

## In extremis

If the above hypotheses are examined closely, it becomes clear that all they amount to is a handful of conjectures, a few statistical links and suggestive analogies. That the elimination of the senses can cause hallucinations is essentially an analogy, just like the depersonalization that can occur during a traumatic event, or the aura before an epileptic seizure. In all these cases, the analogy is still incomplete, so that every conclusion along the lines of 'panoramic memory is nothing but...' is misplaced. If the mental or neuropharmacological mechanisms used in the explanation really had the causal force its advocates attribute to it, then the question arises why it is that not everyone in life-threatening danger experiences panoramic memory. Even in the circumstances most conducive to panoramic memory such as near-drowning, only a minority experiences it.

Modern explanations often have their roots in nineteenth-century medical and neurological work. That is true of the consolatory power of youthful memories in the hour of death (Winslow), but also of the power of hallucinations (Hughlings Jackson), or the links with epileptic symptoms (Féré). Later investigations have substantiated these suggestions and in some cases rendered them experimentally verifiable. Discoveries such as the presence of natural opiates in the brain and their influence on the emotions have here and there led to the convergence of apparently disparate theories. Pfister's psychoanalytical explanation included no endorphins or spontaneously firing neurons, any more than banished kings and hotel doormen figure in the neurophysiological explanation. Yet both explanations predict that the first moment of dread will be followed by a sense of relaxed well-being. Perhaps Pfister with his colourful personifications has brought out the psychological side of the feverish pharmaceutical activities of a brain in crisis.

Anyone who believes he is going to die in a few moments suddenly has very little future and a great deal of past. From one moment to the next he becomes a man *in extremis*. In some people consciousness seems to take flight under these circumstances. Their memories are endowed with an intensity not experienced before. They 'see' memories in a place where they have never been seen before – in front of their eyes, outwardly, externally. So many pictures fly past in a very short time that the usual sense of duration and tempo is thrown out of gear. Memories no longer have their familiar emotional colour and meaning; even tragic recollections share in the peaceful mood of the moment. With all these differences from ordinary experience, the normal, everyday means of expression have become inadequate. Beaufort wrote that his mental activity had been invigorated 'in a ratio which defies all description', and that the rapid flow of his thoughts was 'not only indescribable but probably inconceivable, by any one who has not himself been in a similar situation'. Words with a similar tenor can be found in practically every report of panoramic memory. Putting it into words seems to introduce a timescale that does not go with the introspective experience.

The metaphors, too, that occur in so many reports betray a measure of impotence. An author can only take his metaphors from a sphere of experience he shares with his readers; at the same time he is fully aware of the discrepancies between the metaphors and his real life. The panorama, the theatrical performance, the fast computer, the 35 mm film, the slide show, the film or the video – all are included in his descriptions while the author makes gestures of apology behind their backs, conveying to the reader that they are clumsy analogies for what is an incomparable experience. Physicians, neurologists and psychiatrists who have taken an interest in panoramic memory share this impotence. They lapse easily into metaphor and analogy, and the satisfaction springing from the explanations given above is aesthetic rather than scientific.

Towards the end of his article, Oskar Pfister, too, tried to convey the wonderful lucidity of panoramic memory by a metaphor that takes the reader back to the mountains in which Heim had his fall and where Pfister, too, had twice been in mortal danger. It is almost evening. Returning from a climb, he sees that darkness has already fallen in the valley below. He can barely make out the flanks of the

mountains in the twilight. Only the peak still catches the last light
of the sun and stands out mysteriously aglow above the darkness.


BIBLIOGRAPHY

The letter in which Beaufort described his near-drowning
experience is included in *An Autobiographical Memoir of Sir
John Barrow*, London, 1847, 398–403. The report can also be
found in William Munk's *Euthanasia: or, Medical Treatment in
Aid of an Easy Death*, London, 1887. Heim described his
experiences during his fall in 'Notizen über den Tod durch
Absturz', *Jahrbuch des Schweizer Alpenklubs* 27 (1891–2), Berne,
1892, 327–37. An almost complete English translation can be
found in R. Noyes, Jr and R. Kletti, 'The experience of dying
from falls', *Omega* 3 (1972), 45–52. The article by O. Pfister
appears in a translation by R. Noyes, Jr and R. Kletti in
'Mental states in mortal danger', *Essence* 5 (1981), 5–20. The
quotations from Pfister are from this translation.
Basford, T. K., *Near-Death Experiences: An Annotated Bibliography*, New
York, 1990.
Blackmore, S., *Dying to Live: Near-Death Experiences*, London, 1993.
De Quincey, T., *Confessions of an English Opium-Eater*. Originally
published in *London Magazine*, 1821.
Egger, V., 'Le moi des mourants. Nouveaux faits', *Revue
Philosophique* 42 (1896), 337–68.
Fechner, G. T., *Das Büchlein vom Leben nach dem Tode* (1836). Quoted
from *Life after Death*, translated by M. C. Wadsworth, New
York, c. 1904.
Féré, C., *Pathologie des émotions*, Paris, 1892.
Friendly, A., *Beaufort of the Admiralty: The Life of Sir Francis Beaufort
1774–1857*, New York, 1977.
Kinnier Wilson, S. A., *Modern Problems in Neurology*, London, 1928.
Moody, R. A., *Life after Life*, Atlanta, 1975.
Noyes, R., Jr, and R. Kletti, 'Panoramic memory: a response to the
threat of death', *Omega* 3 (1977), 181–94.
Noyes, R., Jr, and D. J. Slymen, 'The subjective response to
life-threatening danger', *Omega* 4 (1978–9), 313–21.
Oettermann, S., *The Panorama: History of a Mass Medium*, New York,
1997.

Pfister, O., 'Schockdenken und Schockphantasien bei höchster Todesgefahr', *Internationale Zeitschrift für Psychoanalyse* 16, 3–4 (1930), 430–55.

Ring, K., *Life at Death: A Scientific Investigation of the Near-Death Experience*, New York, 1980.

Rosen, D. H., 'Suicide survivors: a follow-up study of persons who survived jumping from the Golden Gate and San Francisco–Oakland Bay bridges', *Western Journal of Medicine* 122 (1975), 289–94.

Winslow, F., *On the Obscure Diseases of the Brain and Disorders of the Mind*, London, 1861.

Zaleski, C., *Otherworld Journeys: Accounts of Near-Death Experience in Medieval and Modern Times*, New York and Oxford, 1987.

# 17    From memory – *Portrait with Still Life*

*For my father*

You will find this *Vanitas still life with portrait of a young painter* in the Lakenhal in Leiden. It was painted by David Bailly, a seventeenth-century Leiden master, and there are good reasons to believe it is a self-portrait; we know from other paintings that this is what Bailly looked like. Not much is known about his life; contemporaries have left hardly any accounts of him. He was born in Leiden in 1584 and decided to become a painter after visiting the shop of the engraver Jacques de Geyn. In the winter of 1608 – he was twenty-four years old at the time – Bailly left for Germany and Italy where he earned his living by painting. After five years, 'weary of travelling', he returned to Leiden, where he quickly made his name as a portraitist. His clients were drawn mainly from university circles.

He married late in life, in 1642, at the age of fifty-eight. The age of his bride, Agneta van Swanenburgh, is not known. In the spring of 1657 the couple made their will, by which time Bailly was too weak to put his signature to the document. His demise, probably during the last days of October, was entered on 5 November 1657 in the parish register of the Pieterskerk. Bailly's death was clearly not considered a significant loss to the community: the entry in the Pieterskerk was not copied into the municipal burial register.

Nowadays, Bailly is chiefly remembered for his *Vanitas still life with portrait of a young painter*. The still life is a depiction of mortality. The diagonal starting from Bailly's head ends in the skull dominating all the other objects displayed on the table. The empty eye sockets point to the sheet of paper hanging from the extreme edge of the table and bearing the text *Vanitas vanitum, et omnia vanitas*. Between head and skull the diagonal cuts a recently snuffed candle from which a wisp of smoke is still escaping. Over the table float soap bubbles: *vita bulla*, life is a soap bubble. The skull is placed among objects underlining the transitory character of earthly things. The rummer has fallen over, the pipe has been extinguished, the roses are faded and overblown, coins and ornaments are scattered over the table. In

Fig. 27   *Vanitas still life with portrait of a young painter* by David Bailly.

an hourglass that is only just visible behind the book, time is nearly up.

A drawing of a lute-player, after Frans Hals, hangs above the palette on the wall. Just in front of the painter lies the end of a recorder. Of all the arts, music was the most transitory, for in the seventeenth century none of it could be preserved. The first artificial memory for sound – the phonograph – was not invented until 1877.

X-rays have brought an intriguing detail to light. It appears that in an earlier design Bailly was pointing his maulstick at a woman's face above the centre of the table. The stick later came to rest on the table, but the woman's face remained vaguely visible, almost like a spectre, behind the fluted glass. For us she is a mystery. Who was she? Why had she been originally assigned so prominent a place? What persuaded Bailly to let her disappear again? And above all, why did he hide her behind layers of paint that still allow her features to shine through?

Bailly's face has a somewhat self-important expression. He seems to be in his late twenties or early thirties, perhaps just back

Fig. 28  Detail from *Vanitas still life with portrait of a young painter* by David Bailly.

from his travels, a young man going up in the world. However the expression of self-satisfaction is tempered by seriousness, something that is amplified by the small portrait of the old man he is holding. Bailly seems to be trying to say that he realizes that he, too, will be an old man one day; he brings the spectator face to face with old age.

*Vanitas still life with portrait of a young painter* conveys the lesson that we must arrange our lives with a view to having to look back on them one last time. And how shall we look back at the values that have determined our life? What good will all the riches, beauty, art, book learning and all the other things we chased after be to us then? As a painting of what life may hold for us, *Vanitas still life with portrait of a young painter* must be read from left to right, from youth to old age, from the past to the future. Like the arrow of time, the painting points to the right.

However, apart from *this* painting, *Vanitas still life with portrait of a young painter* also presents us with *another* painting. And in order to see that other painting you have to know two things. First, on the same sheet of paper that contains the *vanitas* text, we can read: 'David Bailly pinxit Ao 1651.' Secondly, in 1651 Bailly was sixty-seven years old.

These two details change everything. The 'real' self-portrait – if we may put it that way – is not of the young man with his maulstick, but of the old man in the oval frame. Bailly painted himself as the man he had been about forty years earlier. In the self-portrait we see not a young man imagining his future but an old man recalling his youth.

In *Vanitas still life with portrait of a young painter* you are now able, with an almost audible click, to allow the perspective of time to shift. In the inversion, the painting does not move forwards but back-wards, from right to left, a movement running counter to the course of time. Bailly's two portraits taken together constitute a gestalt, not in space but in time: it is possible to see both, but not both at once.

Strangely enough, the message remains intact even with this inversion, because both – the memory of youth and the prospect of old age – point to the passage of time. Is that what Bailly himself tried to express in his painting? A hankering after youth lovingly remembered but now gone? The well-spent course of a life in which so much craftsmanship is gathered that this still-life can be painted in the end? Or the ultimate vanity of all effort? Did he want to hand down to us a monument to the art of painting, the art that can bestow durability upon transience? Bailly has left us no other reports of his intentions than this silent painting; his motives can never now be deduced.

The oval portrait of the old Bailly is placed at the crossing of the diagonals. Resting on the table, it is part of the *vanitas* still life. But it is also grasped, and grasped tenderly I imagine, by the young Bailly, who painted it 'from memory'. Thus six years before his death, David Bailly placed the memory where it belongs: halfway between the enduring and the transient.

BIBLIOGRAPHY

Bruyn, J., 'David Bailly, "fort bon peintre en pourtaicts et en vie coye"', *Oud-Holland* 66 (1951), 148–64, 212–27.

Draaisma, D., '"Naer 't onthoud". Bij het *Portret met stilleven* van David Bailly', *Feit & Fictie* 3 (1996), 79–83.

Popper-Voskuil, N., 'Self-portraiture and vanitas still-life painting in 17th century Holland in reference to David Bailly's vanitas oeuvre', *Pantheon* 31 (1973), 58–74.

Wurfbain, M. L., 'Vanitas-stilleven David Bailly (1584–1657)', *Openbaar Kunstbezit* 13 (1967), 76.

# Index of names

# Index of names